A linguistic Insight into Legislative Drafting

Linguistic Insights

Studies in Language and Communication

Edited by Maurizio Gotti,
Emeritus Professor,
University of Bergamo (Italy).

Volume 302

Giulia Adriana Pennisi

A linguistic Insight into Legislative Drafting

Tradition and Change in the UK Legislation

PETER LANG
Lausanne - Berlin - Bruxelles - Chennai - New York - Oxford

Bibliographic information published by die Deutsche Nationalbibliothek
Die Deutsche Nationalbibliothek lists this publication in the Deutsche Nationalbibliografie; detailed bibliographic data is available on the Internet at ‹http://dnb.d-nb.de›.

Library of Congress Cataloging-in-Publication Data
A CIP catalog record for this book has been applied for at the Library of Congress.

Published with the support of
the Department of Political Science and
International Relations of the University of Palermo

ISSN 1424-8689
ISBN 978-3-0343-4700-6 (Print)
E-ISBN 978-3-0343-4748-8 (E-PDF)
E-ISBN 978-3-0343-4749-5 (EPUB)
DOI 10.3726/b20973

Published by
Peter Lang Group AG, Lausanne, Switzerland

info@peterlang.com
http://www.peterlang.com/

Contents

Acknowledgements 9

Introduction 11

1. Law and language 15
   1.1 The origins of legal English 15
   1.2 Legal texts: Linguistic conventions and constraints 21
   1.3 Legislative provisions in context 27
   1.4 What is legislative drafting all about? 28

2. Professional discourse and legislation 39
   2.1 Professional discourse and legislative drafting 39
   2.2 The contextual frameworks 44
   2.3 A theoretical model for the contextual analysis of legislative drafting 50
      2.3.1 Legislative drafting and the situated communicative event 59
      2.3.2 Legislative drafting and the aim(s) of legislative texts 61
   2.4 Legislative drafting and comprehensibility 63

3. The UK Parliament 69
   3.1 Westminster Palace 69
      3.1.1 Magna Carta 71
      3.1.2 Burgess inclusion and selection 72
      3.1.3 'Model Parliament' 73
      3.1.4 Good Parliament 73
      3.1.5 House of Lords 74
      3.1.6 House of Commons 75
      3.1.7 Elizabethan Parliaments 76

3.1.8 The 17th century 77
3.1.9 The UK Parliament today 78
3.2 UK legislation 79
3.2.1 Parliaments and jurisdictions 81
3.2.2 Geographical extent 82
3.2.3 The UK Parliament and the legislative process 83
3.3 Guide to making legislation 86
3.3.1 Legislative drafting players 90
3.3.2 OPC 92
3.3.3 Good law 93

4. Legislative drafting process 97
4.1 What does legislative drafting mean? 97
4.2 Modern drafting techniques 104
4.2.1 Preliminary provisions 106
4.2.1.1 Long title 106
4.2.1.2 Preamble 108
4.2.1.3 Enacting formula 111
4.2.1.4 Application 113
4.2.1.5 Interpretation section 115
4.2.2 Main body of an Act and principal provisions 118
4.2.2.1 Principal provisions 118
4.2.3 Final provisions 125
4.2.3.1 Repeals and consequential amendments 125
4.2.3.2 Short title 127
4.2.3.3 Commencement 129
4.2.3.4 Schedules 131
4.2.3.5 Explanatory notes 136
4.3 Future perspectives 141

5. Improving legal communication 143
5.1 Plain language 143
5.2 Legislative provisions in context 149

5.2.1 Simplification strategies 153
5.2.2 'Easification' strategies 160
5.3 Gender neutrality in legislative drafting 168
5.3.1 Language and gender 169
5.3.2 The English language and gender 172
5.3.3 He/his/him and the 'masculine rule' 174
5.3.4 Reforming gender language 175
5.3.5 English-language jurisdictions and gender-neutral drafting 179
5.3.6 UK 'Guide to Gender-Neutral Drafting (2019)' 191
5.3.7 'Good law' and UK legislative drafting 192

Conclusions 195

References 201

Appendix 213

Index 269

Acknowledgements

This book results from a long-lasting research interest of mine in specialized discourse and, particularly, legal language and legislation. Over the last ten years, I have explored legislative texts in English-speaking countries and carried out several studies in the UK and European legislation both at the Department of Political Science at the University of Palermo (Italy) and the Institute of Advanced Legal Studies (IALS) – at the University of London (UK). Students and colleagues have been involved in many of the research projects which I have directed at these universities. It would take quite some time to enumerate all the persons and scholars in different parts of the world with whom I have had inspiring conversations and correspondence, but I would like to thank them all for the contributions they have made.

Introduction

Legal English originates from different sources that have influenced its style. Historically speaking, legal English evolved over the three-century period between the 1470s (the setting up of the first printing press in England) and the 1770s (the American Declaration of Independence). Unsurprisingly, its terminology and style are still in the form they had reached by the early years of the 19th century. Traditional legal language has been increasingly challenged in all the major English-speaking countries, and this questioning has brought about important changes in the length and layout of legal documents (e.g., normative texts). Many of these changes have been stimulated by the Plain Language Movement of the latter decades of the 20th century. Despite these important transformations, legal language has remained largely frozen in time.

The main lexico-grammatical features of legal writing are usually characterized as follows: inclusion of archaic words and foreign expressions especially from Latin and French; frequent repetition of fixed syntactic structures; long and convoluted sentences with intricate patterns of coordination and subordination; a highly impersonal style of writing and a tendency towards nominalization.[1] Written legal texts do not necessarily contain all the features mentioned above, though many of them do, and the compound effect often makes deciphering them extremely difficult without specific training (Williams 2004). Indeed, certain types of legal writing present features that render the texts so peculiar at times that they are incomprehensible to anyone except legal experts.

Much of the criticism that legal English has attracted is clearly reasonable in that it is objectively difficult for the layperson to understand it, particularly when they are dealing with legislative texts and norms. There are inherent factors that make it difficult to convey the intentions

1 The Oxford English Dictionary defines nominalization 'a type of word formation in which a verb or an adjective or other part of a speech is used as or transformed into a noun'.

of the legislator and ensure there are no ambiguities in the words and expressions chosen by the legislative drafter (Mousmouti 2019). Complex societies make increasing political demands to produce legislation quickly and efficiently, whereas the lack of effective consultations between policy makers and drafters certainly affect the language used and the underlying function of the text.

The need to produce better legislation cannot be met without the help of other disciplines such as Linguistics, with profitable cooperation between linguists and legislative drafters, a careful analysis of several aspects of the drafting process, and the application of linguistic tools when formulating legal provisions that aim to be communicatively effective (Bhatia 2010, 2014; Engberg 2013b; Gotti 2014; Endicott 2022).

Legislative drafting is a very complex task, given that the formulation of legal norms is conditioned by the different cultural, linguistic and legal environments that inform them. In the case of common law systems, their adversarial nature is reflected in the drafters' stylistic choices featuring very long sentences traditionally consisting of three (or more) main clauses, each modified by many subordinate clauses (Gotti 2014). The need for provisions to be all-inclusive, precise and clear (Bhatia 1987, 1993, 2004; Campbell 1996; Tiersma 1999) results in an increase in sentence length, the great number of inserted parts, detailed terminological explanations, and the use of past-participle clauses to state clearly the source of the qualification of a term. For instance, the intention to cover as many specific cases and interpretations as possible is evident in the number of definitions and explanations normally present, combined with the explicit indication of the limits of applicability of the norm. In the last few decades, the Plain Language Movement has strongly influenced legislation in common law systems, as can be seen in the formulation of norms and regulations instructing legislative drafters to adopt simpler and clearer writing.[2] An increasing number of guidelines for better legislative drafting have been provided with the purpose of achieving a greater degree of clarity and consistency, and these have been exceedingly influential in introducing

2 For example, some Offices of Parliamentary Counsel of various English-speaking countries (e.g. Australia, New Zealand, Scotland) specify in their websites that their drafters adopt plain language techniques.

significant innovations in law-making with a consequent improvement in the quality of legislation. Thanks to criteria such as a smaller number of words per sentence, the extensive use of simple and compound sentences, and the adoption of a common lexis, to name just a few, laws have become more accessible to laypeople.

The adoption of these practices, though, is not in itself a guarantee of a completely successful result. Legislative drafters deal with an unlimited universe of human behaviour, in the sense that it is impossible to predict exactly what may happen in the real world (Bhatia 2021; Endicott 2022). Law-making embraces the whole process ranging from the conceptualization of legislation until its very implementation, whereas legislative drafting is limited only to the drafting process. This does not mean to say that drafting is completely foreign to the legislative process. In fact, the drafting process is part of the legislative process, which in turn is part of the policy process (Stefanou 2011; Xanthaki 2014). At this point, it becomes crucial to consider the context of a legal document, and/or the legislative discourse, in order to shed light upon ambiguous and obscure provisions.

The purpose of this book is to explore firstly, the origin of legislative drafting in common law tradition, i.e., Westminster and the UK Parliament, and the organization of the drafting process, in order to acknowledge how policy decisions originate and are finally transformed into legislation and written norms. If we consider, on the other hand, legislative process in relation to 'context' at different levels, such as the situated communicative event, the environmental framework (i.e., the workplace, the organization, the discipline), and the societal framework (i.e., the legal-political, socio-cultural, and linguistic frameworks), it becomes possible to reach a deeper understanding of the development and constant change of the final product, viz., normative texts, over the last fifty years.

The book is divided into six chapters. After an introductory section, Chapter 1 deals with the topic of providing definitions of the legislative drafting, outlining some trends in discourse analysis, sociolinguistics and textual analysis, and suggesting interesting features of the legislative process in relation to contexts at different levels. Chapter 2 presents a methodology to explore legislative drafting as a professional language/professional discourse in relation to the (i) situated communicative event, (ii) the environmental framework, and (iii) the societal frameworks. Chapter 3 explores the origin of legislative drafting within the common law tradition and its subsequent growth at the Westminster Parliament (i.e., Office of the Parliamentary Counsel, hereafter OPC). Chapter 4 delves into the analysis of the drafting process 'tout court' and the modern drafting techniques adopted for the UK Primary legislation. Chapter 5 considers the recent development that legislative drafting has undergone due to the pressure of the Plain Language Movement at international level, and the 'good law project' at the UK (i.e., Westminster Parliament) level, focusing on the linguistic features of the final product, i.e. a corpus of legislative texts (UK Primary and Secondary legislation). Finally, Chapter 6 summarizes the findings and presents some final remarks for future research.

1 Law and language

1.1 The origins of legal English

Legal English originates from different sources that have influenced its style. Historically speaking, legal English evolved over the three-century period between the 1470s (the setting up of the first printing press in England) and the 1770s (the American Declaration of Independence). Unsurprisingly, its terminology and style are still in the form they had reached by the early years of the 19th century. Traditional legal language has been increasingly challenged in all major English-speaking countries, and this questioning has brought about important changes in the length and layout of legal documents (e.g., normative texts). Many of these changes have been stimulated by the Plain Language Movement of the latter decades of the 20th century.[3] Despite these important transformations, legal language has remained largely frozen in time. In this regard, a concise, though extremely precise account of the history of legal English has been provided by Durant and Leung (2016: 6–8) who identify six important moments/phases in development of legal English,

---

3 Particularly relevant was the rise in the 1960s of Western consumer movements which were concerned with empowering laymen so they could defend their rights against private companies and government bodies. Isolated attempts had been made during the first half of the 20th century, for example in the United States, to introduce measures to make legal English less convoluted. Across the Atlantic, in Liverpool, the plain English campaign was born in 1979 and by the mid-1980s it was already possible to speak of a 'Plain Language Movement' operating in all major English-speaking countries, including Canada, Australia, New Zealand, and, by the early 1990s, in South Africa.

starting from the very beginning of the contact between different languages and the birth of legal language.

The first phase started in AD 410 when the Romans withdrew from Britain, and Latin almost died out, being revived under the influence of St. Augustine for use in Christian ceremonies after AD 597.[4]

The second phase took place immediately after the retreat of the Romans. The Anglo-Saxons invaded Britain and introduced a Germanic language otherwise known as Old English or Anglo-Saxon. In the earlier period of Roman occupation, Old English existed mainly in oral culture. By that time, the enforcement of social order implied superstitious practices based on a ritualistic legal culture that influenced most words of modern legal English.[5] Furthermore, the use of the literary device of alliteration, with the repetition of the consonant sound at the beginning of two or more adjacent words, was a linguistic strategy to create memorable formulae, such as *rest, residue and remainder*, i.e. 'the residuary estate of a testator'[6] (example 1) and typically used in wills and *hold harmless*, which is a clause used in business transactions or commercial activities where a party may be exposed to financial risk or personal danger[7] (example 2):

(1) All the rest, residue and remainder of my property and estate, both real and personal, including my interest in premises [. . .]. I give unto my Trustee, herein named, IN TRUST NEVERTHELESS, for my son [. . .];

(2) The Contractor agrees to defend, indemnify, and hold harmless the Owner and [any other parties] from liability and claim for damages due to bodily injury, death, property [. . .].

---

4 There is little continuity between the Latin brought by the Romans in 43 BC and later influence of Latin on legal English (Durant and Leung 2016).

5 For instance, words like *bequeath*, *guilt*, *manslaughter*, *murder*, *oath*, *right*, *sheriff*, *steal*, *swear*, *theft*, *thief*, *witness* and *writ*, have historically narrowed or altered in meaning (Durant and Leung 2016: 8).

6 Merriam-Webster Dictionary.

7 A provision in an agreement under which one or both parties agree not to hold the other party responsible for any damage, loss, or legal liability. In effect, this clause secures the parties on a unilateral or reciprocal basis. According to Merriam-Webster 'of, relating to, or being an agreement between parties in which one assumes the potential liability for injury that may arise from a situation and thus relieves the other of liability'.

After a widespread adoption of Christianity in the 7th century, the Anglo-Saxon made Latin as the principal language of religion, scholarship, and the language for legal thinking.

The third phase corresponds to the period AD 800–1050, when Vikings from Norway and Denmark established a geographical jurisdiction known as the Dane law in north-eastern England. This invasion had a significant linguistic and political impact that contributed to the development of modern English, as well as legal English.

The fourth phase follows the invasion of Britain by the Normans from northern France in 1066. Migrating themselves from France, they were speakers of Norman French.[8] Due to increased isolation from France and the increased interest in commercial activities with the Anglo-Saxons, significant changes took place in Old English. By the late 13th century, Middle English comes about as a distinct phase in the history of language, with the prevalence of less inflected forms and more structures that were dependent on word order.[9] Notwithstanding the enactment by Parliament of the *Statute of Pleading in 1362*, which censured the fact that parties in most legal actions could not understand the proceedings and required pleas to be made in English Statutes in English, it only really appeared in the late 15th century. Interestingly enough, the same *Statute*, which required the use of English, was itself written in French.

The fifth phase started from the 16th century onwards, with the birth and later development of Early Modern English.

From a mere dialect spoken in The Midlands,[10] English gradually emerged as a standard variety, especially following the introduction of printing in England by Caxton in the 1470s. After the decline of Latin

---

8 In England, Norman French was the language spoken by members of the aristocracy, and used for government documents, administrative and military purposes. The Anglo-Norman language developed as a contact language, adapting in response to the bilingual context. Latin became the language in use for scholarship and religious matters (Tiersma 1999).

9 This made French the language of power and Latin, at least initially, the language of law (Mellinkoff 1963; Baker 2002).

10 Midlands is the region of Central England and commonly subdivided into the East and the West Midlands (Encyclopaedia Britannica).

in the 16th and mid-17th centuries,[11] the English language gained status thanks to the popularity of literary writing in the 17th century. Within this context, the development of legal English was rather unusual (Durant and Leung 2016: 9) for the reason that French in legislation and in legal documents was in use at the time when Anglo-French was in decline outside the legal domain. In fact, a specialized variety of law French survived the *1650 Act: An Act for turning the Books of the Law, and all Process and Proceedings in Courts of Justice, into English*, being finally in demise by the 1730s,

> November, 1650 [22 November, 1650.]
>
> *All Report-Books, and other Law-Books to be in English.*
>
> The Parliament have thought fit to Declare and Enact, and be it Declared and Enacted by this present Parliament, and by the Authority of the same, That all the Report-Books of the Resolutions of Judges, and other Books of the Law of England, shall be Translated into the English Tongue: And that from and after the First day of January, 1650, all Report-Books of the Resolutions of Judges, and all other Books of the Law of England, which shall be Printed, shall be in the English Tongue onely.
>
> *All Writs, Pleadings, Patents, &c. to be in English.*
>
> And be it further Enacted by the Authority aforesaid, That from and after the first Return of Easter Term, which shall be in the year One thousand six hundred fifty and one, all Writs, Proces and Returns thereof, and all Pleadings, Rules, Orders, Indictments, Inquisitions, Certificates; and all Patents, Commissions, Records, Judgements, Statutes, Recognizances, Rolls, Entries, and Proceedings of Courts Leet, Courts Baron, and Customary Courts, and all Proceedings whatsoever in any Courts of Justice within this Commonwealth, and which concerns the Law, and Administration of Justice, shall be in the English Tongue onely, and not in Latine or French, or any other Language then English, Any Law, Custom or Usage heretofore to the contrary notwithstanding. And that the same, and every of them, shall be written in an ordinary, usual and legible Hand and Character, and not in any Hand commonly called Court-hand.[12]

---

11 This was the result of the Reformation and then, consequence of the hostility towards Latin during and after the English Civil War (Durant and Leung 2016).

12 Acts and Ordinances of the Interregnum | British History Online (british-history.ac.uk).

Actually, French law expressions are still present in modern legal English, including the use of adjectives that follow rather than precede nouns (e.g. *attorney general*, *court martial*, *notary public*) and an extensive use of technical terminology, such as:

Adjournament - To postpone the case, either to a fixed date or without fixing one, according to the circumstances.

Defendant - The person who has been accused of a crime.

Evidence - The material that indicates whether someone is guilty of a crime.

Gré à gré - Transfer of a right or property by the freely expressed will of the parties.

Parole - The conditional release of prisoners before they complete their sentence. Paroled prisoners are supervised by a public official, usually called a parole officer. If paroled prisoners violate the conditions of their release, they may be returned to prison.

Plea - The defendant's response of either "guilty" or "innocent" for a crime they are accused of.

Sue - To start legal procedures against someone in order to obtain compensation or payment for damages or wrongdoing.

Verdict - The final decision in the courtroom as to whether or not the defendant is guilty or innocent.

During this period, Latin was used as the language of court records and writs, such as the *habeas corpus*, and then it was used as the language of legislation. Being the language of scholarship of the period, learned English judges and lawyers integrated Latin quotations and maxims of law into their discourse (Solan 1993). There follows a few examples of the most recurrent Latin quotations and maxims still used in legal English today:

Actione legis – Law suits.

Ceteris paribus – Other things being equal.

Ex gratia – Out of kindness, voluntary.

In esse – In extistence.

Lex non deficere postest in justitia exhibenda – The law cannot fail in dispensing justice.

Mens rea – guilty state of mind.

Nemo debet esse judex in propria causa – No one can be judge in his own case.

Non sequitur – An inconsistent statement, it does not follow.

Quod necessitas cogit, defendit – What necessity forces it justifies.

Stare decisis – To stand by decisions (precedents).

Ubi jus ibi remedium est – Where there is a right there is a remedy.[13]

In most cases, the low proficiency in Latin of clerks and scribes led them to include French legal terms with Latin when needed.

During the fifth phase, other significant features of the modern legal English took shape, such as the textual construction of long and grammatically complex sentences (a practice inherited from the Latin prose and passed on to French law), and the use of *binomials* or phrases resulting from two words linked by the conjunction *and*, as in the case of the formula *by and with the advice and consent*[14] [my emphasis here and there].

(3) Be it enacted by the [Queen's] most Excellent Majesty, *by and with the advice and consent* of the Commons in this present Parliament assembled, in accordance with the provisions of the Parliament Acts 1911 and 1949, and by the authority of the same, as follows [...],

Gustafsson (1975: 18) believes that the '[p]artial phonetic identity between the members in the form of alliteration, rhyme and assonance, increases the power of a binomial and operates as an effective mnemonic aid', which explains the perdurance of many binomials in modern legal English.

Durant and Leung (2016) acknowledge that another factor having a huge impact on modern legal English was the invention of printing (Harvey 2015). Given the wider dissemination of printed texts,

> an increased number of uniform versions of legal texts, and legal proceedings changed in the balance they demanded between oral and written pleading. [...]

---

13 Latin Legal Maxims, Writs and Expressions – I | InRebus.

14 The enacting formula is a short paragraph which precedes the clauses of the Bill. This formula was developed in the 15th century for Bills presented for Royal Assent under the Parliament Acts 1911 and 1949 <https://erskinemay.parliament.uk/section/4978/enacting-formula/>.

> Crucial for issues of legal authority, too, the shift from oral to written involved a change from viewing written documents as mere reports of an oral event or ceremony through to seeing written documents as the authoritative statements. Deeper still, fixation of discourse in writing consolidated the legal doctrine of precedent and introduced a textual and more interpretive, 'legalistic' dimension into adversarial litigation (Durant and Leung 2016: 10).

The sixth phase embraced various stages in the history of English, from the invasion and colonization of Britain by others, to Britain itself invading countries, with all stages being characterized by language contact and language change. Needless to say, the imperial expansion by Britain led to the use of English as the language of administration and education in the country's overseas possessions. Combined with the US economic and political influence through the 20th century, this has resulted in English becoming the international lingua franca and reflected in the systematic use of the language in postcolonial national legal systems, as well as in international political and legal institutions and commerce. Notwithstanding the significant expansion of vocabulary arising from its use in modern and industrial societies, legal English is still characterized by the persistence of linguistic archaisms due to its conservative doctrinal values (i.e., considering preceding judgements as authority on the meaning to be assigned to legal terminology).

1.2 Legal texts: Linguistic conventions and constraints

Generally speaking, the main lexico-grammatical features of legal writing are usually characterized as follows: inclusion of archaic words and foreign expressions especially from Latin and French; frequent repetition of fixed syntactic structures; long and convoluted sentences with intricate patterns of coordination and subordination; a highly impersonal style of writing and a tendency towards nominalization.[15] Written

15 The Oxford English Dictionary (OED) defines nominalization 'a type of word formation in which a verb or an adjective or other part of a speech is used as or transformed into a noun'.

legal texts do not necessarily contain all the features mentioned above, though many of them do, and the compound effect often makes deciphering them extremely difficult without specific training (Williams 2004, 2022). Indeed, certain types of legal writing present features that render the texts so peculiar at times that they are incomprehensible to anyone except legal experts. Describing legal English as 'mysterious in form and expression', Butt (2013: 1–2) argues that

> Some infelicities of expression, some overlooked nuances, some grammatical slips, can be forgiven. Lawyers are only human, and in day-to-day practice of law they face an overwhelming weight of words. What cannot be forgiven, however, is the legal profession's systematic mangling of the English language, perpetrated in the name of tradition and precision.

Much of the criticism that legal English has attracted is clearly reasonable in that it is objectively difficult for the layperson to understand it, particularly when they are dealing with legislative texts and norms. There are inherent factors that make it difficult to convey the intentions of the legislator and ensure there are no ambiguities in the words and expressions chosen by the legislative drafter (Fjeld 2001). Complex societies make increasing political demands to produce legislation quickly and efficiently, whereas the lack of effective consultations between policy makers and drafters certainly affect the language used and the underlying function of the text. On the occasion of the Sir William Dale Memorial Lecture[16] for 2005, Geoffrey Bowman (2006: 3) said, 'It is not the drafter's job to make up the policy, and that it should not be his job', though actually 'it is part of his job to offer workable solutions when possible'. In this regard, a few considerations of eminent scholars in the field of law and language do shed some meaningful light on the complex relationship between legislation and drafting:

16 Sir William Dale Centre for Legislative Studies (Institute of Advanced Legal Studies – University of London) organizes the *Annual Sir William Dale Memorial Lecture*. Prestigious speakers from the UK and abroad explore the latest developments on issues related to legislative drafting <SirWilliamDaleMemorialLecture|IALS (sas.ac.uk)>.

- the operation of legislation can only be fully understood in terms of its context or 'sites of engagement' (Scollon 2001). If an instrumental position is taken, the background can be seen to include recognition of a 'problem', determination of objectives, and the choice of means for their achievement (Fairclough 2003; van Dijk 2005, 2007);
- there are 'inherent difficulties in the drafting of legislation'. Legislation is the product of a dialogue between the actors of the drafting process (i.e., policy, legal, and drafting experts), the discipline involved in the process (i.e., policy, substantive law, legislative drafting), and the language used by the experts in their own discipline (i.e., policy, law, and drafting) (Xanthaki 2014);
- the implementation of legislation can be enormously affected by various 'filtering agents' – rule enforcers, rule interpreters, and the population to whom the legislation is directed (Stefanou 2011). They can constrain, adapt and modify the intentions and policies that may have motivated the passage of legislation in the first place (Barnes 2006);
- if the lawmaker or someone else wishes to test how the law in question has been drafted and the extent to which the goals of legislation have been met, the investigation will benefit from the adoption of a broadly 'scientific' approach (Galdia 2009; Solan 2005; Gunnarsson 2009; Solan and Tiersma 2012).

Among the significant features that are typical of legal English, there is the linguistic variation that might occur either by text type, or genre. Genre consists of interconnected elements that together realize a specific purpose. In the legal domain, specific genres serve defined roles, such as to prohibit something, impose duties and orders, make promises, advocate a course of action, etc. Overall, genre concerns the uniqueness of legal text types within the class of texts that all display legal register. On the other hand, register consists in stylistic variation applied across legal text types. In other words, significant variable features tend to occur regularly within a text. This is, for instance, the case of passive grammatical constructions that are used more frequently than active ones:

(4) Liability of insures

Where –

(a) *an accident is caused by an automated vehicle* when driving itself on a road or other public place [. . .].[17]

In this extract (example n. 4) the 'writer backs into sentence', as Garner (2014) observes when describing the use of the passive voice in legal language. Generally speaking, the passive voice is often wordier than the active voice, with the actor performing the action behind the scenes.

Other significant variable features that occur in legal texts are the distinctive use of modals, such as the third person *shall:*

(5) Where -

(a) the appropriate records authority receives a request for information which relates to information which is, or if it existed would be, contained in a transferred public record, and

(b) either of the conditions in subsection (2) is satisfied in relation to any of that information,
that authority *shall*, within the period for complying with section 1(1), send a copy of the request to the responsible authority (Section 15 - *Freedom of Information Act 2000*)[18]

and the absence of contracted forms, such as *it's. . .*, *doesn't. . .*, etc., that occur in situations where a choice is available (Biber and Conrad 2009), as is shown in the following example:

(6) If the school is a selective school and is to be converted into an Academy school, section 1A(1)(c) (requirement to provide education for pupils of different abilities) *does not apply* in relation to any Academy arrangements to be entered into in relation to the school or an educational institution that replaces it (Section 6 - *Academies Act 2010*).[19]

Genre markers are structural, because features that define a text often occur towards the beginning or the end of texts. In the case of legal genre, the genre markers typical of documents, include the layout and

17 Section 2 – *Automated and Electric Vehicles Act 2018* <https://www.legislation.gov.uk/ukpga/2018/18/section/2>.

18 https://www.legislation.gov.uk/ukpga/2000/36/section/15

19 https://www.legislation.gov.uk/ukpga/2010/32/section/6

textual organization (i.e., sections, chapters, paragraphs, etc.), headings and titles, opening and closing statements, signatures and dates when required. These features work together to provide the necessary structure of legal texts, and the absence of one of these essential markers makes the text unable to fulfil its final objective.

In general, three main types of legal texts can be identified (Durant and Leung 2016: 12), where each text type has a specific legal task, and is governed by rules and conventions that vary among legal systems:

> 1st type includes treaties, constitutions, statutes, statutory instruments, by-laws, regulatory codes, that might define 'legislative' documents;
>
> 2nd type consists of contracts, orders, deeds, wills, leases, conveyances, mortgage documents, building contracts, and represent 'private law' documents;
>
> 3rd type includes the opening speech in a trial, cross-examination, summing-up speech, jury direction, etc., and may be defined as 'procedural' documents.

Whereas the first two types are typically written genres, the third type consists of legal text mostly realized in speech (for example during court proceedings). Genre becomes particularly important in relation to legal text types because legal systems function through a hierarchy of different actors involved in the production of legal texts. This is the case of the 1st type of legal documents, i.e., the 'legislative' documents, that build on the multifaceted process of legislation through which policy documents progress into legislative drafting, are published as statutes, regulations, etc., and are further applied by the courts, contested in litigation, and later amended or codified.

Certainly, legislative drafting is a very complex task, given that the formulation of legal norms is conditioned by the different cultural, linguistic and legal environments that form them. In the case of common law systems, their adversarial nature is reflected in the drafters' stylistic choices featuring very long sentences traditionally consisting of three (or more) main clauses, each modified by many subordinate clauses (Gotti 2014). The need for provisions to be all-inclusive, precise and clear (Bhatia 1987, 1993, 2004; Campbell 1996; Tiersma 1999) results in an increase in sentence length, the great number of inserted parts, detailed terminological explanations, and the use of past-participle clauses to state clearly the source of the qualification of a term. For instance, the intention to cover as many specific cases and interpretations as possible is evident in the number of definitions and explanations normally present, combined with the explicit indication of the limits of applicability of the norm.

Particularly in the last few decades, the Plain Language Movement has strongly influenced legislation in common law systems, as can be seen in the formulation of norms and regulations instructing legislative drafters to adopt simpler and clearer writing.[20] An increasing number of guidelines for better legislative drafting have been provided with the purpose of achieving a greater degree of clarity and consistency, and these have been exceedingly influential in introducing significant innovations in law-making with a consequent improvement in the quality of legislation. Thanks to criteria such as a smaller number of words per sentence, the extensive use of simple and compound sentences, and the adoption of a common lexis to name just a few, laws have become more accessible to laypeople. The adoption of these practices, though, is not in itself a guarantee of a completely successful result.

Legislative drafting is often perceived as a practical skill that one learns on the job. Legislative drafting has evolved to become the foundation of political, economic and social transformation. It is still, however, relatively unexplored as an academic discipline and for this reason this volume examines issues related to both the legislative process and the drafting process. The need to produce better legislation cannot be met without the help of other disciplines such as Linguistics, with profitable cooperation between linguists and legislative drafters, a careful analysis of several aspects of the drafting process, and the application of linguistic tools when formulating legal provisions that aim to be communicatively effective (Bhatia 2010, 2014; Engberg 2013a; Gotti 2014; Endicott 2022).

20 For example, some Offices of Parliamentary Counsel of various English-speaking countries (e.g. Australia, New Zealand, Scotland) specify in their websites that their drafters adopt plain language techniques.

1.3 Legislative provisions in context

Legislative drafters deal with an unlimited universe of human behaviour, in the sense that it is impossible to predict exactly what may happen in the real world (Bhatia 2021; Endicott 2022).

Law-making embraces the whole process ranging from the conceptualization of legislation up to its very implementation, whereas legislative drafting is limited only to the drafting process. This does not mean to say that drafting is completely foreign to the legislative process. In fact, the drafting process is part of the legislative process, which in turn is part of the policy process (Stefanou 2011; Xanthaki 2014). At this point, it becomes crucial to consider the context of a legal document, and/or the legislative discourse in order to shed light upon ambiguous and obscure provisions. In linguistics, 'discourse' means the construction and organization of the segments of language above and below the sentence.[21] The meaning is always beyond the sentence (Fowler et al. 1979; Fairclough 1989, 1995, 2003; van Dijk 1985, 1997). The elements of grammar, lexis, and phonology play a fundamental role, but they are reconsidered as a part of a multilayered cognitive, social, and cultural phenomenon (Fairclough 1989; Langacker 1991; Geeraerts 1995; Lakoff and Johnson 1998; Wodak and Meyer 2001).

The purpose of this book is to explore the origin of legislative drafting in common law tradition, i.e., Westminster and the UK Parliament, and the organization of the drafting process, in order to acknowledge how policy decisions originate and are finally transformed into legislations and written norms. The theoretical basis of the analysis conducted in this book derives from a range of disciplines, mainly discourse analysis (van Dijk 2005, 2007; Fairclough 2003; Chafe 2008), genre analysis (Swales 1990; Swales and Rogers 1995; Bhatia 2004, 2014, 2021), sociolinguistics (Tannen 2005; Blommaert 2007), and legal linguistics (Langton 2005; Mattila 2006; Galdia 2009; Goddard 2010; Solan and

21 The Oxford English Dictionary (OED) defines discourse analysis 'a method of analysing the structure of texts or utterances longer than one sentence, taking into account both their linguistic content and their sociolinguistic context; analysis performed using this method.'

Tiersma 2012; Engberg 2013b). The main assumption is that legislative drafting represents an example of professional discourse, where the propositions of specialized information, or knowledge of the actors participating in the legislative process, is translated into meanings, and such meanings are given as input to the rules and strategies of grammatical formulation. Professional knowledge, such as academic, scholarly, scientific, technical, and other kinds of knowledge which require specialized education or training, is a type of group knowledge as defined above. It is acquired, shared, and used among members of various kinds of scholarly or other specialized communities. These specialized communities are defined not only by their specialized knowledge, but also by their specialized social practices, including their specialized discourse and communication, as well as by a complex network of organizations and institutions such as universities, professional groups, and associations, to name just a few. There seems to be a straightforward relation between specialized knowledge and specialized discourse if the latter is merely defined as the verbal expression of the former (Haspelmath et al. 2005; van Dijk 2007; Gunnarsson 2009; Gotti 2011). If we consider, on the other hand, legislative process in relation to 'context' at different levels, such as the situated communicative event, the environmental framework (i.e., the workplace, the organization, the discipline), and the societal framework (i.e., the legal-political, socio-cultural, and linguistic frameworks), it becomes possible to reach a deeper understanding of the development and constant change of the final product, viz., the normative texts.

1.4 What is legislative drafting all about?

In the occasion of the *Sir William Dale Memorial*,[22] Geoffrey Bowman explained that he was invited to discuss the maxim that drafting is more an art than a science. In doing so, he started talking about the

22 See note 16, p. 22.

'philosophy of drafting' and quoted Francis Bacons' expression 'As for the philosophers, they make imaginary laws for imaginary commonwealths; and their discourses are as the stars, which give little light, because they are so high'.[23] Then, he made it clear that 'the basic idea is to find out what the client wants, analyze it to ensure that it stands up, and express what is needed in language that is as precise and clear as possible' (2006: 2).

In this regard, Haack (2014) observes that today, more than four centuries later, 'Bacon's complaint still resonates. Now, as then, the writings of philosophers – even of philosophers of law, who might be expected to be a little more grounded in the real world – all too often "give little light, because they are so high". Yet, epistemological ideas really can illuminate real-life legal issues'.

Recalling what Agobard of Lyons[24] commented on in the different laws prevailing in much of Europe in the 9th century, Bowman concluded that

> it is true that there would normally be little of substance that differed between the drafts. And we would rarely feel that a colleagues efforts were plain wrong. But we might well say, 'I would not have done it that way'. Now, if five different drafters would produce five different Bills, it suggests that legislative drafting is an art rather than a precise science (2006: 2).

As he plainly affirms, one reason why drafting is an art is that all Bills are different. Whereas private legal instruments (e.g., contracts, leases, etc.) are often based on precedents, legislative drafters can very rarely draw on a precedent because each Bill has to be approached as a unique product. This can be observed since the early stages of a Bill, when legislative drafters carry out their function of discovering the department's intention and analyzing the proposed policy (Stefanou 2011). The drafter has to be careful, because it is not the drafters' job to make up the policy; yet, it is part of their job to offer workable solutions when

---

23 Francis Bacon, The Advancement of Learning (1605), in Basil Montagu, ed., *The Works of Francis Bacon,* vol. 2 (London: William Pickering, 1825) at 295 [Bacon], quoted in Bowman (2006: 2).

24 Saint Agobard | archbishop of Lyon | Britannica.

possible. The course that this iterative process takes is different for each normative text, and it is not predictable.

It is generally accepted that legal concepts and legal documents are often difficult to understand. In the case of legislative drafting the position is complicated by other factors, such as the addresses of the normative act, i.e., the legislative audience on the one hand, and the nature of legislation, i.e., the types of normative texts, on the other. Generally speaking, the administrative and legal civil servants, ministers, members of the Houses of Parliament, barristers and solicitors and judges represent the legislative audience, and the people affected by the specific normative text(s). They may range over a wide area, depending on the nature of the Bill, from specialists in a given field such as tax accountants, pension experts, scientists, etc., and laymen. When drafting any given Bill, an element of compromise and balance is at stake. Being himself a legislative drafter, Bowman recalls that

> in drafting a provision to block a sophisticated tax avoidance scheme the drafter's main concern will be to achieve certainty. That may involve sacrifice a degree of ready intelligibility so far as (say) members of Parliament are concerned. Striking the right balance in a given case involves a good deal of judgment. And this is another reason why scholars and experts in legislation believe that legislative drafting is an art rather than a precise science (2006: 4).

In this regard, the nature of legislation was clearly explained by Sir Christopher Jenkins, then the First Parliamentary Counsel, in 1997 in a memorandum to the select committee on the modernization of the House of Commons.[25]

> Memorandum submitted by the First Parliamentary Counsel.
>
> 1. Legislation is often criticised as obscure or in any event difficult to read. There are many factors, apart from the fallibility of the drafters and policy-makers, which contribute to this situation.
>   - Certainty is a prime objective: it can make for long and detailed legislation.
>   - Society and the economy have become more complex, meaning that legislation has had to become more elaborate to cater for a wider and more complex range of circumstances.

25 https://publications.parliament.uk/pa/cm199798/cmselect/cmmodern/190i/md0108.htm

- The law accumulated on the statute book is long and complicated, which means that legislation to extend or amend it tends to be long and complicated too.
- Many Bills are produced too quickly to get the policy and drafting right, or to allow time for public consultation, before they are introduced into Parliament.
- Heavy amendment of a Bill as it goes through Parliament often distorts its structure.

2. Addressing these problems is easier in some cases than in others. But many of the most promising solutions involve increasing the time and care spent on the detailed development of policy and on drafting; and the establishment of better procedures for examining proposals. There have been some useful recent initiatives.

3. There is now increased emphasis on the production of draft legislation for consultation and on the practice of announcing in the Queen's Speech not only the programme for the new session but also some of the candidates for the next. Both these developments should help to increase the time available for getting policy and drafting right before Bills are introduced. There will always be situations where legislation cannot be drafted early; but the more regularly that can be done, the better the general quality of Bills will be.

4. The Inland Revenue has embarked on a major project to improve and simplify tax law. And of course the Law Commission has for over 30 years been making proposals for consolidation and for law reform. The work being done by these two bodies will make existing law easier to use.

5. However, developments of these kinds will not address directly a crucial factor affecting the readability of Bills. That factor is the unique nature of legislation. Unlike other forms of writing, a Bill is not there to inform, to explain, to entertain or to perform any of the other usual functions of literature. A Bill's sole reason for existence is to change the law. The resulting Act *is* the law.

6. A consequence of this unique function is that a Bill cannot set about communicating with the reader in the same way that other forms of writing do. It cannot use the same range of tools. In particular, it cannot repeat important points simply to emphasise their importance or safely explain itself by restating a proposition in different words. To do so would risk creating doubts and ambiguities that would fuel litigation. As a result, legislation speaks in a monotone and its language is compressed. It is less easy for readers to get their bearings and to assimilate quickly what they are being told than it would be if conventional methods of helping the reader were freely available to the drafter.

7. This difficulty is compounded if drafting and lay-out are poor. But even the best drafting and best lay-out cannot eliminate it. It is therefore important to find other ways of helping the reader.

8. The Committee may therefore like to consider how Members and subsequent readers of Bills and Acts could be helped by material which does not itself form part of the law, but is provided alongside the law.
9. Examples of this kind of help already exist. The explanatory memorandum on the front of a Government Bill is one. Notes on Clauses are another, and these are increasingly being made available to Members and sometimes to a wider audience. Again, the Law Commission, when reporting on a law reform project, habitually publishes a draft Bill with notes explaining its provisions. "Explanatory Notes Finance Bill 1997" published by HM Treasury in January illustrates a further approach.
10. The Committee may like to consider whether any of these examples, or variants of them, could be used more widely and consistently; and whether there are other ways of providing help to the reader. Both conventional and electronic means of doing the job are likely to be within the inquiry. *23 June 1997.*[26]

From this clear discussion about the nature of laws, it derives that an Act is not designed to offer the things that other forms of writing offer, information, explanation, argument, etc. A normative text cannot employ all the usual techniques of writing, as in the case of writing the same word, phrase or sentence twice with the purpose of emphasizing them. As a consequence, the language of legislative texts is fixed and clear, with every word assumed to have a purpose, with all words assumed to count and have an equal weight. Nonetheless, as Bowman observes

> in the case of many Bills there is no 'right' structure. There are often several possible ones, and the choice is up to the drafter. He will take pains to present the material in a way that is logical and that puts the reader to as little trouble as possible (2006: 5).

This is all the more evident in the case of the language used. In 2004 the House of Lords Select Committee on the Constitution highly praised the efforts of parliamentary counsel in rendering bills in a more accessible language, as we read in *14th Report of Session 2003–04*, Chapter 4, The Legislative Process, Sections 76 and 77:

26 https://publications.parliament.uk/pa/cm199798/cmselect/cmmodern/190i/md0108.htm

76. For Parliament to examine bills effectively, it needs to understand them. That encompasses the purpose of the bill and the provisions designed to achieve that purpose. For many years, the way in which bills were brought before Parliament was not conducive to aiding understanding. Bills were often drafted in fairly obscure language with no accompanying material to explain the provisions and no clear explanation of the effect of provisions that substituted words for those in earlier Acts. Members were dependent on the Minister's speech on Second Reading and explanations offered in response to probing amendments.

77. Recent years have seen some notable and very welcome changes. One has been in the drafting of legislation. There has been far greater emphasis on the accessibility of language, while ensuring that the language is such as to be amenable to judicial interpretation. We recognise the balance to be drawn between, as Baroness Amos put it, legal accuracy and user-friendly language (Q 21). We commend the efforts of parliamentary counsel in rendering bills in more accessible language.[27]

and Chapter 6 – Connecting with the Public, Sections 194 and 195:

194. We have emphasised that Parliament does not act in a vacuum and that it is crucial that the views of informed opinion and those affected by a bill— categories that are not mutually exclusive—are heard when the measure is being considered, rather than simply after it has taken effect. The natural source for representing those views will continue to be Members of Parliament, alerted by constituents or bodies inside or outside their constituencies. Not all parliamentarians, though, will have the time or resources to pursue every matter drawn to their attention. Indeed, the more they are lobbied, the greater the difficulty in finding time to do justice to all the representations made to them. We believe that it is desirable to ensure that complementary means exist for citizens to be able to make their views known when a bill is being considered.

195. There is clearly a problem in terms of enabling citizens to be involved. As the Hansard Society reminded us, citizens, whether working individually or as part of a group or network, rarely participate in the process. There were, they suggested, various reasons for this lack of involvement. These included: very limited public knowledge of the lawmaking process; consultations are not well advertised; the language throughout the legislative process is often prohibitively obtuse and technical; and there is no established mechanism for public concerns to be placed on the parliamentary agenda (Vol. II, p. 130, para. 22).[28]

27 https://publications.parliament.uk/pa/ld200304/ldselect/ldconst/173/173.pdf
28 *Ibid.*

The general idea behind this Report is the need to express policy decisions in language that is as precise, clear and simple as the circumstances allow.

Over the last decades, guidance on drafting have been proposed and various developments are taking place in the legislative drafting within the UK institutions. Claiming that 'in using the techniques that are available to him, there is no automatic solution and everything requires judgment. Language and techniques change all the time, and I hope they always will. In short, legislative drafting is more an art than a precise science' (2006: 8), Bowman concluded that a golden rule is that drafters should think about each case, and the corresponding text, on its merits.

Until recent times, legislative drafting has been viewed as a mere skill served by government lawyers. In the enlightening article 'Legislative drafting: a new sub-discipline of law is born' written by Helen Xanthaki (2013) and which recollects most of the her long-lasting research done in the field of drafters, legislative drafting and techniques, she provides useful information about the development of drafting legislation over the last decades and offers an interesting perspective from which the real nature of legislative drafting might be considered. Historically, as she claims,

> the idea was that the drafting of legislation was nothing more but know-how learnt via mentoring by brilliant lawyers whose was to basically switch the table round from the normal lawyer's task of statutory interpretation of existing legislation to the extra-ordinary task of drafting legislation with a vision on how this would be interpreted by the others. But things have changed. Legislation became the focus of regulation, replacing the common law in the preference of regulators (2013: 57).

Among the probable causes that produced this change is the sudden popularity of legislative enactments[29] produced by an increasing legal

29 *Statutory Law* is 'the law that exists in legislatively enacted statutes especially as distinguished from common law' (Merriam-Webster Dictionary). *Statutory Law* is the term used to define written laws, usually enacted by a legislative body. Statutory laws vary from regulatory or administrative laws that are passed by executive agencies, and common law, or the law created by prior court decisions. Unlike common law, which is subject to interpretation in its application by the

globalization leading to an emphasis on international statutory law (i.e., treaties etc., and the subsequent national implementation via national statutory law) and the fact that statutory law has become the main method of regulation. This new regulatory environment has invited a detailed study of statutory law from its conceptualization to its implementation, with new questions such as the nature of legislative drafting as a new discipline, its main characteristics and main elements.

The definition of legislative drafting continues to be under debate. Is it an art, an intellectual activity, a technique, or something more? Given the fact that legislative drafting entails both elements of art and elements of science, drafters first should identify all relevant circumstances and rules for each of the cases that need to be regulated and then, they should propose the most appropriate rule for that case or situation.

In this respect, Xanthaki (2014) identifies *phronesis,* i.e., the human intellectuality that Aristotle[30] defines the praxis of subjective decision making on factual circumstances, as the practical knowledge that responds to a concrete situation, doing better than abstract or general theories that conventionally prescribe what is right or wrong. In this way, practical knowledge relies on a kind of immediate insight, rather than more formal inferential processes (Cheng and Holoyoak 1985;

court, statutory laws are generally strictly construed by courts. Strict construction means that courts are generally not able to read between the lines of a statute in order to liberalize its application. Rather, they will be bound by its express terms. As legislative enactments, statutory laws follow the usual process of legislation. A Bill is proposed in the legislature and voted upon. If approved, it passes to the executive branch (either a governor at the state level or the president at the federal level). If the executive signs the Bill it passes into law as a statute. If the executive fails or refuses to sign the Bill, it can be vetoed and sent back to the legislature. In most instances, if the legislature again passes the Bill by a set margin it becomes a statute. Statutes are also recorded, or codified, in writing and published. Statutory law usually becomes effective on a set date written into the Bill. Statutes can be overturned by a later legislative enactment or if found unconstitutional by a court of competent jurisdiction <Statutory Law - HG.org>.

30 Aristotle defines all human intellectuality or science as *episteme*, art as *techne*, and *phronesis* the praxis of subjective decision making on factual circumstances or the practical knowledge of the subjective classification of factual circumstances to principals, and knowledge as *episteme* (Kenny 2010).

Seel 2012). The drafter chooses the appropriate rule and convention that reaches the aimed results according to the specific and practical context at any given time. In order to perform this task, Xanthaki (2013: 65) suggests legislative drafters to: (i) be aware of existing sets of rules and conventions, particularly those disciplining similar cases; (ii) identify the most relevant set of circumstances applicable to the problem; (iii) have the theoretical knowledge and practical experience to promote the rule or convention that best applies under the specific characteristics of the case. As she clearly states,

> let us clarify which are the rules of drafting, and what is the basis of the drafter's subjective choice when selecting the most appropriate one. In other words, which is the ultimate criterion whose correct application leads the drafter to the appropriate choice between rules and drafting conventions? What is quality of legislation? My definition of quality is neither technical, nor empirical. My definition of quality in legislation is functional. [. . .] And ultimately quality in legislation is effectiveness. Effectiveness is the criterion that drafters use when selecting the most appropriate drafting rule for the problem before them. This qualitative definition of quality in legislation respects and embraces the subjectivity and flexibility of both drafting rules and conventions and, ultimately, of *phronetic* legislative drafting (2013: 65).

Generally speaking, normative texts cannot produce adequate regulatory results without the synergy from the other actors of the policy process. The government seeks to implement its agendas by use of the policy process and the legislative process comes into play. It is within the legislative process that drafters go through each one of Thornton's five stages of drafting legislation (the author will consider this in Chapter 4). By taking this holistic picture of legislative process as a tool for regulation into account, one recognizes that the goal of both government and drafters is to achieve quality in legislation. And this statement reflects the key role of the drafter in the whole of the governing process, and strengthens the view that legislation is one of the key instruments offered to governments in their attempt to regulate. If we consider, on the other hand, the legislative process in relation to 'context' at different levels, such as the situated communicative event, the environmental framework (i.e., the workplace, the organization, the discipline), and the societal framework (i.e., the legal-political, socio-cultural, and linguistic frameworks), it becomes possible to reach a deeper understanding of the development and constant change of the final product, viz., the normative texts, over time.

On the basis of the premises developed here, the contextual level of the legislative process and the different, though interrelated, frameworks or levels will be considered in much more detail in the following chapter.

2 Professional discourse and legislation

2.1 Professional discourse and legislative drafting

The main assumption proposed in this book is that legislative drafting represents an example of professional discourse, where the propositions of specialized information, or knowledge of the actors participating in the legislative process, is translated into meanings, and such meanings are given as input to the rules and strategies of grammatical formulation. Discourse is the construction and organization of the segments of language above as well as below the sentence. It is units of language which may be bigger or smaller than a single sentence, but the meaning is always beyond the sentence (Fowler et al. 1979; Fairclough 1989, 1995, 2003; van Dijk 1997). The elements of grammar, lexis, and phonology still play a fundamental role, but they are reconsidered as a part of that multi-layered cognitive and socio-cultural phenomenon defined as 'discourse'. As Bhatia (2010) observes, this is particularly true within common law jurisdictions. Legislative drafters deal with a universe of human behaviour which is unlimited, in the sense that it is impossible to predict exactly what may happen within the human universe. Legislative drafting is a narrower concept to the civil law equivalent of law-making: law-making embraces the whole process of conceptualization of legislation until its very implementation and thus reflects the legislative process, whereas legislative drafting reflects the drafting process only. This does not imply that drafting is completely foreign to the legislative process. In fact, the drafting process is part of the legislative process, which in turn is part of the policy process (Stefanou 2011). Furthermore, the context of a legal document is often scrutinized to shed light upon the meaning of an ambiguous or obscure provision so that it may be interpreted as its government intended initially to be.

The aim is to make provisions that are as clear, precise, unambiguous, and all-inclusive as possible, whereas the nature and function of participant organization unsurprisingly influence the legislative actions. The implementation of legislation may be significantly influenced by a range of filtering agents at whom legislation is directed and who may constrain, adapt, and (possibly) modify the intentions that form the basis of the legislation approved in the first place. In this regard, modern legislative theory urges legislative drafters to bare the text from preliminary provisions and to start as early as possible with the regulatory message that the government is trying to convey to citizens. And, so, the pursuit of modern drafters is to share that message with the users of the legislation in a manner that gets them to be heard loud and clear (Stefanou and Xanthaki 2008).

It, therefore, becomes crucial to explore how linguistics may be of some help for the legislative drafters who want to know how a piece of legislation is structured in terms of lexico-grammatical and discoursal features. In this regard, pragmatics has achieved great progress forming an independent research field concerning the study of language use. As Gunnarsson (2009: 38) observes, 'The pragmatic analysis relates language practices to psychological, social and situational factors, thus also providing a basis for multidimensional understanding of linguistic actions'. For our purposes, it is interesting to recall how Habermas defines 'universal pragmatics' or 'formal pragmatics' based on the relationship between human communication and social evolution, placing language use in the scope of the universal human experience on communication (Thompson 1982).

Indeed, diverse ways of understanding pragmatics and, hence, many different definitions have been proposed to delimitate the meaning and scope of this discipline. Among them, the most comprehensive ways of understanding pragmatics is the 'perspective view' proposed by Verschueren (1999). He defines pragmatics as a general functional perspective concerning the whole complexity of linguistic behaviour. Thus, pragmatics concerns the multiple levels and aspects of language use. According to Verschueren (1999: 59–61), any communicative event is a process of choice making based upon three interrelated properties of language, namely, *variability, negotiability* and *adaptability*. More specifically,

- *variability* defines the range of possibilities from which choices can be made;
- *negotiability* is responsible for the fact that choices are made on the basis of flexible principles and strategies;
- *adaptability* enables linguistic choices from a variable range of possibilities that are defined contextual correlates of adaptability, such as the *structural objects of adaptability* (i.e., linguistic organization of communicative events), *the dynamics of adaptability* (i.e., the dynamic generation of meaning/content in communicative events), and *the salience of adaptation process* (some linguistic choices are made intentionally while others are almost automatic) (Verschueren 1999: 76).

Generally speaking, there seems to be a straightforward relation between specialized knowledge and specialized discourse if the latter is defined as the verbal expression of the former (Haspelmath et al. 2005; van Dijk 2007; Gunnarsson 2009; Gotti 2011). Professional knowledge or *phronesis* that requires specialized education or training, such legislative drafting, is a type of group knowledge as defined above. It is acquired, shared, and used among members of various kinds of scholarly or other specialized communities. These specialized communities are defined not only by their specialized knowledge, but also by their specialized social practices, including their specialized discourse and communication, as well as by a complex network of organizations and institutions such as governments, and professional groups such as the legislative drafters.

The methodology I present below is mostly inspired by Gunnarsson's (2009) analysis of professional discourse. In order to make it useful for the analysis of legislative drafting, I have modified and expanded her model. In particular, I rely on Gunnarsson (2009: 5) to define the term professional discourse, an expression that covers the texts produced and deployed in professional contexts and for professional purposes. This means that professional discourse includes written texts produced by professionals and intended for a multitude of recipients, such as other professionals with the same or different expertise, for semi-professionals, i.e., learners, or for non-professionals, i.e. laypeople.

Indeed, there are a number of features that are typical of professional discourse and differentiate it from non-professional discourse:

- professional discourse is situated and goal-oriented;
- professional discourse has a conventionalized form;
- professional discourse is produced within a socially ordered group;
- professional discourse on various societal framework systems;
- professional discourse dynamically changes.

Professional activities involve domain-specific knowledge and skills that are reflected in language and discourse (Swales 1985, 1990, 2016). From a pragmatic perspective, professional discourse can be analyzed in relation to the specific goal that it aims to achieve. In general, it takes place in situations that are specified in terms of communicative events, participants and place. As Gunnarsson clarifies,

> specialized, goal-oriented situated discourse can also, and not infrequently does, lead to asymmetries between the participants in the event: between experts and lay people, between experts and learners, between experts in different areas. Asymmetries have been analysed in many studies within applied linguistics, in particular asymmetries which cause comprehension problems, e.g. in communication between experts and lay people (2009: 7).

Being a part of a socially organized and structured set of activities within a specific workplace context, professional discourse might be seen as the product of collective process(es) characterized by a collective responsibility. In this respect, Gunnarsson (2009: 9) explores the construction of professional discourse in relation to cognitive, social and societal dimensions and its constant reconstruction in relation to various contextual layers, namely, the situated frame, the environmental framework and four societal frameworks. In the case of the societal frameworks, she identifies: (i) legal-political framework, (ii) technical-economic framework, (iii) socio-cultural framework, and (iv) a linguistic framework. More specifically,

- *a legal-political framework*: here, specific genres are attached to specific professional activities in given situations, which often also requires conventionalized discourse patterns to be used;
- *technical-economical framework*: technological progress is important for the dynamism within communities and organizations of various kinds, forcing them to develop a competitive and flexible structure, also in relation to the language used;

- *socio-cultural framework*: cultural patterns, attitudes and social values are constantly playing a key role in professional communication;
- *linguistic framework*: the language choice and language policy for work-related communication are even more crucial in shaping professional discourse.

From this perspective, professional discourse comes about as a structured set of activities performed by professionals from different levels within an organization, who share to a large extent a collective responsibility in each of the workplace unit. Diagram 1 illustrates the three dimensions in the construction of professional language and discourse, and their corresponding relation to:

- the 'domain of use' in the case of the cognitive dimension;
- the 'actors and group' in the case of the social dimension;
- the 'power and status' in the case of the societal dimension.

The cognitive, social and societal dimensions play a key role in the creation and change of language and discourse in the professions.

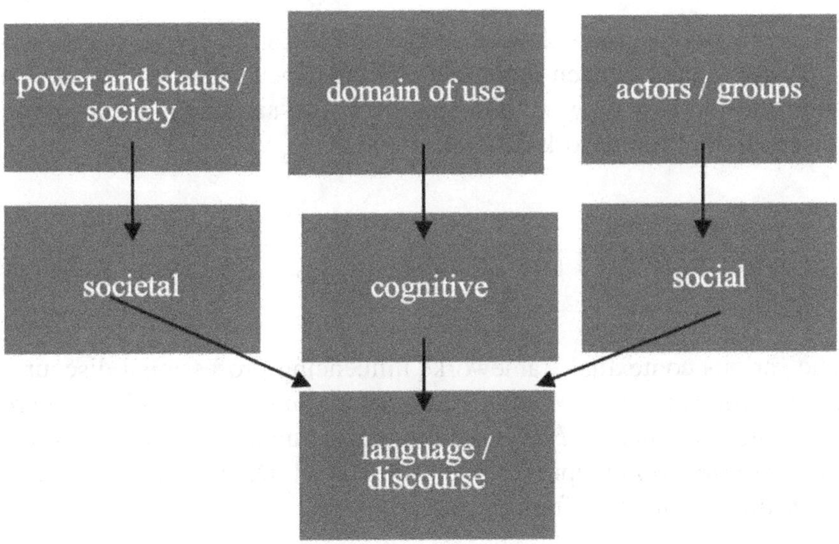

Diagram 1. Model of construction of professional language and discourse (Adapted from Figure 2.1 in Gunnarsson 2009: 20).

Much professional discourse is the result of the roles that cognitive, social and societal dimensions play in the construction of professional language. More specifically, the cognitive dimension is at play when the professional group constructs its own professional language that highlights aspects of the world in a specific way. Every professional group is formed by the organization of an internal role structure, group attitudes and group norms that are built into the cognitive structure specific to that professional group. In the case of legislation, for instance, the legal perspective entails rules and models concerning what is legally acceptable. And, legal language has developed a specialized terminology, sentence structures, text patterns, discourse content, etc., to deal with reality in a way that suits the purposes of the law:

(i) the social dimension is recognisable in the relationships every professional group develops with the surrounding world, that is, the functions it puts forth and the role played by its members in relation to the other actors and/or professional groups in society. This set of societal functions constructs and gives shapes to the discourse of each professional group;

(ii) the societal dimension deals with political and economic factors, such as power relations and status patterns.

According to the model developed by Gunnarsson (2009), these dimensions are related to each other, are context-dependent and also show a complex interplay between different levels that are recognizable within the contextual framework they operate in.

2.2 The contextual frameworks

The various contextual frameworks influencing professional discourse can be grouped into three levels: the *situated frame* representing a micro level, the *environmental framework* representing a macro level, and the *societal frameworks* representing a supra level. Diagram 2 below illustrates these contextual frameworks.

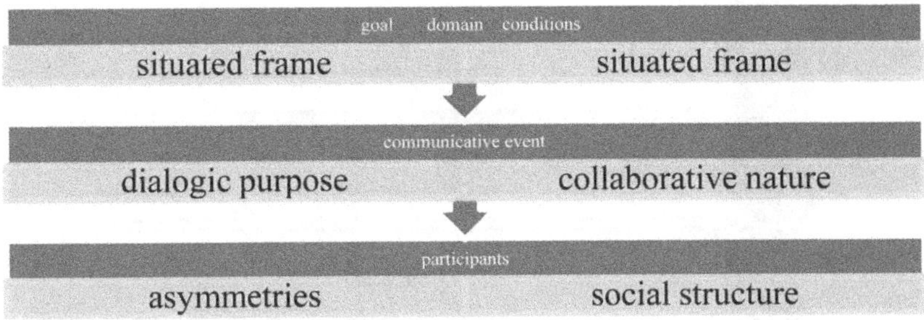

Diagram 2. Contextual frameworks.

Professional discourse is strongly influenced by the surrounding context in which it occurs. The domain of use, i.e. the professional context and the professional purpose, are thus constitutive of a situated frame. The analysis, therefore, is conducted at a micro level and is focused on the communicative event involving one or several participants taking place in the communicative event. We should notice that:

- a professional communicative event can involve one or several participants;
- professional activities often entail a shared, collective responsibility for the end-product, for instance, the legislative text, etc.;
- communicative events that are related to a common goal, form a communicative chain;
- possible asymmetries (i.e., power relations, status patterns, etc.) between the participants represent another structural feature.

At micro level, the analysis of professional discourse should include cognitive and social dimensions and as well as an account of the particular conditions of the situation. The reconstruction of professional discourse should also include the analysis at a macro level, that is, the environmental framework(s) or chains of events that are held together by common goals and constitute the communicative events. At a macro level, the analysis of professional discourse eventually should include both a social dimension and a societal/organizational dimension, as shown in Diagram 3 below.

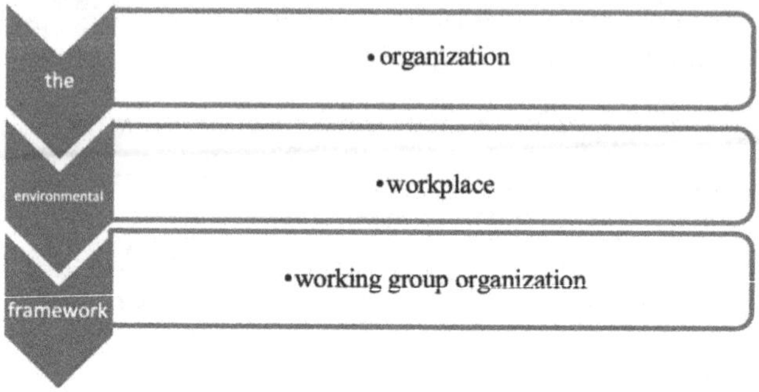

Diagram 3. The environmental framework.

To a large extent, professional discourse is regulated and moulded by other societal sub-frames or framework systems (FSs), such as the legal-political sub-frame (SF 1), technical-economical sub-frame, socio-cultural sub-frame, and a linguistic sub-frame. While at the same time it is an essential part of the construction of them, the relationship between professional discourse and the framework systems is thus dual. These framework systems constrain the text(s) produced within the context of professional discourse in different, thought interconnecting ways. Diagram 4 illustrates the relationship between the four frameworks and the corresponding levels, that is: politics, legislation, education, welfare and the press (FS 1); culture, ideologies, ethics, societal values (FS 2); economy, technology, production, job market (FS 3); linguistic rules, language conventions, language dominance (FS 4).

Beginning from FS 1 (Diagram 4), professional discourse is constrained by the legal system and by the political framework at local, national and supranational levels. Politics and legislative traditions are reflected in legislation, laws and regulations which regulate professional discourse (Zamboni 2018; Malyuga 2020). In the case of the political framework, three dimensions play a crucial role: (i) the institutional dimension, (ii) the normative dimension, and (iii) the process-related dimension. The institutional dimension brings about the action of various institutional and non-institutional actors such as the legislature, the government, political parties, social movements, public media, etc. The normative dimension entails the definition of basic societal values and objectives geared towards a practical realization through normative

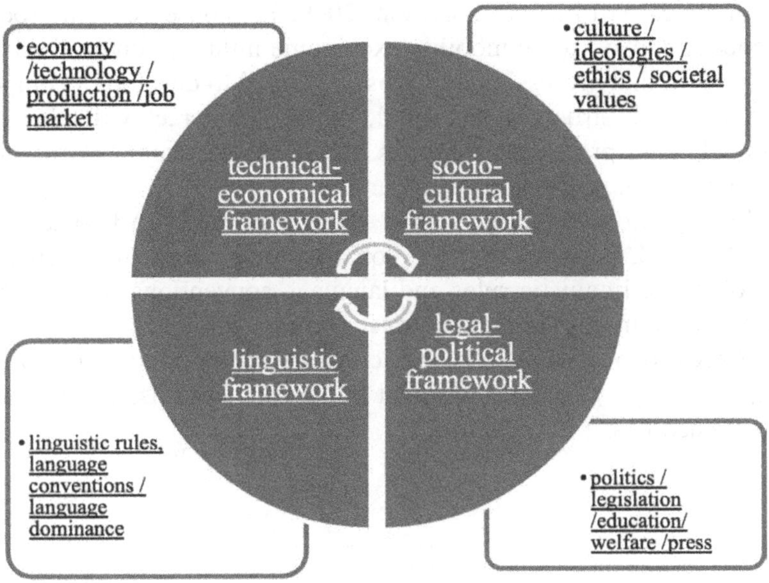

Diagram 4. The Framework Systems: legal-political (FS1), socio-cultural (FS2), technical-economic (FS3), linguistic (FS4).

texts. Then, the process-related dimension involves the formation of the political ideas and purposes through the implementation of the social power and authority and, eventually, generating conflict and consensus. If we attempt to analyze laws and regulations through the above mentioned three dimensions, we can see that from an institutional perspective, the professional discourse is expressed primarily through two factors: the establishment of specific state bodies legitimized by means of their specific organizational structure and, functioning, and legislative traditions where legal solutions are formed through the functioning of state bodies and individuals.

All the same, professional discourse is constrained by FS2 where culturally formed ideas, ethical codes adopted in a particular professional environment reflect, to a large extent, ideologies and ethics which form the backbone of the societal ethical system and these are in turn reflected in the social values of professionals and of professional groups at various levels (Swales and Rogers 1995; Talmy 2017).

In the case of FS3, Gunnarsson (2009: 126) observes that product advances and workforce mobility exert some influence on professional discourse in that professional groups are forced to develop 'a competitive and flexible structure' that should be able to interact with other professional, semi-professional groups and laypeople using an attractive and competitive professional discourse.

Finally, professional discourse strongly depends on FS4 to relate with the local, national and the global language community creating and following linguistic rules and language conventions which (either directly or indirectly) influence text in professions.

Professional discourse is thus constructed and reconstructed in a complex interplay between different framework systems, as Diagram 5 below illustrates.

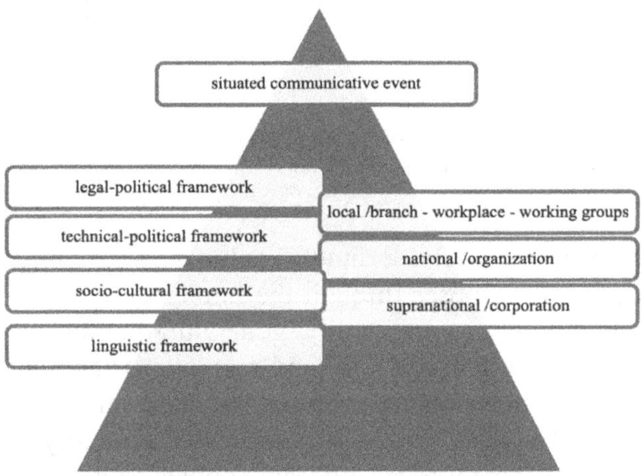

Diagram 5. The contextual reconstruction of professional discourse.

All the linguistic and non-linguistic factors related to a communicative event are within the field of context.

Generally speaking, the context within which social interaction occurs, largely shapes the communicative event participants are involved in. Furthermore, people construct versions of their social world through the instrumentality and functionality of language (Potter and Wetherell 1987; Billig 1997; Taylor 2001; Potter 2003; Willig 2013). In conversational analyses, the concept of positioning has been a key concept in understanding the role context and culture play in social interactions (Davies and Harré 1990; Harré and Moghaddam 2003). Clusters of rights and duties are available to participants involved in social interactions that shape their discourses in professional contexts and assign them specific roles to play (Tirado and Galvez 2008). Yet, these positioning roles in discourse are not static and can change according to the context within which participants take part, such as the discourse environment, time, space and circumstances (Baffour Adjei 2013).

From the point of view of the analysis developed here, professional discourse results as a context-dependent product because it is strongly influenced by legal-political, technical-political, socio-cultural, and linguistic frameworks that interact at a different level within a situated communicative event.

Among the specificities of professional discourse that will be considered in the following chapters, one needs to pay particular attention. Gunnarsson labels this characteristic 'the conventionalized form of professional discourse', where 'practices established within a profession are created to attain professional goals in specific situations, which means that they become strongly conventionalized' (2009: 7). In this regard, legislative texts represent a typical example of professional discourse which is highly conventionalized. Here, a specific genre is attached to legislative professional activities, that requires conventional discourse patterns. To some extent, these patterns come from the rules shaping discourse that have been issued by the legal system of the state governing the professional activity, i.e., the legislative drafting. Not only is the content organization of normative texts to a great extent conventionalized, but also the structure of argumentation is by the members of the drafters' community learnt and internalized. In other words, the way in which they organize and structure the normative text follows specific discourse patterns that are recognized as proper for the normative texts and accepted by members of the participant at the communicative event (e.g., government, legislative drafters, agencies, administrators, laypeople, etc.).

Legislative drafters deal with an unlimited universe of human behaviour, in a sense that it is impossible to predict exactly what may happen in the real world (Bhatia 2021; Endicott 2022). Law-making embraces the whole process ranging from the conceptualization of legislation until its very implementation, whereas legislative drafting is limited only to the drafting process. This does not mean to say that drafting is completely foreign to the legislative process. In fact, the drafting process is part of the legislative process, which in turn is part of the policy process (Stefanou 2011; Xanthaki 2014). At this point, it becomes crucial to consider the context of a legal document, and/or the legislative discourse, in order to shed light upon ambiguous and obscure provisions. In linguistics, 'discourse' means the construction and organization of the segments of language above and below the sentence.[31] The meaning is always beyond the sentence (Fowler et al. 1979; Fairclough 1989, 1995, 2003; van Dijk 1985, 1997, Goddard 2009). The elements of grammar, lexis, and phonology play a fundamental role, but they are reconsidered as a part of a multilayered cognitive, social, and cultural phenomenon (Fairclough 1989; Wodak and Meyer 2001; Geeraerts and Cuyckens 2010).

2.3 A theoretical model for the contextual analysis of legislative drafting

Over the last few decades, scholars analyzing communicative events in professional settings (Candlin 1997; Wenger 1998; Mertz 2007; Candlin et al. 2017) generally agree on the idea that professional discourse consists in any spoken, written or visual form constitutive of social and domain-specific contexts, and formed and used by professionals with special training in order to perform interactional and normative functions (Kong 2014).

Professional discourse is highly conventionalized and this aspect makes any professional group different and unique from any other

31 The Oxford English Dictionary (OED) defines discourse analysis 'a method of analyzing the structure of texts or utterances longer than one sentence, taking into account both their linguistic content and their sociolinguistic context; analysis performed using this method.'

professional group. As clearly observed by Eckert and McConnell-Ginet (1992: 464) a community of practice is 'an aggregate of people who come together around mutual engagement in an endeavour. Ways of doing things, ways of talking, beliefs, values, power relations – in short, practices – emerge in the course of this mutual endeavor'. Needless to say, a doctor does not use the same type of discourse as an engineer. All the same, the conventionalized trait of their communicative messages is also part of what distinguishes professional discourse from the language used in everyday life; for instance, we do not expect doctors, who are presenting the results of their research on the occasion of a medical conference, to use language in the same way as they do when they chat with family and friends during their leisure time.

In the case of legislative texts, there is a plurality of actors with specific abilities who intervene in different stages of the production of norms as the result of the legal expression of a public policy. Among them, one of the most challenging roles is that of the legislative drafter (Zapatero Gómez 2019). The description of the variety of actors playing a role throughout the legislative process and the context base of the UK legislation will be provided in Chapter 3.

Constrained by the legal-political framework at local, national and supranational levels, legislative drafting is deemed to be strongly influenced by government policy and the legislative traditions that are reflected in the laws and regulations which regulate professional discourse. Looking at the text-formation and its end result, i.e., the normative text, there is more than a mere linguistic product. In reality, 'the linguistic factor', Gunnarsson observes

> is very much intermingled with other factors. Writing, or rather text production, is constrained by so many social and societal factors that the linguistic factor seems to be a minor one (2009: 124).

She believes that also the composition of the working team groups and the various contextual frameworks in which the text is constructed, make the text more or less readable, more or less comprehensible. In this regard, I start from Gunnarsson's (2009) claim that the analysis of a collective writing process, such as law-drafting, should consider both cognitive-rhetorical aspects and sociolinguistic factors.

This study provides the assumption that legislative writing, like other types of text writing, is surrounded by a consistent variety of situational factors, such as:

- why a legislative text is produced;
- when a legislative text is produced;
- whom the legislative text is addressed to;
- which form/way (i.e., formal, elaborate, etc.) a legislative text takes from its conception till its final production.

Though more formal and elaborate, the writing process involved in normative texts might be assumed to be similar to those involved in writing a poem, an article, or a letter: thoughts must be generated, mentally organized, and translated into a text. Then, texts must be assessed and eventually revised. Being a consistent collective writing process, legislative drafting needs to be analyzed in its own social and societal contexts. More specifically, the factors that have to be considered can be listed in:

- social variables at group level, i.e., the professional and social background of the members of the drafting committees and the formal and informal social order within the groups;
- contextual frameworks surrounding the legislative drafting process that represent the particular conditions under which normative texts are produced;
- the target readers of the normative texts.

Thus, a sociolinguistic analysis of law-drafting needs to consider who the actors involved in the legislative drafting view as their targeted readers, and this view might be related to the attitudes among professionals and experts to comprehensibility issues and to their readership. As Durant and Leung (2016) observe, social aspects, such as class, job, age, geographical area, etc., eventually overlap within the context of language use. This is all the more evident in the case of legal language:

> The relative difficulty involved in acquiring legal language as a variety also matters, because law is not simply a semantic field such as the weather or geometry, but a professional practice steeped in tradition, subject to intense educational selectivity, and respectful of accentuated hierarchy. Law as a field exhibits complex

> shadings of language use among different institutions, topics, practitioners and purposes. Such semiotic micro-variation signals professional and social relationships both within law and between the legal system and the wider public who are subject to law in a given legal jurisdiction (Durant and Leung 2016: 5–6).

The societal frameworks that influence and constrain legislative discourse can be found in the linguistic and socio-cultural aspects of a specific legal and political context. Furthermore, it is possible to distinguish between macro- and micro-societal factors: the whole legislative process governing any given system and its language represent the macro-societal factors, whereas micro-societal factors might be seen in the specific and, perhaps contingent, situation surrounding the group of professionals working on the legislative process. More specifically,

- starting from the macro-societal factors, it is important to look at the drafting system governing the legislative process. In other words, questions like the following have to be posed and answered: How is this system constructed? Does it progress in a series of distinct stages? Is it a collective writing process or not? Is the normative text written by lawyers? Do groups outside of the legislative process influence the drafting process? How much value is attached to tradition? How are normative texts published? The first macro-societal factors to be considered are the legal system and the political structure governing the legislative process. For instance, looking at the role politicians play in drafting normative texts. Then, it is important to recognize the influence exerted by other actors (i.e., groups of interest, representatives of different social classes, etc.) in the drafting process. To complete the picture on macro-societal factors, we need to consider the role played by the linguistic factors. When writing normative texts, professional groups taking part in the drafting process operate within the linguistic system (lexico-grammar components, textual structures, vocabulary, etc.) available and applicable in that professional context;
- in the case of micro-societal frameworks, the attention is directed towards the particular situation in which legislative documents are produced. Needless to say, the temporary political, economic and social context might lead to controversial decisions that will end in different kinds of laws. Even the drafting situation might vary, with

some normative texts made and passed with urgency, and others taking years to be done. In the case of most normative texts there exist similar related laws in the country or antecedent laws. Looking at the linguistic choices, we might find certain traits unique to each law, or at least to each field of law (e.g. the language of contracts and the language of labour law and taxation law); eventually, the attitudes towards language change tend to be different among lawyers with different areas of expertise (Tiersma 1999; Bhatia 2021).

The analysis conducted here on the legislative drafting process of UK Primary legislation[32] (i.e., Acts of Parliament) combines cognitive-rhetorical and sociolinguistic traditions (Flower and Hayes 1981, 1984; Xanthaki 2014). The five stages of text production within classical rhetoric (invention, arrangement, style, memory and delivery) have been adapted to modern cognitive theories (Talmy 2006; Gunnarsson 2009). According to sociolinguistic theories (van Dijk 1993; Hudson 1996; Fairclough and Wodak 1997; Wodak and Meyer 2001), talking and speaking involve a continuous adaptation to the 'local group' and, to a large extent, to the 'discourse community'. In this regard, Swales (2016: 11) writes,

> The term *discourse community* has been widely used and discussed (sometimes critically) by scholars in applied language studies as a way of recognizing that communications largely operate within conventions and expectations established by communities of various kinds. As this interest in the concept has proliferated, we have come to see that these communities are, in fact, differentiated by various factors, such as how localized they are, what origins they have had, and what types of activity are central to their existence.

When producing a text, there occurs a relatively conscious or unconscious adaptation to the norms and attitudes of the discourse community which the members are part of. In the case of a text produced in different steps by various groups of professionals, i.e. collective writing, additional negotiations about the content structuring, wording, layout, etc., happen during the drafting process. This implies that not only does

32 UK Primary legislation is the general term used to describe the main laws passed by the legislative bodies of the UK, including the UK Parliament <https://www.parliament.uk/site-information/glossary/>.

the final text reflect the aims, knowledge, norms and attitudes of the members of professional groups involved in the process, but also the interaction among them throughout the same process. In this regard, Gunnarsson (2009: 133) uses the expression 'legal working group' when referring to a group formed by the committee members, where the members involved consist of both professionals and semi-professionals in relation to legislation. From Gunnarsson's (2009) perspective, legislative writing involves an adaptation to the professional group and, more generally, to the legal 'communicative community'[33] which is the expression she uses to indicate the 'discourse community', and within the same community to those who operate in the public sphere. In particular, she proposes a three-step cognitive-rhetorical approach. More specifically,

- Step 1 consists in the construction of a text, and includes both generating ideas and transposing them into words. In the case of the legislative drafting process, the members of the professional community become involved in a continuous discussion on the content of the draft, with different formulations representing different contents;
- Step 2 consists in editing the text and covers the whole legislative drafting process, from the written notes and explanations to the final normative text;
- The third and final Step consists in the act of considering the final draft again in order to asses it, to make changes to it, the so-called *reviewing* process that also occurs in normal writing procedures (Flower and Hayes 1984).

It needs to be stressed that in the case of professional writing done collectively by various groups within the same discourse community, the drafting process consists in a continuous adaptation to the various groups and the public sphere of the discourse community. The drafting

33 As Gunnarsson (2009: 133) explains, she uses 'the term "communicative community" (instead of "speech community" or "discourse community") to mark that both spoken and written communication, as well as both contact and distant communication, are referred to'.

of normative texts, for instance, is a collective process where 'the preparation of the draft text is done by one person, in most cases the secretary, who assumes the role of interpreter and combiner of different ideas. Then, the representation of the text is made collectively by the members of the drafting commission. The chairperson and the politicians have decisive roles, and the members of the commission contribute by reviewing the issue from their perspectives and possibly extending the content of the text' (Gunnarsson 2009: 134).

By a comparison between individual writing and collective writing, the main differences consist in that: (i) the topic is considered from a multitude of angles, (ii) different concepts and various versions of the draft are explored, and (iii) different goals and potential outcomes are considered. A clear description of this scenario can be found in Gunnarsson (2009: 136), where she observes that

> construction of the text thus becomes a multifaceted exploration of reality and imagining what might take place in the future. All of the representatives try to get the others to accept their perspectives. They argue for their own points of view, by presenting different experienced or imagined cases. They build up whole scenarios. It is a time-consuming matter to construct a collective text representation.

As the following description of professional writing will show (Diagram 6), various groups of professionals crowd the discourse

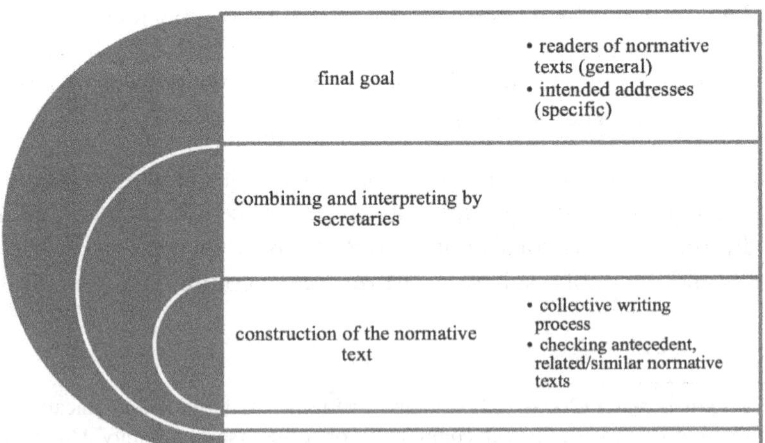

Diagram 6. Professional writing – the collective legislative drafting process.

community governing the legislative process. Lawyers, politicians, representatives of different public organizations, and drafters play a role in this process, and they actively take part in the construction, editing and reviewing phases of the final text.

In this model, the legislative drafters have to achieve some goal. They need to direct the text towards a specific group of people, the intended readers of the normative text. Yet, normative texts are produced in compliance with different actors playing their role at different levels of the drafting process, such as the government responsible for the policy decisions, and the departmental teams, who are staffed with the professionals performing the tasks of preparing legislation and taking it through Parliament.

Looking more closely at professional documents, we find that another key element is the comprehensibility problem that results in various comprehension levels depending on the properties of the text. In this regard, Gunnarsson (2009: 101) identifies: (i) a superficial level represented by typography and syntax, (ii) an intermediate level represented by semantics, and (iii) a deeper level represented by pragmatic factors, such as 'perspective and function-orientation'. As far as the superficial level is concerned, Gunnarsson provides an interesting correspondence between text level and comprehension level (Table 1).

Table 1. Text and comprehension levels.

Text level	**Comprehension level**
Superficial level: typography Superficial level: syntax	The addressee / The reader recognizes the letters The addressee / The reader comprehends the individual words / the syntactic relationships
Intermediate level: semantics	The addressee / The reader comprehends the individual sentence in terms of its structural and conventional meaning / sentence-semantic
Deeper level pragmatic: function-orientation and perspective	The addressee / The reader understands what actions the text should direct towards

Likewise, different reading purposes may direct the reading process towards different text levels. As Table 2 shows, the reading purpose directs the process towards a focus on different text levels. The processing of more superficial levels is overtaken by deeper text levels, and different text levels are responsible for the diverse levels of comprehension.

Table 2. Processing text levels and reading purposes (Adapted from Gunnarsson 2009: 102).

Text level	Reading purpose	Reading process
Word semantics and syntax processed primarily. Typography auxiliary level	text and layout	the correct wording is related to the words and phrase structure
Syntax and sentence-semantics processed primarily. Typography auxiliary level	text content	the text is related to the message in itself
perspective processed primarily / semantics, syntax and typography auxiliary level	text producer's world description	the text is related to or induces a notion of the text producer's situation and their perception of the world
perspective processed primarily / semantics, syntax and typography auxiliary levels	action-oriented comprehension → indirect purpose	the text is related primarily to the addressee's own situation
function-orientation processed primarily / semantics, syntax and typography auxiliary level	action-oriented comprehension → direct purpose	the text is related primarily to the addressee's own situation, their perception of the world and alternative courses of action

Table 2 illustrates that the more superficial text level the addressee focuses on, the less important reading purpose they aim at. The theory Gunnarsson (2009) suggests is based upon a strong relationship between linguistic factors, such as typography, syntax and word-semantics, with the addressee's reading purpose and the corresponding reading process. This method of analysis becomes particularly useful when taking into account professional texts and, in particular, the comprehensibility of action-oriented texts such as legislative texts.

2.3.1 Legislative drafting and the situated communicative event

Legislation represents the main form of regulatory tools used by governments, either elected, appointed, or otherwise established. Its adoption by a 'formally authorized legislature'(Xanthaki 2014: 3) allows the policy process to commence the legislative process, being first translated into legal concepts and then transformed into normative texts. Legislation could aim at changing or preserving the existing structures at the political, economic, cultural or social level. Given the fact that these structures are the results of the actions of individuals or groups, legislation aims at directing people's actions as well. Eventually, legislation is one of the choices at the disposal of governments to implement their policy.

In the case of normative texts, the comprehension of the text by the addressees will require a *general legal knowledge,* such as lexico-grammar and textual conventions (i.e., the structuring of law texts, legal terminology, etc.), and a *specific knowledge* for the law text in question. With regard to the background knowledge, a further distinction does exist among the readers of legislative texts; the one between lawyer (legal representatives, administrative staff, public officer, etc.) and lay-people. In this regard, legislative texts can be read in order to obtain an overall picture of their content, to know how to act under specific circumstances, or to judge in specific situations. Table 3 illustrates the setting and the possible reasons for reading legislative texts in terms of the 'situational context', the 'reading purpose' and the subsequent 'outcomes'.

Table 3. Reasons for and outcomes from reading legislative texts (Adapted from Gunnarsson 2009: 106).

Situational context (SC)	Purposes (P) of reading legislative	Outcomes (O) from reading legislative texts
SC1. readers come across the normative text and want *to acquire knowledge* about it	P1. *the normative text is read in all its parts* in order to know the cases it regulates, the rights it assigns, and the duties it imposes	O1. *readers get some knowledge* about the normative text, for instance, they can use this knowledge for subsequent action

Continued

Table 3. Continued

Situational context (SC)	**Purposes (P) of reading legislative**	**Outcomes (O) from reading legislative texts**
SC2. readers encounter *a concrete case* and want to know how it is regulated by the legislation (for instance, a dispute between a dealer and a customer)	P2. *the normative text is not read entirely*. Readers look at the parts that discipline the concrete case they have encountered (for instance, the customer's rights and duties, the dealer's rights and duties, what exceptions are provided in the texts for both of them, etc.)	O2. *readers proceed in accordance with the provisions of the normative text*. They know what the normative text regulates in the concrete case they have encountered and/or might encounter

The setting in which the reading of legislative texts takes place, i.e. the situational context, can occur when one comes across a piece of legislation and wants to acquire knowledge about its content; for instance the cases it regulates, the categories of citizens it is aimed at, the rights and duties it assigns and imposes, etc., and eventually wants to use the information for subsequent actions. On the other hand, the situational context might be a concrete case which motivates the search for the normative text regulating it, reading the parts (Articles, Sections, etc.) in the text that discipline it, and operating in accordance with the provisions in the normative text that discipline the concrete case that have motivated the reading in the first place. Comprehension, therefore, is strongly linked to the situational contexts that orientate the reading to the entire text or some of its parts.

In the case of the rules provided in the normative text, a further distinction can made between the sphere of application of the rules and the rules of action or conduct they impose. The comprehension of the text requires the potential reader to link up the sphere of application of the rules with their own situational context. In other words, they should be able to identify the relevant rule(s) (P1 and P2), refer back to it when dealing with their own situational context (SC1 and SC2), and drawing the right conclusion for the subsequent action (O1 and O2).

Thus, the reading process of normative texts involves two main processes: the search process that consists in reading the text in order to find the general content (P1) or the relevant part/section of the text (P2), and the conclusion process that consists in obtaining some knowledge of a piece of legislation (O1), or knowing about the consequences deriving from the concrete situation that has motivated the reading in the first place.

2.3.2 Legislative drafting and the aim(s) of legislative texts

Legislative texts represent a means of shaping societal progress. At a micro level the aim of legislation is to either influence and/or direct people's actions. At a macro level the aim of legislation can be to maintain and/or alter the existing political, economic, and socio-cultural structures. As these structures are the product of actions performed by people or groups of individuals, if legislation aims at changing people's norms of behaviour, it thus represents an instrument of reform. On the other hand, if legislation aims at preservation, it maintains people's norms of behaviour from changing. If this latter is the case, legislative texts have the purpose of codifying the existing norms of society.

Taking Fillmore and Baker's (2009) description of the content base of texts that is mainly based on the implications coming from the performance of an action, Gunnarsson (2009) identifies three types of rules (Table 4).

Table 4. Types of rules (Adapted from Gunnarsson 2009: 101).

Rule class	**Field of application**	**Directions**			
		core	***type***	***content***	***addressee***
action rule	framework situation	acting party	right, duty prohibition recommendation, etc.	action + possible conditions	other party
definition rule	the whole legislative text (parts of the act)	concept	definition	content of the definition	acting party and/or other party
stipulation rule	framework situation	concept	provisions	–	acting and/or other party

More specifically:

- *action rules* describe the framework situation; that is, identify who is to perform the action (acting party), state the type of action(s) (right, duty, prohibition, etc.), describe the content (action, possible conditions), and indicate the addressee of the action performed (other party);
- *definition rules* indicate the various parts of the legislative text, express the idea behind the action, give the definition of the action, the content of the definition itself, and provide the identification of both the acting party and the addressee(s);
- *stipulation rules* describe the framework situation; that is, identify the overall legal concept behind the action, the implications (provisions), and provide the classification of both the acting party and the addressee(s).

The *field of application* and the *directions,* i.e. *core, type, content* and *addressee,* are explicitly stated for each class of rules. Then, the different types of rules are distinguished when the schema is applied to the Act by different verbs, such as modal verbs. For instance,

- in the case of action rules, *may...*, *is entitled to..*, *is authorized to.., has the discretion to...*, etc. are mostly present when giving a right; *shall* (archaic form)[34]..., *has a duty to...*, are typically used when imposing a duty or obligation; *may not*...are mostly present when imposing prohibition; *need not*... can be found in the case of stating exemptions, and *should*... are typically present in the case of recommendations;
- in the case of definition rules, *is meant* is a typically used verb;
- in the case of stipulation rules, typical verbs used are *shall apply...*, *shall not apply...*

At this point, it is worth mentioning that the modern trend among experts in legal drafting is to eliminate *shall* and replace it with *must* when imposing obligation (Garner 2011, 2013). Yet, some modern legal

34 When imposing obligation, the modern trend among experts in legal drafting is to eliminate *shall* and replace it with *must* (Butt 2013: 269).

writers still believe that *shall* has a place in legislative documents. In particular, they make a distinction between rules that express a 'command' and rules that are 'merely directory', that is, rules or provisions that require a certain course of action to be taken but that do not impose any sanction for breach (i.e., breach gives no rise to legal consequences). For this reason, they suggest legislative drafters to use *must* for obligation and *shall* for directory provisions (Butt 2013: 268–269).

Overall, this scheme could be of some help when analyzing the structure of legislative texts.

2.4 Legislative drafting and comprehensibility

Generally speaking, one of the main goals of legislative drafters is to pursue quality in legislation (De Benedetto et al. 2011; Xanthaki 2014). This idea encapsulates two important assumptions, in that the drafters play a crucial role in the governing process, and legislation is one of the 'last and least choices' (Weatherhill 2007) at the government's disposal to implement regulation. In order to pursue quality in governmental regulation, Xanthaki (2014) suggests visualizing legislative drafting as a pyramid whose levels represent different subgoals that are involved in achieving efficacy, i.e. the ultimate and larger goal that drafters should aim for is the 'efficacy' of legislation. Diagram 7 below shows the hierarchical position of the Xanthaki's 'virtues' (2014: 5) or subgoals to the efficacy of normative texts.

Situated at the bottom of the pyramidal representation of the subgoals for the legislative drafters there is *simplicity*. In Xanthaki's representation, simplicity of normative texts implies the use of plain language. As she explains (2014: 9)

> Plain English takes into account design and layout, as well as language, and means analysing and deciding what information readers need to make informed decisions, before words, sentences or paragraphs are considered. A plain language document uses words economically and at a level that the audience of the particular texts can understand. Sentence structure is tight. The tone is welcoming and direct. The design is visually appealing.

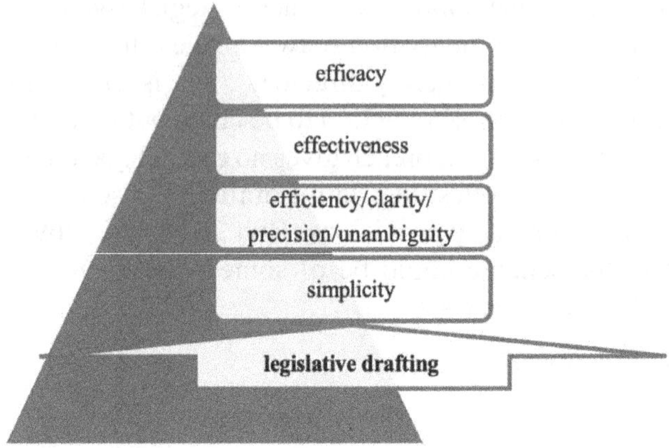

Diagram 7. Legislative drafting virtues (Adapted from Xanthaki 2014: 5).

The main problems usually identified by the Plain Language Movement are lengthy sentences, archaisms, passive constructions, superfluous words and unnecessary doublets (Gustafsson 1984; Gotti 2011, 2014; Gibbon and Griffiths 2017).[35] According to Eagleson et al. (1997), a plain language text uses only as many words as is necessary, avoids ambiguous wording, pompous expressions and convoluted sentence structure. Butt (2013: 102) indentifies the main features of plain language in three key features:

- clear and simple writing style;
- the grammatical use of English that most effectively presents the idea to the reader;
- a writing style that readers can understand in one reading and combines clear, concise expressions, an effective structure and good document design.

Claiming that the expression 'plain language' is rather inappropriate, because it might suggest 'a kindergarten style of language – on which

35 Legal doublets are two near-synonyms joined by a conjunction and used together as one term in legal language. They tend to retain the same word order – for example, *each and every*; each word in the doublet has roots in a different medieval language (Germanic Old English, Norman French, or Latin); they are often alliterative (*part and parcel*, *testament and will*, *freely and voluntary*).

patronises adult readers' (2013: 102), Butt describes plain language being more than simplified English. The phrase 'clear and effective for the intended audience' is the key assumption upon which plain language lies. The reader's level of understanding becomes an important issue to be considered in the final structure and language of normative texts.

Immediately above the first and lowest subgoal, i.e. *simplicity*, we find *efficiency, clarity* and *precision*. Literally speaking, *efficiency* means the capability of producing desired results with little or no waste (Merriam-Webster Dictionary). In the context of legislative drafting, efficiency means the ability of achieving the best benefits of legislative action with little or minimal cost. Not only does *efficiency* refer to the choice of the most financially appropriate solution, but also it is 'a quality *sine qua non* of the regulation, and consequently the legislation that has been selected as the tool for the achievement of the regulatory goals' (Xanthaki 2014: 8).

On the same level of the pyramidal representation of subgoals, and next to *efficiency* we find *clarity*, *precision* and *unambiguity*. More specifically,

- *clarity* means the quality of normative texts of being clear, coherent and intelligible;
- *precision* is the quality of normative texts of being exact and accurate in the use of terms and expressions or details;
- *unambiguity* means the lack of ambiguity in normative texts at the level of syntax (i.e., clear sentence structure and adequate organization of phrases and clauses) and at the level of the meaning of words (i.e., possession of one clear meaning for words).

Clarity, precision and *unambiguity* turn normative texts into comprehensible pieces of legislation for the final reader who, according to the specific situational context, comes across the normative text and wants to acquire knowledge about it or encounters a concrete case and wants to know how it is regulated by the legislation[36] (see Section 1.4).

36 Xanthaki (2013, 2014) claims that *clarity, precision* and *unambiguity* make normative texts more predictable and, for this reason, comprehensible for those who have the task of implementing legislation (i.e., administrative officers, courts of justice, etc.).

Thanks to the previous subgoals, i.e. *simplicity, clarity, precision* and *unambiguity*, a normative text can reach *effectiveness*, a quality that can be tested when the same text is produced

- predicting the possible results coming from the legislative text and considering them throughout the drafting and formulation process;
- providing a clear definition of the normative text's objectives and purposes;
- specifying the appropriate enforcement measures.

Hence, *effectiveness* results from a good balance between the normative text and its effects, and an 'effective normative text' is a law that is implemented and/or respected.

Then, the main goal for legislation is *efficacy*, which is placed at the top of the pyramidal representation of the legislative drafting virtues. Often confused with *effectiveness*,

> from the narrow point of legislative drafting [*efficacy*] can be defined as the capacity of a piece of legislation to achieve the regulatory aims that it is set to address (Xanthaki 2014: 6).

It might occur that a legislative text, though it matches the desired regulatory effects, decided in the first instance by the governmental policy, is wrongly implemented or improperly applied by the courts of justice. And one might conclude that the wrong implementation, as well as the improper judicial application, depends on the poor quality of the text produced by the legislative drafters. All the same, it might be possible that the poor quality of the text is a consequence of 'a fault in the content of the pursued policy' Xanthaki (2014: 6) or in a flawed consideration of the regulatory impact coming from its implementation and/or judicial application.

As *efficacy* is the final goal of the legislative process, legislative drafters can contribute by producing texts that are evaluated via the quality of *effectiveness*. And effectiveness in normative texts is assessed by testing their *simplicity, clarity, precision* and *unambiguity*. In this regard, the use of plain language and the more recent linguistic transformation (i.e., 'singular they') and textual reorganization of normative texts, which the author considers in Chapter 4, represent important tools for the achievement of *clarity*, *precision* and *unambiguity* in legislation.

Finally, Xanthaki's (2014) pyramidal representation of the legislative drafting qualities constitutes an interesting and useful tool for the description of the main principles of drafting and their position throughout the organizational representation of the legislative drafting process in the UK.

3 The UK Parliament

3.1 Westminster Palace

This chapter gives an account of the development of parliamentary sovereignty and the Palace of Westminster which has been the centre of power for over 900 years, beginning from the absolute rule by the sovereign, to Parliament claiming its authority over the UK Monarchy, and the modern democratic legislature of the present day.[37]

The origins of the modern UK Parliament stretch back to the Anglo-Saxon government from the 8th to 11th centuries. These are particularly evident in the *Witan* and the *Moot*. *Witan,* a word that belongs to the Old English,[38] also called *Witenagemot*, was the council of the Anglo-Saxon kings in and of England, whose composition and time of meeting were determined by the King. Attended by the greater nobles and Bishops, the *Witan* did not represent a popular assembly. Among its important duties, was to advise the king on all matters on which he chose to ask its opinion. Indeed, the *Witan* has the function of confirming the King's grants of land to both churches and laymen, giving its consent to the King's issue of new laws or new statements of ancient custom, and helping him deal with rebels and persons suspected of hostility. However, it cannot considered a popular assembly. Given its composition and duties, it closely resembled its successor, the *commune concilium* of the Anglo-Norman kings, with this latter body composed of baronial councillors who were bound to the King by feudal ties.[39] This larger

---

37 https://www.parliament.uk/about/living-heritage/evolutionofparliament/

38 Merriam-Webster Dictionary.

39 Witan | Anglo-Saxon council | Britannica.

group of noble advisors was later known as the *Great Council* and it formed the basis for the modern upper House of Parliament, today the House of Lords.

Moots, or regular meetings, for each county or shire were held under the Anglo-Saxons to hear and discuss local matters. More specifically, the *Shire Moot* was attended by the local lords and Bishops, the sheriff, and four representatives of each village and introduced the idea of representative government at a local level. After the Conquest, this meeting became known as the *County Court.*

Eventually the noble councillors of the *Great Council* and the local spokesmen of the *County Court* joined to form a Parliament of two Houses, the aristocratic House of Lords and the locally representative House of Commons.

The most important members in the Commons were the knights of the shire, who primarily expressed the interests of the gentry (i.e., the landed elite). During the 15th and 16th centuries, important institutional developments in Parliament took place, in particular in, its organization and record keeping. For instance, the records of Parliament, such as the business, votes and decisions of each day in the House of Lords have been recorded since 1510, and this official daily account, i.e., 'the Lords Journal', is still produced today.

In the case of the House of Commons, the official record known as 'the Commons Journal', started in 1547. Since the 18th century, the Journals of the two Houses of Parliament have been available since they were first printed and, nowadays, they are in most cases available online. They still represent the official record of Parliament.

The Westminster Parliament developed over one-thousand years from the Anglo-Saxon *Witan* to the reign of Elizabeth I. The political needs of the English King and his government are considered the main reasons for a natural development of Parliament that went through short periods of quick development. Today, the British Parliament is one of the oldest permanent representative assemblies in the world.[40]

The medieval Parliament met at the old Palace of Westminster. It burned down in a fire in 1834, and only a few buildings from the

40 https://www.parliament.uk/about/living-heritage/evolutionofparliament/originsofparliament/birthofparliament/

medieval palace remain. Westminster Hall is the most significant among the extant buildings, and it is still the largest medieval hall in England. Historically, it was the location of the most important law courts of England, and it was not used primarily for parliamentary meetings. The Commons did not meet in the Palace for over two centuries.

Eventually, the Westminster Parliament developed throughout Middle Ages from the meetings of the *Witan* to the Reformation of Law.[41] In this Chapter, the following Subsections provide a brief summary of the most significant moments in time of the parliamentary historical development.

3.1.1 Magna Carta

A general overview of the body that today represents the UK legislative body cannot start without mentioning the Great Charter and the role it played in the relations between the English Monarchy and influential powers in England in the 13th century. From the 7th century to the 11th century, councils of Barons and Bishops were called together by Monarchs to advise them on how to rule. Historians consider those councils as the prototype of the modern Parliament.

In England, relations between the King and these powerful advisers became a struggle for control. In 1215, King John was forced to agree to a Great Charter – Magna Carta in Latin – which limited the Monarch's authority. This was the first time an English Monarch formally recognized that their subjects had proper legal rights, such as the right not to be condemned without a trial. Magna Carta gave Barons and Bishops the right to be consulted before new taxes could be levied.

The very first example of a parliament in which representatives from towns and counties (mostly in England) were summoned together to discuss issues of national concern, was Simon De Montfort's Parliament. The Earl of Leicester, the French noble Simon de Montfort came to England in the 1230s and received lands from King Henry III, and married the King's sister becoming one of King Henry's main

41 https://www.parliament.uk/about/living-heritage/evolutionofparliament/originsofparliament/birthofparliament/

advisers. Simon De Montfort's Parliament is considered the earliest prototype of the modern Parliament because of its inclusion of both Knights and Burgesses, which extended the categories of people represented at a high level and allowed to take part in questions of the nation's concern.[42] The following is a brief account of the most salient changes and innovations in the historical development of the Westminster Parliament.

3.1.2 Burgess inclusion and selection

In the 14th century, Burgesses were the larger group in the Commons known as a Borough. The selection of burgesses depended on the will of the King who could turn a town into a parliamentary borough by means of a royal charter. Indeed, this practice could be established for any settlement, regardless of its size or importance and also influenced the ways in which local representatives might be elected for each borough (i.e., only those who had the franchise would be elected). In 1413 a statute regulated this practice by declaring that only the burgesses inhabiting the boroughs might be elected. As acknowledge by the historical reports of that time, Peers and landowners were still capable of influencing the selection of the representatives in the boroughs notwithstanding the enforcement of the statute.[43]

Members of the aristocracy kept their influence on the elections, of both knights and burgesses in the following centuries, while the growing cities of the industrial revolution had no representatives in Parliament. The burgesses' complaints for reform of Parliament in 1832 were mostly based on this lack of representation in the legislative body.

42 In 2015, the Houses of Parliament commemorated 750 years since the Simon de Montfort Parliament (1265) <https://www.parliament.uk/2015/>.

43 In 1422, the perpetration of this trend is confirmed by the fact that one-quarter of the elected burgesses was not living in the borough where they were elected <https://www.kent.gov.uk/leisure-and-community/history-and-heritage/kent-archives-and-local-history>.

3.1.3 'Model Parliament'

The first Parliament was officially summoned in 1275, when the then King Edward I convened his nobles and churchmen, and issued orders (i.e., writs) for the election of two representatives (called the 'knights of the shire') from each county and two representatives (known as 'burgesses') from each city and/or town. The main assignment of the representatives of the counties and towns was to listen to and approve the King's plan for new taxation. From this point on, King Edward I made Parliament's meetings a frequent event (at least for almost twenty years) and the official records of its proceedings and decisions were written up and sewn together into long scrolls called the *Rolls of Parliament*.[44] The Parliament of that time was called 'Model Parliament' as the attendance of two representatives from each county and two representatives from each city or town, became regular for (almost) all future Parliaments.

When Edward II, Edward I's son, was removed from the throne in 1327, Parliament started including representatives of the people.

3.1.4 Good Parliament

By the 14th century, the representatives of the counties and of the towns became an established component of Parliament.[45] Sitting together in one chamber and deliberating separately from the King and his nobles, they were known as the House of Commons. The then King Edward III issued a resolution establishing that a Parliament should be summoned annually. Throughout the 14th century, the Commons participated more actively in government, instead of simply accepting the taxation decisions of the King. In 1376, the Common's choice of Sir Peter de la Mare to act as the Common's spokesman before the King in joining its complaints with that of the Lords led him to be considered the precursor of the office of Speaker of the House of Commons.

In 1376, an important event occurred in the history of the UK Parliament: the Commons prosecuted before the nobles some of the

44 Parliament Rolls of Medieval England | British History Online (british-history.ac.uk).

45 Edward III came to the throne in 1327.

King's corrupt ministers, a process that was identified as impeachment. Since then, this procedure became frequent as Parliament acted against Edward III's heir Richard II, and for this reason Parliament was known as 'Good Parliament'.

3.1.5 House of Lords

In the 14th century, two types of Lords were sitting in Parliament: (i) the Lords Spiritual, and (ii) the Lords Temporal. Bishops and Abbots[46] formed the Lords Spiritual, even though not many Abbots were ever summoned to Parliament and most who were never attended. From 1305, two Archbishops and nineteen Bishops, later increased to twenty-four Bishops, were all summoned to every Parliament until they were excluded from Parliament in 1642 and eventually restored in 1661. They still sit in the House of Lords today. The Lords Temporal consisted of a small number of Earls and a much larger number of Barons. According to historical records,[47] the first reference to the nobility as Peers can be found in 1321. By the middle of the 15th century the Lords Temporal were further divided into five ranks, in descending order: Dukes, Marquises, Earls, Viscounts, and Barons. The Lords Temporal also insisted that a summons to the Lords was an honour due to their noble status, not just an expression of the King's will, which should be transferable to their inheritors in perpetuity.

For hundreds of years, membership of the House of Lords usually passed from father to son. Members were known as Hereditary Peers because they had inherited their position. By the 1950s, it was accepted that this needed to change. The *Life Peerages Act 1958* allowed Peers to be appointed for life rather than on a hereditary basis. The Act also allowed women to become members of the House of Lords. The proportion of Life Peers in the Lords increased dramatically when the House of Lords Act 1999 ended the right of Hereditary Peers to sit and vote

46 The superior of a monastery for men (i.e., the Abbot), no longer existed after Henry VIII abolished all the monasteries in the 1530s.

47 History of the House of Lords – UK Parliament.

in the Lords. The aim was to make the House of Lords more democratic and more representative.[48] In 2000, the independent House of Lords Appointments Commission was set up to recommend people for appointment as Life Peers.

It is important to mention that the first volume of the House of Lords Journal, appeared on 21 January 1510. Compiled during the first year of the reign of Henry VIII, this Journal has continued to be produced as the official record of the business and proceedings of the House ever since. Mainly written in Latin for the first half of the century, English was increasingly used after 1550.[49] The early versions of the Journal consisted of daily entries of Bills read and business done. From 1510, the Journal began to include lists of Lords present.

In 2003 the Clerk of the Parliaments made the decision to completely omit Latin entries from the Journal.[50]

3.1.6 House of Commons

In 1348, the Commons claimed financial primacy on the reason that it (not the House of Lords) represented the people.

In the 15th century, the House of Commons was recognized as having equal responsibility in making laws. From its inception, one of the main roles of Parliament was to act as a forum for hearing private petitions, such as requests for help or favours from the people, which were previously submitted to the King and Lords. Gradually, the Commons became the principal petitioners to the House of Lords, submitting petitions and addressing general problems which could be resolved by the King through new laws, i.e., the statutes. For this reason, petitioners

48 House of Lords Reform 1997–2010: A Chronology <https://www.parliament.uk/globalassets/documents/lords-information-office/house-of-lords-reform-1997-2010---28--june-2010.pdf>.

49 Until 1886, Norman-French was used for entries concerning Receivers and Triers of Petitions.

50 By this time Latin was only used to describe the sitting day and the date and the list of members present <https://www.parliament.uk/about/living-heritage/evolutionofparliament/originsofparliament/birthofparliament/collections/modernlordsjournal/>.

began to submit their complaints and requests first to the House of Commons, which wrote draft statutes (i.e., Bills) based on these petitions, to be then presented to the House of Lords.

In 1414, under pressure by the House of Commons, it was decided that neither the King nor the House of Lords should change the wording of any of the Bills submitted by the House of Commons, nor should any Bill become an Act (i.e., a statute), without the agreement of this latter. The development of Parliament has been characterized by the idea that the Commons rather than the Lords should have the final say on tax-raising powers since the very inception of the House of Commons. By the 19th century, though, the Lords had begun to challenge it.

In 1911, Members of the House of Commons argued that the people had voted for them, and, the *Parliament Act 1911* removed the House of Lords' authority to veto legislation on taxation and spending.

3.1.7 Elizabethan Parliaments

At this point it is worth mentioning the various interpretations historians have given to the developments of Parliament in the 16th century, especially concerning the Parliaments of Elizabeth I.

During the reign of Elizabeth I, Peter Wentworth became a famous Member of Parliament after he was arrested for arguing that the Commons should have the freedom to discuss whatever it wished, as in the case of the controversial topic of religion, without fear of retaliation from the Queen.

Some historians see in Wentworth an indication of the increasing importance of the House of Commons which was developing an organized oppositional stance to the Crown by that time. On the contrary, other historians have looked more carefully at the daily business of Parliament and do not see in it any sign of an extensive opposition, organization or ideology. In fact, under Elizabeth I, Parliament was summoned by the Queen and was a branch of royal government. Eventually, a few historians consider Wentworth and others like him as the symbol of the oppositional voices within the context of the 16th century where Members of Parliament mostly acted as the Monarch's servants.

3.1.8 The 17th century

The 17th century was characterized by a series of significant events. In 1625, Charles I became King. Believing that he could reign without the advice and consent of the legislative body, the King tried to rule without Parliament from 1629 to 1640. This led inevitably to clashes and, eventually, relations between Charles I and Parliament broke down in 1641. An episode worth mentioning is the one that occurred on 4 January 1642, when Charles I came to the House of Commons with soldiers to arrest a group of Members of Parliament (hereafter MPs) who he considered his political opponents. The Speaker at the time, William Lenthall, refused to tell the King where they were, saying

> I have, Sir, neither eyes to see, nor tongue to speak, in this place, but as the house is pleased to direct me, whose servant I am here; and I humbly ask pardon that I cannot give any other answer to what your majesty is pleased to demand of me.[51]

After this incident, the struggle between the King and Parliament led to the Civil War. Eventually, Charles was executed in 1649, with the subsequent abolition of the Monarchy and the House of Lords. Oliver Cromwell, commander of the army, took charge and ruled as Lord Protector (i.e., head of state) of the new republic (i.e., Cromwell Republic) for nearly 10 years. In particular, he found the House of Commons unmanageable and brought it to an end in 1653. Two years after his death, Parliament and the Monarchy were restored (this was not until 1660).

In 1689, the *Bill of Rights* set out exactly what was expected of the Monarch. It is an original Act of the English Parliament that limited royal power and established the supremacy of Parliament. In other words, the Monarch could not suspend or make laws, levy taxes or raise a standing army without Parliament's consent. Furthermore, people were allowed to petition the Monarch without fear of prosecution and have just treatment by the courts. Parliament was summoned regularly, with the declaration of the principles of free elections and freedom of speech within Parliament. The *Bill of Rights 1689* was used as

51 Oxford Dictionary of National Biography (oxforddnb.com).

a model for the US *Bill of Rights 1789*.[52] The main principles of the *Bill of Rights 1689* are still in force today (for instance, they are cited in legal cases).

3.1.9 The UK Parliament today

Today, the main functions of Parliament consists in examining the governmental actions through questioning ministers, debating and committee work, making new laws, holding the power to set taxes and debating current issues. Parliament is made up of three central elements: (i) the House of Commons, (ii) the House of Lords and formally (iii) the Monarchy.[53] In general, the decisions made in one House have to be approved by the other. When a Bill (i.e., a proposal for a new law, or a proposal to significantly change an existing law) has been approved in the same form by a majority in the House of Commons and the House of Lords it is formally agreed to by the Crown. This formal approval is known as Royal Assent. This transforms a Bill into an Act of Parliament, allowing it to become an 'Act of Parliament', that is a 'law in the UK'.

Before Bills are introduced into Parliament, there is often consultation or discussion with interested parties such as professional bodies, pressure groups and voluntary organizations.[54]

An Act of Parliament (i.e., a Bill that has been approved by both the House of Commons and the House of Lords and been given Royal Assent by the Monarch) creates a new law or changes an existing law. Taken together, Acts of Parliament make up what is known as Statute Law in the UK. Changes to the law happen through the passing of another Act or delegated legislation.[55]

---

52 Its influence can also be seen in other documents establishing the rights of humans, such as the *United Nations Declaration of Human Rights* and the *European Convention on Human Rights* <Bill of Rights 1689 – UK Parliament>.

53 Time has reduced the power of the Monarchy, and today it is broadly ceremonial.

54 Consultation paper – UK Parliament.

55 An Act can be repealed so that its provisions no longer apply. This happens when parliamentary committees examine UK laws and recommend the removal of out of date or obsolete legislation.

Even though new laws can originate from an MP or a Lord, most plans for new laws are introduced by Government. The King's Speech[56] at the opening of each parliamentary session includes many of them, as well as changes to existing laws.

In 1849, the UK Parliament changed from handwriting original Acts of Parliament to printing them. Texts of most Acts of Parliament as originally passed by Parliament since 1800 are available on the legislation.gov.uk website, as well as almost all current Acts of Parliament.

3.2 UK legislation

The first important distinction that needs to be considered when analyzing modern UK legislation and its legislative process, is the difference between Primary legislation and Secondary legislation.

'Primary legislation' describes the main laws passed by the legislative bodies of the UK, namely, Acts of the UK Parliament, Scottish Parliament, Welsh Parliament and Northern Ireland Assembly.[57] It also includes Acts passed by historical parliaments, other Primary legislation for Northern Ireland and Church of England Measures.[58] These types of legislation are generally named 'statutes' and the expression 'the statute

56 The King's Speech is the speech that the King reads out in the Lords Chamber on the occasion of the State Opening of Parliament. It sets out the programme of legislation that the Government intends to pursue in the forthcoming parliamentary session <King's Speech – UK Parliament>.

57 The analysis developed in this book relates to the Acts of the UK Parliament, mostly the 'Primary legislation'.

58 The Primary legislation for the Church of England Measures refers to the General Synod, which is the national assembly of the Church of England. Established in 1970 under the Synodical Government Measure 1969, the General Synod approves legislation affecting the Church of England, formulates new forms of worship and discusses matters of national and international importance (including the annual budget for the work of the Church at national level) <About General Synod | The Church of England>.

book' refers to the whole of the statute law presently in force. Certain legislative instruments called 'Prerogative Orders' are also referred to as Primary Legislation.[59]

'Secondary legislation', also called 'Subordinate legislation', is delegated legislation made by a person or body under authority included in 'Primary legislation'. In this case, ministers, the Crown or public bodies have powers conferred on them to make Secondary legislation. Statutory Instruments, Statutory Rules and Orders, and Church Instruments[60] belong to 'Secondary legislation'. 'Orders', 'Regulations', 'Rules' are the three main types of the UK Statutory Instruments.[61] Even though serving different functions, the Statutory Instruments all have the same legislative force. More specifically,

- the legislative instruments made since 1999 under authority contained in Acts of the Scottish Parliament are called 'Scottish Statutory Instruments'. Similar to the UK Statutory Instruments, the main types of Scottish Statutory Instruments are 'Orders', 'Regulations' and 'Rules'. Also, the 'Acts of Sederunt' and 'Acts of Adjournal' are rules of courts contained in Scottish Statutory Instruments;[62]
- 'Welsh Statutory Instruments' relate specifically to Wales. They are Statutory instruments which may be enclosed in Acts of the UK Parliament, Measures of the National Assembly for Wales or Acts of

59 'Prerogative Orders' are made by the Crown and the Privy Council under the royal prerogative. 'The Privy Council is the mechanism through which interdepartmental agreement is reached on those items of Government business which, for historical or other reasons, fall to Ministers as Privy Counsellors rather than as Departmental Ministers' <https://privycouncil.independent.gov.uk/>.

60 'Church Instruments' are issued by the Archbishops of Canterbury and York. Sometimes called 'Archbishops Instruments', they are referred to in annotations to the revised legislation and are mainly for the purpose of implementing Church Measures.

61 Indeed, no limit is imposed on the descriptions that may be given to Statutory Instruments. For example, 'Scheme', 'Direction' and 'Declaration' are typical Statutory Instruments. Prior to 1948, 'Statutory Instruments' were known as 'Statutory Rules and Orders'.

62 https://www.parliament.scot/

the National Assembly for Wales or Acts of Senedd Cymru.[63] Welsh Statutory Instruments are published in both English and Welsh languages;[64]

- 'Statutory Instruments for Northern Ireland', also called Statutory Rules of Northern Ireland, can be contained in Acts of the Northern Ireland Assembly and in exercise of powers granted in Primary legislation. They may also be made under authority contained in Acts of the UK Parliament or in the Orders in Council containing the Primary legislation for Northern Ireland.[65]

3.2.1 Parliaments and jurisdictions

At this point, it is important to give a brief account of the Parliaments and jurisdictions that are involved in the making of the UK Primary and Secondary legislation.

- The UK Parliament

To begin with, most of the Acts passed by the UK Parliament are *Public General Acts*. These Acts deal with issues of general public interest. Then, a small number of Acts constitute the *Private Acts*, which are further sub-divided into *Local Acts* (i.e., Acts dealing with matters of local interest) and *Personal Acts* (i.e., Act relating to specific persons, and are very rare in current legislation).

The UK Parliament provides laws (i.e., *Public General Acts*) for the whole of the UK, namely England, Wales, Scotland and Northern Ireland. Individually, Wales Scotland, and Northern Ireland have powers to make legislation for their own jurisdiction.[66]

---

63 The Welsh Ministers make subordinate legislation using powers given to them in enabling acts such as Senedd Acts, Assembly Measures and Acts of the UK Parliament.

64 https://senedd.wales/senedd-business/legislation/subordinate-legislation/

65 Typically, this event occurs during periods of direct rule by the UK government and it is still used for matters that have not been devolved to the Assembly <http://www.niassembly.gov.uk/>.

66 https://www.parliament.uk/

- The Welsh Parliament

The Welsh Parliament makes laws for Wales on specific issues and subject areas.[67] *Measures of the National Assembly for Wales* (passed from 2008 to 2011), *Acts of the National Assembly for Wales* (passed from 2011 to 2020) *Acts of Senedd Cymru* (passed from May 2020 onwards), and are published in both English and Welsh languages.[68]

- The Scottish Parliament

The *Scotland Act 1998* established the Scottish Parliament with the aim of debating issues that are known as devolved matters, and making laws for Scotland.[69] The *Scotland Act 2016* transfers further powers to the Scottish Parliament in areas such as taxation, welfare and elections.[70]

- The Northern Ireland Assembly

The Belfast Agreement of 10 April 1998 established the Northern Ireland Assembly.[71] One year later, the *Northern Ireland Act 1998* gave legal force to the Agreement. Afterwards, the Northern Ireland Assembly as well as a series of interrelated bodies were created. With the exception of reserved matters that remain the responsibility of the Westminster Parliament, the Northern Ireland Assembly has legislative and executive authority for all matters that are known as transferred matters.

3.2.2 Geographical extent

The expression 'Geographical Extent' describes the geographical area within the UK to which a piece of legislation (or part/section of a piece of legislation) applies. In the context of legislation, 'extent' is a synonym for 'jurisdiction'. For instance, the extent may be the whole of the

67 The UK government (or different bodies like local authorities) makes laws that apply to Wales in all the other subject areas <Home | GOV.WALES>.

68 https://senedd.wales/

69 Some issues remain the responsibility of the UK Parliament alone, and are known as 'Reserved Matters' <Devolved Parliaments and Assemblies – UK Parliament>.

70 https://www.parliament.scot/about/how-parliament-works

71 https://www.gov.uk/government/organisations/northern-ireland-office

UK territory or one or more of the three jurisdictions within the UK, i.e., England and Wales (which are not separate jurisdictions), Scotland, and Northern Ireland.

In more recent legislation, the word 'extent' is placed mainly to help readers find legislation relevant to each of the four geographical parts of the UK. Currently, each extent is represented by one of, or a combination of, England (E), Wales (W), Scotland (S) and Northern Ireland (NI). This information is usually displayed within revised legislation.[72] Without going into further detail on this topic, it suffices to say that, if there is a substitution of legislative text in a provision that extends to the whole of the UK, but the substitution affects Wales only, two versions result: one for the provision as amended to cover Wales only, and one for the provision in its unamended condition to cover England, Scotland and Northern Ireland.[73]

3.2.3 The UK Parliament and the legislative process

In order to make an outline of the parliamentary stages, one should begin from the introduction of a Bill in either the House of Commons, or the House of Lords. Overall, there are five key stages in each House. In the summary of the parliamentary stages which is reported below, the author puts forward a Bill that has been introduced in the House of Commons:

> 1st stage: First Reading (House of Commons, hereafter Commons)
>
> During the First Reading there is a formal presentation of the Bill. In other words, the title of the Bill is read out, the minister responsible for its introduction nods. After these formal passages, the Bill is deemed to have had its initial reading. During the First reading no debate is allowed, and the final text of the Bill is supplied by Parliamentary Counsel to the Public Bill Office the day before introduction and ahead of publication.[74]

72 https://www.legislation.gov.uk/search/extent

73 https://www.legislation.gov.uk/help#editorialPracticeGuide

74 There is a certain number of documents which support the Introduction of a Bill, such as the publication of an impact assessment for ensuring the appropriate availability of relevant older papers and revised editions of Acts.

The Office of the Parliamentary Counsel consists of experienced barristers and solicitors who assist government departments in preparing Bills. Government departments' proposals for new laws are sent to the Counsel who produce draft versions of the Bill for the department to approve. At times, several drafts are needed before the Bill is finally prepared and ready to be introduced in the First Reading.

2nd stage: Second Reading (Commons)

In the Second Reading, the MPs debate on general principles of the Bill. According to a traditional convention, the debate will not usually take place until two week-ends have passed following the First Reading. Usually, the minister responsible for the Introduction of the Bill will prepare the notes and briefing and will open and wind up the debate. Programme motions are normally taken immediately after the Second Reading without debate, and are prepared by the Parliamentary Counsel.[75]

3rd stage: Committee Stage (Commons)

During the Committee Stage the Bill is examined line-by-line, with the consideration of amendments, oral evidence heard and written evidence (eventually) published. Such detailed scrutiny and amendment of the Bill usually begin the week after Second Reading and takes place in a public Bill committee known as Standing Committee(s). In most cases evidence from experts and interest groups are taken, including those gathered from the minister responsible for the introduction of the Bill (and other officials) and before beginning clause-by-clause scrutiny of the Bill according to the programme resolution.[76]

4th stage: Report Stage (Commons)

Further opportunity to consider amendments made in Committee and to amend the Bill can be taken during the Report Stage. This can take place anytime from a week after Committee Stage. Being the final amending stage in the Commons, the debate and discussion have to be confined to amendments selected for debate, rather than a clause-by-clause examination of the Bill.

5th stage: Third Reading (Commons)

---

75 A programme motion can be used by the government to timetable a Bill's progress through the House of Commons by setting out the time allowed for debate at each of its stages. The motion is usually put forward for agreement immediately after a Government Bill has passed its Second Reading <Glossary – UK Parliament>.

76 The Committee Stage can also take place in 'Committee of the whole House', which is usually for Bills of a financial or constitutional nature or for 'emergency' legislation that is being taken forward under the so-called fast-track procedure <Glossary – UK Parliament>.

Third Reading consists in a final consideration. As a rule, it takes place immediately after Report Stage and represents a further chance for the House of Commons to consider whether the Bill, as a whole, should proceed (in the light of amendments proposed at Committee and Report Stages). No amendments are permitted at Third Reading.[77] At the end of the debate, the House decides (i.e., votes on) whether to approve the Third Reading of the Bill.

When a Bill is passed by the Commons, it is taken to the Lords by a Commons Clerk[78] for its First Reading:

1st stage. First Reading (House of Lords, hereafter Lords)

The First Reading is moved straight away without debate and the Bill is printed.[79] Where a Bill starts its passage in the Lords, the minister responsible for the introduction of the Bill reads out the title of the Bill at First Reading.

2nd stage: Second Reading (Lords)

Customarily, the Second Reading takes place two weekends after the introduction of the Bill. The procedure is rather similar to that taking place in the House of Commons, with some minor differences, including that the House of Lords does not vote on Second Reading, and no programme motion is taken in the Lords.

3rd stage: Committee Stage (Lords)

The Committee Stage begins once two weeks have elapsed since Second Reading. The requirement for producing notes and background for ministers on clauses and/or amendments is the same as in the House of Commons. As regards the suggested amendments, the government cannot restrict the subjects under discussion or impose a time limit. This is a major difference with procedure in the House of Commons.

4th stage: Report Stage (Lords)

During Report Stage, the House of Lords has a further opportunity to examine and make amendments or changes to a Bill. Usually, this begins fourteen days after Committee Stage has concluded and can be spread over several days. It is generally shorter than the Committee Stage because the debate is limited to amendments before the House of Lords, with no need to debate each clause.

---

77 In exceptional occasions, 'purely verbal' amendments are permitted <Glossary – UK Parliament>.

78 The Clerk of the House is the principal constitutional adviser to the House, and adviser on all its procedure and business <Glossary – UK Parliament >.

79 Where a Bill starts its passage in the Lords, the Bill minister reads out the long title of the Bill at First Reading.

5th stage: Third Reading (Lords)

Unlike in the House of Commons, amendments at Third Reading in the House of Lords can only be made if the issue has not been fully considered and voted on during either Committee or Report Stage. It is often used to clarify specific parts of the Bill. If the Bill was first introduced in the House of Commons, it is sent back after Third Reading in the Lords for consideration of the Lords amendments. If there have been no amendments in the House of Lords, the Bill is sent to the Monarch to receive the Royal Assent and become an Act of Parliament.

In case the of a Bill that begins in the House of Lords, it goes to the House of Commons for its First Reading. Then, the House of Commons reprints the Bill with the Lords amendments.[80]

On completion of the parliamentary stages in both Houses, the Bill is sent to the Monarch to receive Royal Assent. This is when the King formally agrees to make the bill into an Act of Parliament (i.e., a law). Although the Monarch has the right to refuse Royal Assent, nowadays this does not happen[81]; the last such occasion was in 1708, and today, Royal Assent is regarded as a formality.

3.3 Guide to making legislation

My discussion now focuses on the stages of the legislative writing process and the composition of the professionals involved.

---

80 If the Bill has been amended in the second House, it goes back to the House of introduction for consideration of the amendments in question (i.e., 'Commons consideration of Lords' amendments', or 'Lords consideration of Commons' amendments'). In this case, the expression *ping-pong* refers to the to and fro of amendments to Bills between the House of Commons and the House of Lords. The first House can accept, reject, amend or suggest an alternative to the amendments (*amendment in lieu*), which the second House will then consider. The matter goes back and forward between the two Houses (*ping pong*) until agreement has been reached. If the House of Commons and the House of Lords cannot reach agreement on part of a Bill (*double insistence*), the Bill will be lost <Glossary – UK Parliament>.

81 The last occasion the Monarch refused to Royal Assent was in 1708, and Royal Assent is regarded today as a formality <Glossary – UK Parliament>.

A detailed and clear description of the variety of actors working throughout the legislative process is provided in the Guide prepared by the Parliamentary Business and Legislation (PBL) Cabinet Committee, a part of the Cabinet Secretariat at the UK Cabinet Office.[82] It covers the procedures to be followed in preparing Primary legislation, taking it through the UK Parliament, and setting out what is required of Bill teams/actors at each stage of the legislative process. Published in 2022, the *Guide to Making Legislation* (hereafter, *Guide 2022*), is aimed at the 'departmental teams' (i.e., the professionals involved in the legislative process) and

> help[s] them manage their work effectively throughout the process of preparing legislation and taking it through Parliament. It describes the main features of the normal legislative process but cannot cover every possible circumstance: every bill is different (*Guide 2022*: 1.3).

Guide 2022 is divided into 8 Sections, each of them dealing with the various procedures to be followed in (i) preparing Primary legislation, (ii) taking it through Parliament, and (iii) setting out what is required of Bill teams at each stage of the process. The different stages are dealt with in chronological order. *Guide 2022* deals mostly with conventional government Bills that represent the part used by most Bill teams, though it also refers to other types of government Bill and private members' Bills in the very two last Sections (G and H).[83]

---

82 This Guide was produced together with the advice of Parliamentary Counsel and the Offices of the Commons Chief Whip, Lords Chief Whip, Leader of the House of Commons, Leader of the House of Lords, the Public Bill Offices of both Houses and officials in other government departments <Guide to making legislation – GOV.UK (www.gov.uk)>. Some parts of *Guide 2022* are reported in the Appendix to this book.

83 Section G deals with certain other types of government Bill: hybrid Bills and consolidation Bills. Section H deals with private members' Bills and will be of use to departmental clerks (UK Parliament) and to policy officials and private secretaries supporting ministers (who are responsible for responding on behalf of the Government) to private members' Bills. <Guide to making legislation – GOV.UK (www.gov.uk)>.

More specifically:

Section A consists in an ‘Introduction to the Legislative Process and Bidding for Legislation’;
Section B describes all the procedure to be followed when ‘Preparing the Bill for Introduction’;
Section C presents the ‘Essential Guidance for Bill Teams’;
Section D explains the ‘Commons Stages’;
Section E explains the ‘Lords Stages’;
Section F is about the ‘Further Action after Completing Commons and Lords Stages and after Royal Assent’;
Section G describes ‘Other Types of Government Bill’;
Section H describes the ‘Private Members’ Bills’.

Guide 2022 is also designed for officials to consult during the legislative process to identify the key points and actions required at each stage. For this reason, the last Section of the *Guide 2022* (i.e. Section H), is followed by six Appendixes that provide:

Appendix A: ‘Glossary’ of key terms and main concepts;
Appendix B: ‘Contact Details’;
Appendix C: ‘Other Guides’;
Appendix D: a ‘Checklist for Each Stage’;
Appendix E: the ‘Codes of Practice and Legislation’;
Appendix F: the procedure to be followed in ‘Securing Legislative Consent Motions in the Devolved Legislatures’.

The key points and checklists for each legislative stage are provided in ‘Appendix D’ to the *Guide 2022*. For our purposes, Table 5 below, reports only the key points of ‘Appendix D’ that are related to the ‘Preparation of the Bill for Introduction’, where the act of drafting Bills actually takes place.

Table 5. 'Appendix D' – preparation of the Bill for introduction.

Before Drafting Legislation
Obtain collective agreement for the policy in the Bill.
Obtain PBL[84] clearance for a slot in the programme and drafting authority for OPC[85] to draft the Bill.
Put in place a Bill team and governance mechanisms.
Have a clear delivery plan for developing the Bill and supporting documents.

During Drafting
Engage the territorial offices and then the devolved administrations on any devolved implications of the Bill.
Work with departments across-government on any implications for their areas.
Update PBL secretariat and the business managers regularly.
Hold early discussions about handling with the Whips offices.
Address any finance, public expenditure or tax implications of the Bill and obtain the agreement of HM Treasury[86] where necessary.
Give the Parliamentary Authorities an opportunity to comment on proposals intended to apply in relation to Parliament or the Parliamentary estate.
Get in touch with the AGO (Attorney's General Office) and LSAG to discuss the key legal issues in the Bill and whether any Law Officer consent will be required. AGO and LSAG (Legal Secretariat to the Advocate General) will require a draft legal issues memorandum (LIM) three weeks before documents are sent to PBL (Parliamentary Business and Legislation). AGO and LSAG officials will need to comment on any draft requests for retrospection or early commencement in good time for the final requests to be sent to AGO and LSAG at least two weeks before PBL consideration.
Contact the United Kingdom Intelligence Community to discuss whether the proposals impact on work of the Agencies.

Continued

84 PBL stands for Parliamentary Business and Legislation (PBL) Secretariat, Cabinet Office <pbl-secretariat@cabinetoffice.gov.uk>.

85 OPC stands for Office of the Parliamentary Counsel <https://www.gov.uk/government/organisations/office-of-the-parliamentary-counsel>.

86 HM Treasury stands for His Majesty's Treasury <HM Treasury – GOV.UK (www.gov.uk)>.

Table 5. Continued

During Drafting
Contact the Data Protection Team in DCMS[87] to discuss whether the proposals which relate to the processing of personal data are compatible with data protection legislation.

During Drafting of the Bill
Clear with lawyers, senior responsible owners and Ministers (where necessary).
Begin work on explanatory notes (using the template), starting with the sections on policy background and legal background.
Provide updates to the Secretariat on explanatory notes preparedness as Bill is updated throughout drafting.
Seek comments from departmental lawyers throughout drafting of the Bill
Consider whether you should consult Parliamentary Counsel on parts of the notes relating to territorial extent and application. If the Bill is to be introduced in the House of Commons you should ask Parliamentary Counsel to provide, or to clear, the wording for the parts of the notes relating to Parliamentary approval for financial costs or charges imposed
Continue consultation with the Territorial Offices and Office of the Advocate General as appropriate in relation to any devolution matters

As explained in the Introduction to *Guide 2022*, the Guide to Making Legislation has been written with the needs of departmental teams in mind, to help them manage their work throughout the process of preparing legislation and taking it through Parliament (*Guide 2022*, 1:1).

Eventually, it is plainly admitted by the *Guide*'s author (i.e., the Cabinet Secretariat at the UK Cabinet Office) that even though describing the main features of the normal legislative process, *Guide 2022* cannot cover every possible circumstance given that every Bill is different and unique to a certain respect.

3.3.1 Legislative drafting players

The main groups of actors across government and their role in the legislative process are those described in Diagram 8.

87 DCMS stands for Data Protection Policy Team <datapcorrespondence@dcms.gov.uk>.

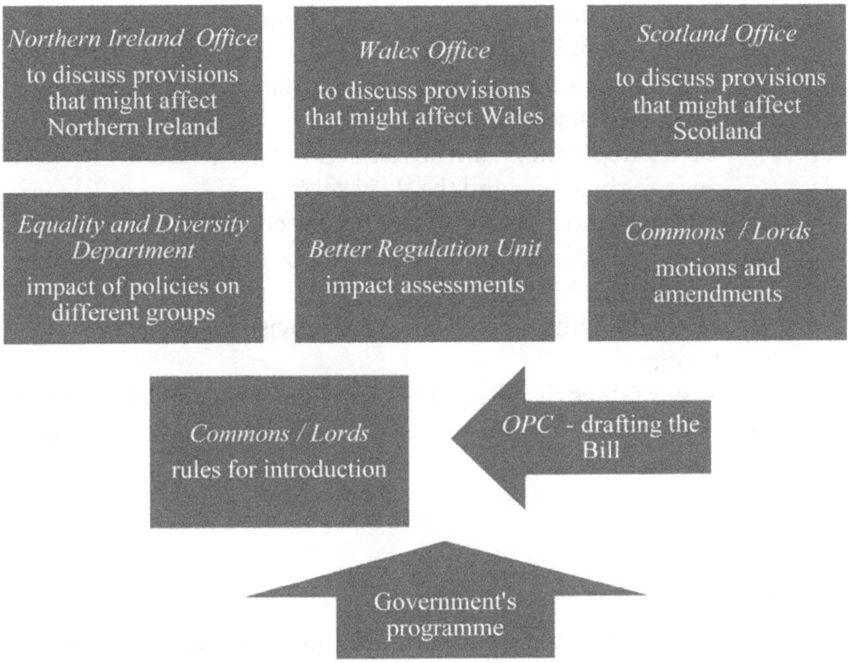

Diagram 8. Groups of players in the legislative process.

More specifically,

(i) legislative drafting process starts with the Parliamentary Business and Legislation (PBL) Committee supporting the management of the Government's programme of legislation and provides advice to ministers on legislative issues;

(ii) Office of the Parliamentary Counsel (OPC) is responsible for drafting the Bill;

(iii) Public and Private Bill Offices of the two Houses support the legislative process in Parliament. In particular, the Clerk of Legislation in the Commons and the Clerk of Legislation in the Lords clear and conform Bills to the rules for introduction of each House;

(iv) Government Whips' Office in the Commons supports the government Whips and on parliamentary procedures for

Bills, on programme motions, timing of legislation. The Government Whips' Office in the Lords negotiates the grouping of amendments, and offers assistance with all aspects of parliamentary procedure;[88]

(v) Better Regulation Unit advises on impact assessments, guidance for business and the third sector;
(vi) Equality and Diversity Department considers the impact of proposed policies on different groups (i.e., in regard to race, gender, disability, etc.);
(vii) Scotland Office discusses any provisions that may affect Scotland;
(viii) Wales Office discusses any provisions that may affect Wales;
(ix) Northern Office discusses any provisions that may affect Northern Ireland.

3.3.2 OPC

From the *Guide*'s checklist reported in Diagram 8 above, the important role played by OPC in the drafting process of Bills becomes apparent. As part of the Cabinet Office,[89] the OPC has about fifty legally qualified drafters who are responsible for drafting all government Bills.[90]

In this regard, it is interesting to mention that OPC is responsible for a range of other matters relating to the legislative drafting. For instance, drafters act as the channel of communication between the Government's departments and officials in Parliament (*Guide 2022:* n.6).

88 Whips are Members of Parliament (MPs) or members of the House of Lords appointed by each party to inform and organize their own members in Parliament. Their main responsibility is to make sure that their members vote in divisions, and vote in line with party policy. It is the party Whips, along with the Leader and Shadow Leaders of each House, that negotiate behind the scenes to arrange the day to day business in Parliament. This process is often referred to as 'the usual channels' <Glossary – UK Parliament>.

89 Cabinet Office supports the Prime Minister and ensures the effective running of government <https://www.gov.uk/government/organisations/cabinet-office>.

90 OPC is also responsible for writing Bills that are to be published in draft for public consultation or pre-legislative scrutiny.

Drafters do not specialize in particular areas of law. As a result, those from within the department who are instructing OPC (i.e., the departmental lawyers) are responsible for providing the drafters of the Bill with the so-called 'instructions'. Normally, drafters in OPC are organized into four teams, each of which is headed by a Team Leader and is allocated the responsibility of drafting Bills for specific departments.

As for the role of drafters in relation to policy-making, it is the governmental department, rather than the drafter, who is responsible for deciding the policy. However, in *Guide 2022,* the valuable contribution drafters can give to policy-making is clearly recognized while respecting the fact that final decisions must be made by the department (*Guide 2022*: 8.8). For instance, OPC can spot potential inconsistencies or flaws in what the governmental department proposes in the instructions, and may suggest other solutions.

Unquestionably, the overall success in drafting Bills depends on good quality instructions given by the governmental department to the OPC.

3.3.3 Good law

In Section 8 *Drafting the Bill*, the *Guide* provides a significant statement about 'good laws':

> 8.1 Everyone working on a bill should keep in mind the essential components of good law. Good law is law which is necessary, clear, coherent, effective and accessible (*Guide 2022*: 48).

By quoting the 'About Us' content in the OPC's webpage, the *Guide* not only reinforces the idea of 'good law' as a guiding principle that should inspire all those involved at different stages and in various capacities in the making of legislation, but also suggests considering it as a part of the new, user-centred approach:

> Mistaken perceptions of what the law requires can encourage risk-aversion and inaction. Good law is: necessary, clear, coherent, effective and accessible (see the Office of the Parliamentary Counsel website). An understanding of 'good law' should underpin the preparation and promotion of legislation. It should be the default, with good law principles guiding all those involved at different stages and in various capacities in the making of legislation. Like open policy-making and

> the strategic use of digital technology, good law should be considered part of the new, user-centred approach across government (*Guide 2022*: 5.3).

What is worth noticing in the extract above, which has been taken from *Guide 2022*, is the attention given to the comprehensibility and accessibility of laws that must be guaranteed to the final readers, that is, both the addressed categories of citizens and groups of law experts ('Good law is: necessary, clear, coherent, effective and accessible. [. . .] good law should be considered part of the new, user-centred approach across government'). Furthermore, *Guide 2022* itself suggests looking at the OPC website to get more information about the techniques to write 'necessary, clear, coherent, effective and accessible' laws.

Indeed, the OPC website provides a drafting guidance (i.e., *Office of the Parliament Drafting Guidance 2020*, hereafter *Guidance 2020*) that has been produced by the Drafting Techniques Group of the Office of the Parliamentary Counsel.[91] *Guidance 2020* is for members of the office only, and it is meant to help them in their mission of making it as easy as possible for readers to understand the Bills that they write. As the 'Introduction' to *Guidance 2020* clarifies, it is not meant to be a comprehensive guide to legislative drafting, in that some things which assist clarity such as layout or typography are outside their control and hence are not discussed. Although it does not represent a guide to statutory interpretation or past drafting practice, *Guidance 2020* includes:

- guidance on clear writing;
- specific wording to use in certain circumstances drafting techniques;
- guidelines on drafting repeals and amendments;
- information on subordinate legislation.

Overall, the fundamental requirement stated in the *Guidance* is that drafts must be accurate and effective. To reach such a goal, an important principle indicated in *Guidance 2020* and discussed in 'Part 1', is that of *Clarity*, which is symbolized with the act of *Telling the story* (Part 1: 1.1.1). Here, OPC suggests drafters to:

91 Office of the Parliamentary Counsel drafting guidance – GOV.UK (www.gov.uk).

- take readers 'by the hand and lead them through the story' they have to inform about (*Guidance 2020*: 1.1.1);
- give readers an overview of the whole story at the outset; in doing so, readers can understand each part in the light of the whole (*Guidance 2020*: 1.1.2);
- in some cases, a Table of Contents can give a suitable overview (*Guidance 2020*: 1.1.3);
- consider that Acts will have readers with different interests (for instance, those directly addressed by its provisions, professional advisers, the courts). Moreover, the readers of a Bill might be diverse again (i.e., ministers, members of the two Houses of Parliament, lobby groups and other interested parties). Such competing interests need to be balanced and given due weight in what they write as a legislative text (*Guidance 2020*: 1.1.4);
- find a clear order in which to tell the story that might spread across a whole Bill, or contained in a single clause (*Guidance 2020*: 1.1.5);
- find a clear and logical order of the material in the Bill, so that later propositions build upon earlier ones (*Guidance 2020*: 1.1.6);
- minimize the use of cross-references. Whenever possible, this can be done by re-ordering the material (*Guidance 2020*: 1.1.7);
- provide for a division in the Bill that reflects the divisions of thought (*Guidance 2020*: 1.1.8);
- preferably, put the main proposition (or at least give the reader some idea of what the clause is about) in the opening subsection of a clause, and not in the middle of the clause (*Guidance 2020*: 1.1.9);
- state the effect before listing the conditions, mostly when the clause produces a particular legal effect if conditions are met. For instance, the sentence 'A notice must be given if . . . (the several conditions)' is probably easier to understand than 'If . . . (several conditions) . . ., a notice must be given' (*Guidance 2020*: 1.1.10);
- write short sentences. In the case of a sentence requiring the reader to retain too much information, it is better to insert one idea per sentence (*Guidance 2020*: 1.1.11);
- consider the fact that a single complex proposition is sometimes best expressed in a single sentence, rather than as a series of short sentences in consecutive subsections which then have to be put back together again to make sense (*Guidance 2020*: 1.1.12);

– avoid unnecessary emphasis that may be distracting, for instance, excessive use of '*But*' at the beginning of a sentence (*Guidance* 2020: 1.1.16).

From the analysis developed in this Chapter, it becomes evident that a Bill is a joint effort, and there are many participants, such as ministers, administrative and legal civil servants, drafters, Members and officials of both Houses, and members of the public affected by the Bill. The drafter's main contact will usually be with the departmental lawyers, who draw up written instructions to the OPC.

As the final reader is likely to be interested in how a Bill changes the law and effects the categories of people to whom it is specifically addressed to, drafting in a way that draws more attention to the structure and mechanics of the Bill itself, than to its effect, is likely to be particularly unhelpful.

Members of the OPC are asked to have regard to the *Guidance.* However, everything in the guidance is subject to the fundamental prerequisite that drafters should write Bills as accurately and effectively as possible. It follows that there might be departures from what *Guidance 2020* itself recommends. Chapter 4 will consider such strategies more closely, paying particular attention to the linguistic features and textual strategies characterizing modern legislative drafting techniques.

4 Legislative drafting process

4.1 What does legislative drafting mean?

As a process of making texts of legislation, legislative drafting needs to be distinguished from a different activity, the so-called 'legal drafting' that involves the production of a text used in the judicial process. All the same, legislative drafting is different from the civil law equivalent practice of 'law-making' in that this latter activity involves the whole process of conceptualization of legislation until the implementation of policy decisions – thus, law-making represents the whole legislative process, whereas legislative drafting reflects the drafting process only.

As a matter of fact, legislative drafting is not completely foreign to the legislative process. In fact, legislative drafting is part of the legislative process, which in turn belongs to the policy process (Stefanou and Xanthaki 2008). A detailed description of the legislative process is that provided by Thornton (1996) who is still considered one of the leading scholars in the field of legislative drafting. According to Thornton, the drafting process is divided into five stages:

1. understanding the proposal;
2. analysing the proposal;
3. designing the law;
4. composing and developing the draft;
5. verifying the draft.[92]

92 Xanthaki 2022.

More specifically,

- in Stage 1 drafters receive the instructions compiled by the policy and legal instructing officers of the department that have requested the drafting of legislation. These drafting instructions are information given to the legislative drafters as a means of assisting them in writing effective legislation within the parameters already decided on by the government. Such government indications, that could be either concise or detailed, aim at providing the drafter with the necessary knowledge about the political decisions that substantiate the coming legislation, and the selection of the legal means that are proposed for achieving that policy. The government indications cannot take the form of a rough draft law. Drawing from Xanthaki's (2014) analysis of the institutional subjects taking part in the UK legislative process, instructions for Primary legislation (i.e., government Bills) are given by Government Departments. The results, which a proposed Bill is intended to achieve, are considered by the Administrators along with some legal advice when necessary.[93] Drafting instructions are prepared by a Legal Advisor, whereas the Administrators prepare the drafting instructions.[94] The Legal Adviser's main tasks are:
  - to consider when and how any changes or additions to the law are needed to give effect to the policy;
  - to provide the drafter with accurate drafting instructions;
  - to discuss with the drafter any difficulties coming from the instructions;
  - to ensure that every draft achieves the desired results and to find possible mistakes, such as wrong internal references, etc.;

93 Administrators are administrative civil servants who are responsible for policy and administration. Legal advisers are based in Government Departments and are familiar with the legal framework (statutory and common law) under which the Department operates (Xanthaki 2014). 'Bill' is the technical word used to indicate a draft of a proposed law presented to parliament for discussion (OED).

94 Detailed instructions prepared by Legal advisers within the Department are sent to the Office of Parliamentary Counsel (OPC), the so-called 'Bill Team'. Furthermore, Private Members' Bills do not, in principle, receive drafting support from the OPC. And delegated legislation is instructed and drafted within each Government Department.

  – to make sure that the final draft corresponds to the drafting instructions and reaches the main results desired.

- In Stage 2 drafters prepare a legislative plan, also known as a legislative research report or plan, which might be either a short or long report, and is based on the drafter's response to the drafting instructions. The legislative plan is aimed at ensuring that the end result of the legislation corresponds to the government's policy. For this reason, the legislative plan includes an analysis of the existing law and the reason for a new legislation.[95]

The analysis of the implications coming from the legislative proposal can be described as shown in Table 6 below.

Table 6. Legislative plan.

Legislative plan	
Step 1	needs, preliminary choices, information, measures, solutions
Step 2	analysis of the solutions, costs and benefits, feedback system
Step 3	implementing provisions, and/or new agencies

In terms of content, the legislative plan is expected to provide the identification of the public need(s) for which a new legislation (or a reforming of existing normative texts) is needed. This implies a process that can be summarized in a three-step route:

(i) some preliminary choices about the scope and the limits of the legislative solution have to be explicitly indicated in the drafting instructions in order to guarantee an effective regulation, such as the behaviour and/or activity to be addressed,

95 Legislative plan means a regulatory tool that can only be used as a solution of last resort where every other regulatory choice would not be effective; analysis of the practical implications of the legislative proposals.

their distinction from other related behaviour and/or activity, some background about the public need(s) for which a new legislation is proposed, information about other solutions proposed and implemented elsewhere (even abroad) and about any analyses conducted at a departmental or academic level;

(ii) the second step involves the description of the proposed legislative solutions and the considerations about the conformity of any subsequent or indirect measures (i.e., civil damages or penalties, punishments, etc.), a cost-benefit analysis, and the identification of the monitoring and feedback systems, such as periodic evaluation of the effectiveness of the Bill;

(iii) finally, the proposed legislative solution has to be justified, particularly in the case of the creation of a new administrative, state or private agency, or when new duties are assigned to an existing agency whose appointment, powers and duties have to be indicated in the legislative plan.

- The structuring of the legislative text takes place in Stage 3, where drafters arrange the order of the provisions by providing a table that shows the headings and the section titles. Generally speaking, the text is divided into parts when the number of sections is too large and it becomes advisable to arrange them in conceptual units. In this regard, Xanthaki (2013) mentions Lord Thring who, at the beginning of the last century, inspired the doctrine with practical indications on the general arrangement of provisions in legislative texts. Interestingly enough, in his book published in 1902, Lord Thring denounces the poor quality of legislative provisions observing that

> statutes, made with great deliberation and by learned and judicious lawyers, have been expressed so obscurely or have been constructed so inaptly that decisions interpretating the sense of these provisions, or supplying and correcting the provisions *ex ratione legis,* have been of necessity heaped upon them by the courts of justice (1902: 3).

Then, Lord Thring suggests a solution represented by five *Rules* indicated below:

> Rule I -Provisions declaring the law should be separated from and take precedence· of provisions relating to the administration of the law [. . .].
> Rule II -The simpler proposition should precede the more complex and in an ascending scale of propositions the less should come before the greater [. . .].
> Rule III - Principal provisions should be separated from subordinate provisions. The latter should be placed towards the end of the Act, while the former should occupy their proper position in the narrative of the occurrence to which they refer. Principal provisions are such as declare the material objects of the Act. Subordinate provisions are such enactments as are required to give effect to the principal provisions by declaring in detail the manner in which they are to be worked out or by adding enactments to complete the operation of the principal provisions [. . .]
> Rule IV - (a) Local or exceptional provisions, (b) temporary provisions, and (c) provisions relating to repeal of Acts should be separated from the other enactments, and placed by themselves under separate headings [. . .].
> Rule V - Procedure and matters of detail should be set apart by themselves, and should not, except under very special circumstances, find any place in the body of the Act (1902: 38–44).

According to Lord Thring (1902), drafters should know the law before any questions of administration might arise; hence, the 'provisions relating to the administration of the law' should be placed after 'the provisions stating the law'. In the case of the language used, 'simpler propositions' should be placed before 'more complex' ones, and 'principal provisions' declaring the objects of the legislative text should be separated from 'subordinate provisions', which are aimed to give effects to the principal ones. Then, the body of legislative texts should not include any indications about administrative matters.

- Stage 4 consists in the drafting of the text. Xanthaki (2013) recommends drafters to write legislative provisions applying the rules for words and grammar in a way that texts are made intelligible (that is, using words that are plain, clear and unambiguous), and the rules for a textual organization (e.g., short sentences, paragraphs, numbering articles, etc.) aimed at producing non-densely packed legislative texts.

In this regard, the traditional legislative drafting theory prescribes that a Bill[96] includes some of the types of provisions that are listed below (Table 7):

Table 7. Type of provisions.

Types of provisions	
Preliminary provisions	Long title, Preamble, Enacting clause, Short title, Commencement, Duration/Expiry, Application, Purpose clause, Definitions, Interpretation
Principal provisions	Substantive provisions, Administrative provisions
Miscellaneous	Offences, time limit for prosecution, continuing offences, offences by corporations, and vicarious responsibility, Supplementary provisions (i.e., evidentiary provisions, a power to make subordinate legislation, service of notices, powers of entry and search, seizure and arrest)
Final provisions	Savings and transitional (if they are long, may be placed in a Schedule), Repeals, Consequential amendments (if the they are numerous, may be placed in an Annex), Schedules, (presented in a tabular form)

More specifically, in the case of the *Preliminary provisions*, partly as an outcome of the Plain Language Movement demanding plainer legislative texts, modern legislative drafting theory recommends legislative drafters to reduce them (i.e. 'Long title', 'Preamble', 'Enacting clause', 'Short title', 'Commencement', 'Duration/Expiry', 'Application', 'Purpose clause', 'Definitions', 'Interpretation' to the most basic information), and begin directly with the regulatory message(s), e.g. rights and duties addressed to citizens and/or specific categories of people. Being the main purpose of policy-makers to give laws that are more comprehensible to the final addresses than it was before, modern drafting theory urges the reduction of the traditional list of *Preliminary provisions*. As the scholars in this field remind us, the 'Long title' maintains both its long-established function (e.g., the description of the law is

96 A Bill is a proposal for a new law, or a proposal to significantly change an existing law <Glossary – UK Parliament>.

being reformed) and its external form (e.g., a quite extensive long sentence). The role traditionally played by the 'Preamble' is reduced to the bare minimum,[97] whereas the 'Enacting clause' remains an important constitutional requirement for the legitimacy of the normative text. The 'Short title' still represents a means of reference to the law in the index of the Statute Book.[98] 'Commencement', 'Duration', 'Expiry', 'Application', and 'Interpretation provisions' are now placed in the *Final provisions* section, as well as the 'Definitions' that could either be placed in *Final provisions* or, rather, in the 'Schedules' at the end of the legislative text.[99]

In the case of the *Principal provisions*, the 'Substantive provisions' establish rights, duties, powers, and protection of persons to be benefited or regulated who are specifically indicated in the normative texts. These provisions are drafted as prescriptions, prohibitions, regulations, or a combination of them. Then, *Final provisions* include 'Savings', 'Transitional provisions', 'Repeals', 'Consequential amendments', and 'Schedules'. As the name might suggest, 'Savings provisions' preserve or save a law, right or privilege that would otherwise be repealed or cease to have effect when an existing law is repealed. 'Transitional provisions' guarantee a smooth transition between the existing law/normative provision and the new one.[100] Deletion of normative provisions or Acts from the Statute Book are given in the 'Repeals provisions'. In

97 In this regard, Xanthaki observes that 'the role of the preamble is diminished to a cosmetic one in the case of archaic or ceremonial laws, or to a transitional one in the case of the confirmation of the legal basis of the law and the observance of the constitutional stages of the legislative process in newer or weaker Democracies' (2013: 61).

98 When a law is on or reaches the Statute Book, it has been formally approved and written down and can be used in a law court (Cambridge Dictionary).

99 Scholars in the legislative drafting have recently noticed a renewed interest in the Purpose clauses that, after having been neglected for many years, are now increasingly inserted in the normative text as Objectives clauses including measurable criteria for the effectiveness of the legislation in regular post-legislative scrutiny cycles (Xanthaki 2022).

100 Xanthaki makes a clear distinction between the meaning and the corresponding function of *Savings* provisions and *Transitional*: 'they are two different species and should carry separate headings. Savings provisions do not relate to time: they simple preserve a circle of persons or activities from the field of application of the

doing so, they must be introduced clearly and explicitly to avoid confusion. Then, 'Schedules' consist in provisions attached to the main text of the law and directly linked to the 'Substantive provisions' within the text. The main function of Schedules is to clarify procedural and other distinct groups of provisions.

- Stage 5. Finally, this stage involves the verification of the legislative text which is conducted firstly within the drafting team, and then by other interested Ministries and affected agencies, in order to improve its clarity and to check its practicability.

Eventually, the verification of the legislative text should be a continuous process throughout the drafting, with drafts subjected to a scrutiny of the legal form, clarity and comprehensibility of text, and the final version of the laws analyzed on the basis of a wider range of matters and tested by legal verifications.

4.2 Modern drafting techniques

The legislative drafting process starts with 'understanding the proposal' (Xanthaki 2013), that is, when the Bill has been allocated a slot in the programme and its policy content has collective agreement. This initial step implies that drafters understand the drafting instructions. And, in order to reach this initial goal, drafters might ask questions, bring about new thoughts, confirm feedback, consider the current status of legislation in the field under review. Eventually, the outcomes of this preliminary work are recorded in the Legislative plan (see Table 6) which will assist the drafting teams in the subsequent steps of the drafting process.

---

new regime; they are long term provisions. Transitional provisions focus on regulating, for the short term, issues that continue to fall within the field of application of both the old and new regimes but the regulation changes with the new regime. They are short term provisions that regulate the transition between the old and the new regime for the same class of subjects, or objects, or activities' (2013: 61).

At this point, drafters go through the third stage of Thornton's (1996: 130) drafting process, that of 'designing the law'. It needs to be said that structuring a text is not merely a mere technical task, as it consists in classifying the provisions and prioritizing them to ensure that the key message of legislative communication is placed at the beginning of the text. If the goal is to ensure that the readers, whoever they might be (laypeople and/or experts in the field of law) immediately understand the message of the legislative text, the expression of the regulatory choice, prohibition, declaration, etc., has to appear immediate and clear. A strategic textual structure, together with appropriate lexico-grammatical choices, can certainly facilitate the attainment of this result. As Xanthaki (2013: 62) observes, aiming at effective legislative texts basically means that the regulatory results of the legislative texts are pursued via the observance of the prescribed behaviour by the final addresses of the legislation. In order to achieve these regulatory results, the final addressees of the new legislation need to understand the content of the regulatory message, that is, what they must, should, and/or can do, and what they must refrain from doing.

A proper textual structure helps identify the key message by placing it in a position of importance throughout the whole text. The following are some useful techniques that have been suggested in the field of modern legislative drafting (Xanthaki 2014; Xanthaki 2022).

In this regard, the first task to be accomplished in drafting legislative texts is to place the prioritization of normative provisions, that is, distinguishing and separating provisions declaring the law (i.e., the regulatory message) from the provisions concerning the administration of the law (i.e., provisions related to the creation of the administrative structure that will implement the law). The first provisions should take precedence over the latter. Indeed, it is the task of the drafting team to classify the provisions and prioritize them.

Among the common law English-speaking jurisdictions,[101] the UK represents a good example of the modern legislative drafting approach that has smoothly departed from the traditional style. In this regard, concerns about plain language have come into play when structuring

101 Other interesting examples of modern legislative drafting techniques that depart from traditional style can be found in Australia, Canada and New Zealand.

legislative texts within the last few decades. Within this context, provisions can be classified as *Preliminary*, *Principal* (*Substantive provisions* and *Administrative provisions*) and *Final provisions*, with further subclassifications among them.

The following subparagraphs of Chapter 4 explain the main linguistic and textual features of each of the possible types of *Provisions* that have been found in the more recent UK Primary legislation (1990s–2023).

4.2.1 Preliminary provisions

The innovative style in the UK prescribes that *Preliminary provisions* are absolutely necessary and must be short. In fact, the main regulatory message (i.e., the object of the normative text), needs to be communicated as close to the beginning of the Act as possible. *Preliminary Provisions* often consist, but not always,[102] of:

- Long title
- Preamble (in most recent Acts it tends to be less present)
- Enacting clause
- Application
- Definitions
- Interpretation

Let us look at each of these components in more detail with the help of some practical examples taken from the UK Acts of Parliament that have been enacted in recent decades.

4.2.1.1 Long title

The 'Long title' usually begins with the expression *An Act to...* and explains briefly the Act's content. Some Long titles are quite detailed and informative, but others are brief and convey little. In most cases, it consists in the description of the main goal of the law reform performed

102 According to Xanthaki (2014: 133), Preliminary provisions in some cases might not include these types of provisions.

by the Act, remains at the beginning of the normative text, and serves as an introduction to the Act, as shown in the extract below:

> Political Parties, Elections and Referendums Act 2000
>
> 2000 CHAPTER 41
>
> An Act to establish an Electoral Commission; to make provision about the registration and finances of political parties; to make provision about donations and expenditure for political purposes; to make provision about election and referendum campaigns and the conduct of referendums; to make provision about election petitions and other legal proceedings in connection with elections; to reduce the qualifying periods set out in sections 1 and 3 of the Representation of the People Act 1985; to make pre-consolidation amendments relating to European Parliamentary Elections; and for connected purposes.
>
> [30th November 2000][103]

Nowadays, the electronic publication of UK legislation has the expression *Introductory Text*:

> *Introductory Text*
>
> PART I THE ELECTORAL COMMISSION
>
> *Establishment of Electoral Commission and bodies with related functions*
>
> 1. Establishment of the Electoral Commission.
> 2. Speaker's Committee.
> 3. Appointment of Electoral Commissioners and Commission chairman.
>
> 3A. Four Electoral Commissioners to be persons put forward by parties
>
> 4. Parliamentary Parties Panel.
>
> *Commission's general functions*

Its main function is to ask the readers to consider quickly whether the Act is relevant to them.

103 Political Parties, Elections and Referendums Act 2000 (legislation.gov.uk).

4.2.1.2 Preamble

Older pieces of legislation often include a 'Preamble' in place of the Long title. A Preamble describes the purpose of an Act, and tends to be more comprehensive than a Long title:

> 1987 No. 1950
>
> AGRICULTURE
>
> HORTICULTURE
>
> The Agriculture Improvement (Amendment) Regulations 1987
>
> *Made 13th November 1987*
>
> *Laid before Parliament 18th November 1987*
>
> *Coming into force 1st January 1988*
>
> The Minister of Agriculture, Fisheries and Food and the Secretary of State, acting jointly, being Ministers designated for the purposes of section 2(2) of the European Communities Act 1972(1) in relation to the common agricultural policy of the European Economic Community(2), in exercise of the powers conferred on them by the said section 2(2) and of all other powers enabling them in that behalf, hereby make the following Regulations: [. . .].[104]

Preambles tend to be less present. When used, their main function is to serve as a means of 'confirmation of constitutionality' (Xanthaki 2013) by explaining the legal basis (and naming the legal authorities) upon which the Act has passed.

In more recent legislation, Preambles (when used) tend to be placed immediately after the Long title. Indeed, Preambles continue to play an important function when legislative drafters need to legitimate the new piece of legislation, such as the case of constitutional measures, international legislation (and the subsequent national implementing instruments), the legislation of new jurisdictions to name just a few. In this context, the addressees of the legislative measure, and any potential reader, need to be reassured about the legitimacy of the constitutional basis of the Act.

104 The Agriculture Improvement (Amendment) Regulations 1987 (legislation.gov.uk).

Elections Act 2022

Energy (Oil and Gas) Profits Levy Act 2022

2022 CHAPTER 40

An Act to make provision for, and in connection with, imposing a charge on ring fence profits of companies.

[14th July 2022].[105]

Most Gracious Sovereign

We, Your Majesty's most dutiful and loyal subjects, the Commons of the United Kingdom in Parliament assembled, towards raising the necessary supplies to defray Your Majesty's public expenses, and making an addition to the public revenue, have freely and voluntarily resolved to give and to grant unto Your Majesty the tax hereinafter mentioned; and do therefore most humbly beseech Your Majesty that it may be enacted, and be it enacted by the Queen's most Excellent Majesty, by and with the advice and consent of the Lords Spiritual and Temporal, and Commons, in this present Parliament assembled, and by the authority of the same, as follows:—

As we see in the extract above, which has been taken from the *Energy (Oil and Gas) Profits Levy Act 2022*, the 'Introductory text' has two parts:

(i) the first contains the most important regulatory message, i.e., the Long title (*An Act to make provision for, and in connection with, imposing a charge on ring fence profits of companies*), plus the indication of the day, month, and year of the enactment of the Act that are reported immediately after in square brackets (i.e. [*14th July 2022*]). The aim is to provide the addressee of the legislative texts, and any potential reader, with the main objectives of the Act;

(ii) the second part, i.e. the Preamble, contains information about the legal basis of the Act and the adherence to the constitutional procedural requirements (*We, Your Majesty's most dutiful and loyal subjects, the Commons of the United Kingdom in Parliament assembled, towards raising the necessary supplies to defray Your Majesty's public expenses, and making an addition to the public revenue, have freely and voluntarily resolved to give and to grant unto Your Majesty*

105 https://www.legislation.gov.uk/ukpga/2022/40/introduction

> *the tax hereinafter mentioned; and do therefore most humbly beseech Your Majesty that it may be enacted, and be it enacted by the Queen's most Excellent Majesty, by and with the advice and consent of the Lords Spiritual and Temporal, and Commons, in this present Parliament assembled, and by the authority of the same, as follows*).
>
> Clearly enough, this second part is rather verbose with archaic expressions such as doublets (*most dutiful and loyal . . ., have freely and voluntary. . ., to give and to grant . . ., by and with the advice and consent*), the frequent use of the 'textual-mapping'[106] by means of adverbials (*hereinafter*) or complex prepositional phrases with very detailed terminological explanations to state clearly the procedural requirements (*by and with the advice and consent of the Lords Spiritual and Temporal, and Commons, in this present Parliament assembled, and by the authority of the same . . .*). Then, it is noticeable that the legal language used emphasizes the pragmatic function of connectives by making meaning more apparent through inclusion in the surface form of a lexeme denoting their illocutionary value (*and do therefore. . .*) and acting as a more transparent paraphrase of a common connective (i.e., simply *and*).

The extract above is a clear example of the need to draft Preambles as clearly as possible, avoiding the insertion of any operative provision. This communicative goal is achieved in the following 'Introductory text' that has been taken from the case of the *Election Act 2022*:

> Election Act 2022
>
> 2022 CHAPTER 37
>
> An Act to make provision about the administration and conduct of elections, including provision designed to strengthen the integrity of the electoral process and provision about the use of the simple majority system in elections for certain offices; about overseas electors; about voting and candidacy rights of EU citizens; about the designation of a strategy and policy statement for the Electoral

106 Bhatia 1987.

> Commission; about the membership of the Speaker's Committee; about the Electoral Commission's functions in relation to criminal proceedings; about financial information to be provided by a political party on applying for registration; for preventing a person being registered as a political party and being a recognised non-party campaigner at the same time; about regulation of expenditure for political purposes; about disqualification of offenders for holding elective offices; about information to be included in electronic campaigning material; and for connected purposes.
>
> [28th April 2022]
>
> Be it enacted by the Queen's most Excellent Majesty, by and with the advice and consent of the Lords Spiritual and Temporal, and Commons, in this present Parliament assembled, and by the authority of the same, as follows: [. . .].[107]

In this case,

(i) the first part (i.e., Long title) contains the most important regulatory message. The aim is to provide the addressee of the legislative texts, and any potential reader, with a detailed description of the main objectives of the Act. Then, information about the day, month and year of the enactment of the Act are reported immediately after in square brackets (i.e. [*28th April 2022*]);
(ii) the second part (i.e., Preamble) basically justifies the Enacting provisions, providing concise information about the necessary constitutional requirements.

4.2.1.3 Enacting formula

The Acts of the UK Parliament are passed by both Houses of Parliament, and have the following 'Enacting formula' *(Be it enacted. . .)*:

> *Be it enacted* by the Queen's most Excellent Majesty, by and with the advice and consent of the Lords Spiritual and Temporal, and Commons, in this present Parliament assembled, and by the authority of the same, as follows: [. . .].[108]

The enacting formula mostly serves to confirm that 'the Act has complied with the procedural requirements for its constitutionality and

107 Elections Act 2022 (legislation.gov.uk).
108 https://www.legislation.gov.uk/ukpga/2022/40/introduction

legality' (Xanthaki 2014: 69), as the following extract taken from the *Energy (Oil and Gas) Profits Levy Act 2022* clearly shows:

> Most Gracious Sovereign
>
> We, Your Majesty's most dutiful and loyal subjects, the Commons of the United Kingdom in Parliament assembled, towards raising the necessary supplies to defray Your Majesty's public expenses, and making an addition to the public revenue, have freely and voluntarily resolved to give and to grant unto Your Majesty the tax hereinafter mentioned; and do therefore most humbly beseech Your Majesty that it *may be enacted*, and *be it enacted* by the Queen's most Excellent Majesty, by and with the advice and consent of the Lords Spiritual and Temporal, and Commons, in this present Parliament assembled, and by the authority of the same, as follows [. . .].[109]

These two extracts show a different drafting style in the construction of the enacting clause. The extract taken from the *Election Act 2022* and reported on page 110 a statement written in plain language describing the legislative authority (*the Queen, The Lords Spiritual and Temporal, the Commons*) who have agreed on the measures that are introduced by the Act.

Quite the opposite, the extract taken from the *Energy (Oil and Gas) Profits Levy Act 2022* presents a quite verbose language (*Most Gracious Sovereign. . ., We, Your Majesty's most dutiful and loyal subjects. . ., most humbly beseech),* a textual-mapping'[110] adverbial *hereinafter,* quite a few doublets (*dutiful and loyal, freely and voluntarily, to give and to grant, by and with*), and some repetitions (*be enacted*), for a total amount of 105 words (67 words more than the other extract that consists of 38 words). Noticeably, these two extracts represent an example of the dilemma faced by modern legislative drafting, that is, finding the right balance between the traditional and more pompous linguistic style on the one hand, and a modern plain language corresponding constructions that, eventually, might 'generate ambiguity as to whether the text is legislative or not' (Xanthaki 2014) on the other.

According to Kurzon (1986) the Enacting clause performs the speech act of enactment. In this regard, it is interesting to observe that the UK parliamentary process does not prescribe a stage, nor a phase

109 Energy (Oil and Gas) Profits Levy Act 2022 (legislation.gov.uk).
110 Bhatia 1987.

where the Enacting formula must be read out or uttered. And one might wonder about the reason of maintaining a drafting convention that stretches back to the 17th century (Thornton 1996).

In order to explain the purpose of the Enacting formula, Jackson (1985) considers the semiotic function performed by the clause and identifies four types of addressees to whom the clause is addressed. More specifically,

- 1st type: the public, i.e. the laypeople and the lawyers who rely on the self-evidence of a standardized expression/phrase as validating the words of the enactment;
- 2nd type: the courts who need to access the authenticated (original) text;
- 3rd type: the legislative officers who administer and control the certification process that leads to the authenticated (original) text;
- 4th type: MPs and Lords who need the enacting formula to offer substantiation and evidence to the first three types of addressee.

Overall, the Enacting formula performs the function of stating officially that the legislative authority (i.e., the Monarch, the Commons and the House of Lords) have been aware of and have agreed on the measures introduced by the new legislative instrument.

4.2.1.4 Application

Application provisions have the function of clarifying the extent of application of the new regulatory means introduced by the legislative text. In most cases, they are used to indicate 'who', 'what', 'when' and 'where' the legislation either regulates or applies to:

(i) 'who' may indicate a specific category of persons to whom the law does or does not apply;
(ii) 'what' may refer to specific areas, and/or parts of regulation;
(iii) 'when' may indicate the specific points in time that are regulated by the legislative text;
(iv) 'where' may specify the geographical extent of the legislative text's bindingness.

The extract below represents an example of typical Application provisions of contemporary UK legislation:

Application of this Part

9 General exclusions

Excluded persons:

(1) Nothing in this Part imposes any criminal or civil liability on an individual who organises activities—
  (a) as the employee of another person
  b) in the course of service as a member of the regular forces
  (c) in the course of service or undertaking training or duties as a member of the reserve forces.

(2) In subsection (1), "regular forces" and "reserve forces" have the same meaning as in the Armed Forces Act 2006 (see section 374 of that Act).

Excluded activities:

(3) In this Act, references to activities do not include—
  (a) the activity of fishing for profit, or
  (b) activities carried out or to be carried out in Antarctica on a vessel or aircraft travelling to an immediate destination outside Antarctica.

(4) In subsection (3)(b) "vessel" has the same meaning as in the Antarctic Act 1994 (see section 31(1) of that Act).

Excluded emergencies:

(5) A person is not guilty of an offence under section 1, or liable under section 2 or 3, in relation to an environmental emergency caused by—
  (a) an act or omission necessary to protect human life or safety
  (b) a natural disaster, where the person had complied with the requirements of section 5(2)(preventative measures) in relation to disasters of that description
  (c) an act of terrorism
  (d) an act of belligerency against the activities of the person
  (e) action which was itself a reasonable response action relating to a prior environmental emergency.

10 The Crown

(1) This Part binds the Crown, except as otherwise expressly provided.

(2) No contravention of any provision of this Part makes the Crown criminally liable; but the High Court or, in Scotland, the Court of Session may on the

application of the Secretary of State declare unlawful any act or omission of the Crown which constitutes such a contravention.

(3) Subsection (2) does not affect the criminal liability of persons in the service of the Crown (but see section 9(1)).

(4) For the purposes of this Part, references to the Crown are to be regarded as including [. . .].[111]

In this extract taken from the *Antarctic Act 2013*, there is a list of *General exclusions*, further subdivided in *excluded persons, excluded activities, excluded emergences*, which indicates the persons, the particular activities, and circumstances to whom specific regulations do not apply. Then, Sec. 2 of Art. 10 provides an indication as to 'where the Crown might be declared criminally liable' (i.e., the geographical extent of the legislative text's exclusions/exceptions).

4.2.1.5 Interpretation section

Nearly all Acts define certain words or expressions so that they have a specific meaning for the purpose of the Act:

PART 3

CORPORATE OFFENCES OF FAILURE TO PREVENT FACILITATION OF TAX EVASION

44 Meaning of relevant body and acting in the capacity of an associated person:

(1) This section defines expressions used in this Part. (2) "Relevant body" means a body corporate or partnership (wherever incorporated or formed). (3) "Partnership" means— (a) a partnership within the meaning of the Partnership Act 1890, or (b) a limited partnership registered under the Limited Partnerships Act 1907, or a firm or entity of a similar character formed under the law of a foreign country. (4) A person (P) acts in the capacity of a person associated with a relevant body (B) if P is— (a) an employee of B who is acting in the capacity of an employee, (b) an agent of B (other than an employee) who is acting in the capacity of an agent, or (c) any other person who performs services for or on behalf of B who is acting in the capacity of a person performing such services. (5) For the purposes of subsection (4)(c) the question whether or not P is a person who provides services for or on behalf of B is to

111 Antarctic Act 2013 (legislation.gov.uk).

> be determined by reference to all the relevant circumstances and not merely by reference to the nature of the relationship between P and B. [. . .].[112]

These definitions and/or clarifications can be found in the 'Interpretation section' at the end of the Act or the relevant Part of the Act. The following extract is taken from the Table of Contents of the *Criminal Finance Act 2017*, and it clearly shows that the Interpretation section (*52. Interpretation of Part 3*) is placed almost at the end of the Act:

Criminal Finances Act 2017

CHAPTER 22

CRIMINAL FINANCES ACT 2017

PART 1

PROCEEDS OF CRIME

CHAPTER 1

INVESTIGATIONS

1. Unexplained wealth orders: England and Wales and Northern Ireland
2. Interim freezing orders
3. External Assistance

[. . .] CHAPTER 5

Part 3 Corporate offences of failure to prevent facilitation of tax evasion.

Preliminary

44. Meaning of relevant body and acting in the capacity of an associated person [. . .]

Consequential amendments and interpretation

51. Consequential amendments

52. Interpretation of Part 3

Part 4 General

53. Minor and consequential amendments

54. Power to make consequential provision

112 Criminal Finances Act 2017 (legislation.gov.uk).

55. Section 54: procedural requirements

56. Financial provision

57. Extent

58. Commencement

59. Short title

[. . .].[113]

In this regard, it is interesting to look more closely at the content of the Interpretation section found below:

52. Interpretation of Part 3

(1) In this Part—

"conduct", *includes* acts and omissions

"foreign country", *means* a country or territory outside the United Kingdom

"foreign tax evasion facilitation offence" *has the meaning* given by section 46(6);

"foreign tax evasion offence" *has the meaning* given by section 46 (5);

"partnership" *has the meaning* given by section 44 (3)

"relevant body" *has the meaning* given by section 44 (2)

"tax" *includes* duty and any other form of taxation (however described)

"UK tax evasion facilitation offence" *has the meaning* given by section 45(5) and (6)

"UK tax evasion offence" *has the meaning* given by section 45(4).[114]

(2) References in this Part to a person acting in the capacity of a person associated with a relevant body are to be construed in accordance with section 44(4).[115]

Here, *has the meaning* is the predominant expression that is used to clarify words and phrases that are present in specific paragraphs or subsections of the Act, whereas the verbs *mean* and *include* are used to

113 Criminal Finances Act 2017 (legislation.gov.uk).
114 Criminal Finances Act 2017 (legislation.gov.uk).
115 https://www.legislation.gov.uk/ukpga/2017/22/section/52

define terms and expressions that are spread throughout the Act without any reference to any specific paragraph or subsection.

4.2.2 Main body of an Act and principal provisions

The main body of an Act is divided into sections (1, 2, 3, etc.), subsections ((1), (2), (3), etc.), paragraphs ((a), (b), (c), etc.) and subparagraphs ((i), (ii), (iii), etc.). The main body of an Act may be divided into Parts if it deals with a number of different topics, and Parts may be further subdivided into Chapters:

> Energy (Oil and Gas) Profits Levy Act 2022
>
> UK Public General Acts 2022 c. 40 - Table of contents
>
> Introductory Text
>
> Charge to tax
>
> 1. Charge to tax
>
> Relief for investment expenditure
>
> 2. Additional expenditure treated as incurred for purposes of *section 1*
> 3. *Section 2:* meaning of "operating expenditure" [. . .].[116]

Each section has a heading, which is intended to indicate what that Section is about and may help the reader to identify the relevant provisions more quickly. The core of the legislative text is constituted by the *Principal provisions.* They are aimed at conveying the regulatory message of the government's institutions by producing the intended law reform. *Principal provisions* consist of 'Substantive provisions' and 'Administrative provisions'.

4.2.2.1. Principal provisions

'Principal provisions' establish rights, duties, powers and privileges for specific categories of people. The corresponding normative prescription takes the technical terms of prescriptions, prohibitions, and

116 Energy (Oil and Gas) Profits Levy Act 2022 (legislation.gov.uk).

or regulations. They carry the regulatory message, that is, they tell the addressee how they are expected to act and/or behave from the enactment of the Act onwards. Principal provisions can be 'substantive' or 'administrative'. Indeed, the distinction is based upon their content: substantive provisions deal with substantive law (i.e., rights and duties of people, organizations, etc.), whereas administrative provisions refer to the procedural arrangements required to put the substantive provisions into effect. Furthermore, the distinction of content between substantive and administrative provisions does not imply any automatic categorization in terms of primary and secondary importance.[117]

In the case of Principal provisions, legislative drafters need to consider carefully the lexico-grammatical structures of the provisions that are going to confer powers and impose duties. In line with the modal revolution in legal writing and the growing tendency of 'shall-free legislation' (Garzone 2013: 69) embraced by the Plain English Movement (Williams 2004), and clearly stated in 'UK Office of Parliamentary Counsel (OPC) Drafting Guidance 2011', *shall* has been increasingly replaced by the modals *may* and *must*.

The role played by *shall* as the hallmark of the traditional writing style has been widely explored by eminent scholars both in the field of law (Mellinkoff 1963; Gustafsson 1975; Gardner 2004; Langton 2005; Butt 2013) and the in the field of linguistics and specialized languages (Tiermsa 1999; Gotti and Dossena 2001; Garzone 2013; Bhatia 2021). For this reason, the intention of the author is simply to recall some of the main conclusions that have come up from these pivotal studies.

To begin with, the indeterminacy of interpretation of *shall* is mainly due to its polysemy. In fact, in order to properly get the meaning of the modals used in normative texts, the reader has to grasp the link between linguistic semantic values and the social pragmatic setting of the legal provisions (Fillmore and Baker 2009). According to the conventional legal writing style, strong obligations were expressed and/or conveyed by the use of the deontic modal auxiliary *shall*. The idea supporting the

117 Xanthaki clarifies that, even though substantive provisions tend to be of primary importance, 'administrative provisions can be equally at home as primary provisions, in legislative texts of a purely or merely administrative content, or as subordinate provisions' (2014: 149).

'overuse of shall' (Butt 2013), as well as the resistance of some legal drafters to feel unable to abandon it, is that the authenticity of legal documents cannot be guaranteed with other substituting modals such as *must* or *is to be / has to be*. Yet, one of the main problems with *shall* is that, in legal writing, it has been traditionally used to serve diverse purposes.

In this regard, Butt (2013) provides a list (though not exhaustive) of the purpose conventionally served by *shall*, which includes the following functions:[118]

– negating / imposing duties

negating duties

Upon the discontinuance of the operation of the Surrey Commercial Docks or the Surrey Canal, *all statutory obligations of the Port Authority* under any local Act (including an Act conforming a Provisional Order) with respect to, or in connection with, the said docks or canal, as the case may be, *shall cease* [. . .]

imposing duties

the Port Authority within one year *shall pay* to such person a sum equal to the amount of the compensation so due less the value of any benefit [. . .]

– granting rights / negating rights

granting rights

Any person who suffers loss by the extinguishment by subsection (2) of this section of any private right, and who makes a claim in writing to the Port Authority within one year from the extinguishment of the private right, *shall be entitled to* compensation [. . .] [119]

negating rights

If the Port Authority decide to discontinue permanently the operation of the Surrey Commercial Docks or the Surrey Canal and if the date of discontinuance there is existence in relation to the said docks or canal so discontinued any private right or obligation, *such right* or obligation *shall* thereupon *be extinguished* [. . .].

– giving directions

the sum payable to such person shall be determined under and in accordance with the Land Compensation Act 1961. [. . .]

118 As Butt (2013: 263) clarifies, 'the categories of *shall* are not closed'.

119 ukla_19700078_en.pdf (legislation.gov.uk).

– stating circumstances

Reference in this Act to any enactment shall be construed as reference to that enactment as re-enacted, extended or amended by, or by virtue of, any enactment, including this Act. [...]

– making a condition precedent / making a condition subsequent

making a condition precedent

Provided that nothing in this subsection shall prejudice the right of the Port Authority to recover any dues or moneys which have accrued due or become payable to them before the date of discontinuance. [...]

making a condition subsequent

Notwithstanding the provisions of section 3 (As to rights and obligations on discontinuance of the Surrey Canal and the Surrey Commercial Docks) of this Act, and the discontinuance of the operation of the Surrey Canal or the use of the land being the site of the Surrey Canal for any purpose other than that of the said canal, *the London Transport Executive and the British Railways Board respectively shall so long as it is required have reasonable access at all times* over the Surrey Canal [...]

– expressing the future

All costs, charges, and expenses of and incidental to the preparing for, obtaining and passing of this Act shall be paid by the Port Authority out of the port fund established under section 16 of the Port of London Act 1908. [...]

According to the old drafting style, it was not unusual to have *shall* performing different functions even in one single document. To demonstrate such a drafting convention, the extracts reported above are taken from the same Act (i.e., *Port of London Act 1970*) and show the different functions performed by *shall* not only within the same legislative text, but also within the same clause.

As scholars and practitioners working in the legal field have incessantly observed, the various functions of *shall* can be a source of wrong or misleading interpretation by the final readers (both professionals and laypeople). Furthermore, this was among the major claims raised by the Plain Language Movement and the main reason for a shall-free legislation produced by modern legislative drafting.

Generally speaking, the indeterminacy of interpretation of modality markers is due to their polysemy. For the purpose of this study, the author will limit the discussion about modality markers in normative texts saying that an adequate use of modals needs to be based on a careful consideration of the relation between linguistic semantic values and the social pragmatic setting of the normative provisions (Gotti and Dossena 2001). In this context, *should* may create uncertainty of meaning because it could be perceived to convey an obligation that is not entirely binding and allow greater discretionality of interpretation and application on the part of the reader of the prescriptive norms. However, a few instances of the use of *should* have been found in normative texts, as can be seen in the following example:

> 18 Control of entry
>
> After paragraph 2A (2) of Schedule 2 to the Immigration Act 1971 (control of entry: persons arriving with leave to enter) insert—
>
> (2A) Where the person's leave to enter derives, by virtue of section 3A (3), from an entry clearance, he may also be examined by an immigration officer for the purpose of establishing whether the leave *should* be cancelled on the grounds that the person's purpose in arriving in the United Kingdom is different from the purpose specified in the entry clearance.[120]

In recent legislation, *shall* has been consistently substituted by the deontic modal auxiliary *must*, as clearly shown in the extract below which has been taken from the *British Sign Language Act 2022*:

> 3 Guidance on use of British Sign Language
>
> (1) The Secretary of State *must* issue guidance, or arrange for guidance to be issued, about the promotion and facilitation of the use of British Sign Language.
>
> (2) Guidance under this section *may* for example include—
>
> (a) advice for relevant government departments on providing information to the Secretary of State in accordance with section 2(4),
> (b) advice on best practice for communicating with British Sign Language users (both when interacting with individuals and when communicating with the public at large), and
> (c) case studies to illustrate the value of providing British Sign Language interpretation in communications with the public.

---

120 https://www.legislation.gov.uk/ukpga/2004/19/section/18

(3) Guidance under this section *must* not include advice or other material which —

(a) relates only to Scotland and does not relate to reserved matters (within the meaning of the Scotland Act 1998)
(b) relates only to Wales and does not relate to reserved matters (within the meaning of the Government of Wales Act 2006).

(4) The Secretary of State *must* arrange for any guidance issued under this section to be published.[121]

Here, the analysis of the extract shows that *must* is used to convey a strong obligation ('The Secretary of State *must* issue guidance, or arrange guidance to...'), whereas *may* is used to express discretion and/or probability ('Guidance under this section *may* for example include...').

The choice between them depends on the regulatory message that the legislative drafter intends to convey. According to the analysis conducted by the author,

(i) the modal *must* replaces *shall* in its mandatory function where the exercise of the power conferred is to be undertaken;
(ii) the modal *may* substitutes *shall* where the power conferred is permissive. In a few cases, the expression *is entitled to* is used to emphasizes the power of right, rather than merely discretion.

In this regard, it is interesting to consider the extract below that has been taken from a quite recent legislation (*Small Business, Enterprise and Employment Act 2015*):

Power to invalidate certain restrictive terms of business contracts:

(1) The appropriate authority *may* by regulations make provision for the purpose of securing that any non-assignment of receivables term of a relevant contract—

(a) has no effect
(b) has no effect in relation to persons of a prescribed description
(c) has effect in relation to persons of a prescribed description only for such purposes as may be prescribed.[122]

121 https://www.legislation.gov.uk/ukpga/2022/34/section/3
122 Small Business, Enterprise and Employment Act 2015 (legislation.gov.uk).

Companies: duty to publish report on payment practices and performance

(1) The Secretary of State *may* by regulations impose a requirement, on such descriptions of companies as *may* be prescribed, to publish, at such intervals and in such manner as *may* be prescribed, prescribed information about—

(a) the company's payment practices and policies relating to relevant contracts of a prescribed description, and
(b) the company's performance by reference to those practices and policies. [. . .]

(3) The regulations *may not* impose a requirement on a company in relation to any time during which—

(a) it qualifies as a micro-entity for the purposes of section 384A of the Companies Act 2006, [. . .]
(b) the small companies regime under that Act applies to it (see section 381 of that Act), or
(c) it qualifies as medium-sized for the purposes of section 465 or 466 of that Act.

(4) "The company's payment practices and policies" has such meaning as *may* be prescribed and the information which *may* be prescribed *may*, in particular, include information—

(a) about the standard payment terms of the company and whether these are part of any code of conduct or code of ethics of the company,
(b) about payment terms of the company which are not standard,
(c) about the processing and payment of invoices,
(d) by reference to such codes of conduct or standards as *may* be prescribed and as are applicable to companies generally or to companies of a prescribed description, [. . .]

(5) The regulations *may* require that information published in accordance with the regulations *must* be approved or signed by such description of person as *may* be prescribed.

(6) The regulations *may* require such of the information required to be published as *may* be prescribed to be given, in such form as *may* be prescribed, to prescribed persons.

(7) The regulations *may* make provision for a prescribed breach by a prescribed description of person of a requirement imposed by the regulations to be an offence punishable on summary conviction [. . .].

(8) Before making regulations under this section the Secretary of State *must* consult such persons as the Secretary of State considers appropriate. [. . .].[123]

123 Small Business, Enterprise and Employment Act 2015 (legislation.gov.uk).

Here, *must* (1 occurrence) substitutes *shall* (0 occurrences) in its mandatory function ('Before making regulations under this section the Secretary of State *must* consult such persons as the Secretary of State considers appropriate'), whereas *may* (14 occurrences) and *may not* (1 occurrence) substitutes *shall* (0 occurrence) to convey a discretionary power granted by the law to act or to work on judgement under certain conditions ('The Secretary of State *may* by regulations impose a requirement, on such descriptions of companies as *may* be prescribed, to publish, at such intervals and in such manner as *may* be prescribed...').

4.2.3 Final provisions

Final provisions come after *Principal provisions* and often consist, but not always, of these provisions:

- Repeals and consequential amendments
- Short title
- Commencement (Duration or Expiry provisions)
- Schedules (definition and interpretation)

Let us look at each of these Final provisions in more detail.

4.2.3.1 Repeals and consequential amendments

Generally speaking, 'Repeals and consequential amendments' produce the obliteration of an Act or some sections of it from the Statute Book.[124] Repeals and consequential amendments can take the form of:

(i) a simple repeal, where the provision is no longer needed; no legislative action is to be taken in order to modify the provision that has been repealed. In this case, the verbs that results as the most appropriate to convey this message are *delete*, *repeal*, and *revoke*

63 Repeal of certain provisions about culverts

124 'When a law is on or reaches the statute book, it has been formally approved and written down and can be used in a law court' (Cambridge Dictionary).

The following provisions of the Public Health Act 1936 *are repealed*—

(a) section 262 (power of local authority to require culverting of watercourses and ditches where building operations in prospect)

(b) section 263 (watercourses in urban districts not to be culverted except in accordance with approved plans) [. . .].[125]

(ii) repeals or re-enactments, where a new provision consolidates the existing law via a deletion of one or more provisions that are substituted by new elements that leaves the existing law largely unchanged. According to the analysis conducted here, the verb mostly used in this type of repeals is insert, as shown in the following extract taken from the *Grocery Code Adjudicator Act 2013*,

Amendments and transition

*Parliamen*tary Commissioner Act *1967 (c. 13)*

(1) In Schedule 2 to the Parliamentary Commissioner Act 1967 (departments etc subject to investigation) at the appropriate place *insert*— " Groceries Code Adjudicator" [. . .].[126]

and the verb *omit*, as shown in the extract below taken from the *Protection of Freedom Act 2012*·

113 Repeal of provisions for conducting certain fraud cases without jury

Omit section 43 of the Criminal Justice Act 2003 (applications by prosecution for certain fraud cases to be conducted without a jury).[127]

(iii) repeals and amendments consist in a replacement, where the existing law is adjusted to meet new cases. The analysis has shown that the verbs more suited to convey this message are *insert* and *substitute*

125 Water Act 2014 (legislation.gov.uk).

126 Groceries Code Adjudicator Act 2013 (legislation.gov.uk).

127 Protection of Freedoms Act 2012 (legislation.gov.uk).

PART 5 Minor and consequential modifications

28 Meaning of certain terms:

(1) Section 98 of the 2009 Act is amended as follows.

(2) For the definition of "annual target", *substitute*—

""annual target" has the meaning given by section 3(6),".

(2) After the definition of "Committee" *insert*—

""current international carbon reporting practice" has the meaning given by section 19(2),".

(3) After the definition of "emissions" *insert*—

""emissions reduction target" means—

(a) an annual target,
(b) an interim target, or
(c) the net-zero emissions target".

(5) After the definition of "energy efficiency" *insert*—

""fair and safe Scottish emissions budget" has the meaning given by section 2B (2)," [. . .]

(9) For the definition of "target year" *substitute*—

""target year" means a year for which an emissions reduction target has been set,".

Overall, the drafter's choice of the most appropriate verb to be used for each type of Repeals and amendments becomes crucial for the purpose of serving certain and clear provisions to the final addressees (i.e., lay-people and lawyers).

4.2.3.2 Short title

'Short title' is the name by which the Act is known and contains the year in which it was passed. In more recent decades, the Short title tends to be placed at the end of the text. This is clearly shown in the Table of Contents of the *UK Public Acts 2022* shown below:

UK Public General Acts 2022 c. 40 - Table of contents

Introductory Text

Charge to tax

1. Charge to tax

Relief for investment expenditure

2. Additional expenditure treated as incurred for purposes of section 1
3. Section 2: meaning of "operating expenditure"
4. Section 2: meaning of "leasing expenditure"
5. Section 2: meaning of "disqualifying purposes"
6. Recycling etc of assets to generate relief
7. When investment expenditure is incurred

Financing and decommissioning costs

8. Meaning of "financing costs" etc
9. Meaning of "decommissioning costs"

Qualifying levy losses

10. Relief for qualifying levy losses

Management and administration etc

11. Application of corporation tax provisions
12. Requirement to provide information about payments
13. Adjustments

Final provisions

14. Consequential provision
15. Transitional provision for accounting periods straddling 26 May 2022
16. Transitional provision for accounting periods straddling 31 December 2025
17. Rules for apportioning profits or loss to separate accounting periods
18. Interpretation
19. *Short title.*[128]

---

128 Energy (Oil and Gas) Profits Levy Act 2022 (legislation.gov.uk).

Furthermore, the Short title represents a statement of reference to the subject matter of the normative text immediately differentiating it from other relevant Acts, as shown here below:

> 76. *Short title*
>
> This Act may be cited as the Statistics and Registration Service Act 2007.[129]

If we look at the example above, Short title must indicate the Act as accurately and distinctively as possible in order to avoid any possible confusion with other similar Acts. Therefore, it always includes the year of enactment of the Act (*2007*) and expresses the topic/matter by which the Act is to be known.

It might happen that Acts need to be distinguished by previous and/ or related Acts on the same topic:

> 19. *Short title*
>
> This Act may be cited as the Energy *(Oil and Gas)* Profits Levy Act 2022.

In this case, specific aspects or details of the Act can be added in the Short title providing that they are inserted in brackets.

4.2.3.3 Commencement

Acts have 'Coming into force' or 'Commencement' provisions. Indeed, the beginning, duration and extension of an Act represent an important regulatory message. Traditionally placed at the beginning of the text, 'Commencement provisions' tend to be placed towards the end of the Act, along with the Short title and Duration or Expiry provisions:

> Courts and Tribunals (Judiciary and Functions of Staff) Act 2018
>
> UK Public General Acts 2018 c. 33 Table of contents
>
> Introductory Text
>
> Judiciary

129 https://www.legislation.gov.uk/ukpga/2007/18/section/76

1. Deployment of judges
2. Alteration of judicial titles

   Functions of staff

3. Authorised court and tribunal staff: legal advice and judicial functions

   Final provisions

4. Short title, *commencement* and extent.[130]

'Commencement' and 'Duration' or Expiry provisions' set out when or how the Act is to take effect, along with the range over which it extends as shown in the extract below:[131]

Short title, commencement and extent

(1) This Act may be cited as the Courts and Tribunals (Judiciary and Functions of Staff) Act 2018.

(2) *Sections 1 and 2 come into force at the end of the period of two months beginning with the day on which this Act is passed.*

(3) *Section 3 and the Schedule come into force on such day as the Secretary of State may by regulations made by statutory instrument appoint.*

(4) Regulations under subsection (3) may—

 (a) appoint different days for different purposes
 (b) appoint different days for different areas
 (c) make transitional, transitory or saving provision.

(5) *This section comes into force on the day on which this Act is passed.*

(6) Any amendment, repeal or revocation made by this Act has *the same extent as* the enactment amended, repealed or revoked.

(7) *The rest of this Act extends* to England and Wales, Scotland and Northern Ireland.[132]

130 Courts and Tribunals (Judiciary and Functions of Staff) Act 2018 (legislation.gov.uk).

131 In the case of the Subordinate legislation, they are set out at the beginning.

132 Courts and Tribunals (Judiciary and Functions of Staff) Act 2018 (legislation.gov.uk).

Placing Commencement and Duration or Expiry provisions in the *Final provisions* help the reader (i.e., laypeople and legal professionals) find the necessary information about the temporal and juridical boundaries of the Act.

4.2.3.4 Schedules

In more recent legislation, definitions of key terms are placed at the beginning of an Act to help the reader understand the provisions that follow (i.e., Substantial definitions). Legislative drafters, resort to Schedules for separating secondary and/or procedural provisions from the main body of the Act. Furthermore, Acts, that present a consistent number of Sections, Subsections and Paragraphs often contain an Index of all terms that are defined, normally in 'Schedules' that come at the end of the Act, as clearly shown in the extract below taken from the Table of Contents of the *Deregulation Act 2015*:

> *Deregulation Act 2015*
>
> UK Public General Acts 2015 c. 20 - Table of contents
>
> [...]
>
> SCHEDULES
>
> SCHEDULE 1 Approved English apprenticeships
>
> SCHEDULE 2 Driving instructors
>
> SCHEDULE 3 Motor insurance industry: certificates of insurance
>
> SCHEDULE 4 Agricultural Holdings Act 1986: resolution of disputes by third party determination
>
> SCHEDULE 5 Auditors ceasing to hold office
>
> SCHEDULE 6 Insolvency and company law
>
> SCHEDULE 7 Ascertainment of rights of way
>
> SCHEDULE 8 Provision of passenger rail services
>
> SCHEDULE 9 Road traffic legislation: use of vehicles in emergency response by NHS
>
> SCHEDULE 10 Regulation of the use of roads and railways
>
> SCHEDULE 11 Enforcement of transport legislation
>
> SCHEDULE 12 Household waste: London

SCHEDULE 13 Other measures relating to animals, food and the environment

SCHEDULE 14 Abolition of office of the Chief Executive of Skills Funding

SCHEDULE 15 Further and higher education: reduction of burdens

SCHEDULE 16 Schools: reduction of burdens

SCHEDULE 17 Part to be inserted as Part 5A of the Licensing Act 2003

SCHEDULE 18 Amendments consequential on section 69

SCHEDULE 19 CLC practitioner services: consequential amendments

SCHEDULE 20 The Council for Licensed Conveyancers: other amendments

SCHEDULE 21 Poisons and explosives precursors

SCHEDULE 22 Removal of consultation requirements

SCHEDULE 23 Legislation no longer of practical use [133]

In some cases, Schedules are subdivided into Parts that generally contains numbered paragraphs (i.e., 'Subsidiary definitions'), as can be seen in the extract taken from 'Schedule 2. Driving Instructors' of the *Deregulation Act 2015*:

SCHEDULE 2 DRIVING INSTRUCTORS

[...]

Part 2

[...]

(9) [...] "Community licence" has the same meaning as in Part 3 of this Act; "disability" means a want of physical ability affecting the driving of motor cars; and

(a) "relevant disability", in relation to a person, means any prescribed disability or any other disability likely to cause the driving of a motor car by him to be a source of danger to the public

(b) "prospective disability", in relation to a person, means any other disability which, at the material time, is not of such a kind that it is a relevant disability but, by virtue of the intermittent or progressive nature of the disability or otherwise, may become a relevant disability in the course of time

"emergency control assessment" and "emergency control certificate" mean an assessment and a certificate under section 133A [...].[134]

---

133 https://www.legislation.gov.uk/ukpga/2015/20/contents

134 https://www.legislation.gov.uk/ukpga/2015/20/schedule/2

Schedules may contain technical details that could interrupt the flow of the text if included in the main body of the Act. When performing this function, they represent a useful device for separating the main body of the Act from issues of secondary regulatory value and making the content of legislation clearer and more effectively communicated. In more recent years, legislative drafters resort to Schedules in order to place procedural and administrative provisions away from the main provisions of the Act. For this reason, Schedules offer useful instructions to the executive officers who will apply the law. Other material that can be inserted in Schedules might include:

- lists of persons and/or places to which the Act applies (or does not apply)

  SCHEDULE 1

  PARTICULAR PURPOSES FOR WHICH PROVISION MAY BE MADE UNDER SECTION 2

  [. . .]

  9. Authorising *the Secretary of State* to make schemes for the charging by regulators of fees or other charges in respect of, or in respect of an application for —

  (a) the grant of a permit,

  (b) the variation of a permit or the conditions to which it is subject, or

  (c) the transfer or surrender of a permit,

  or in respect of the subsistence of a permit.

  9 (A)(1) Authorising *the Secretary of State* to make schemes for the charging by regulators of charges, as respects functions in relation to offshore installations, corresponding to those that may be prescribed under section 41A of the Environment Act 1995.

  (2) *Subsections (2) to (5) of section 41A of that Act apply in relation to the Secretary of State* and a charging scheme made by virtue of this paragraph as they apply in relation to *the Scottish Environment Protection Agency* and a charging scheme made by that Agency under the 1995 Act. [. . .][135]

- the composition of a body set up or established by the Act

---

135 Pollution Prevention and Control Act 1999 (legislation.gov.uk).

SCHEDULE 5

THE BOARD OF THE PENSION PROTECTION FUND

1. *The chairman of the Board is to be appointed* by the Secretary of State [. . .]

Appointment of ordinary members

2.(1) *The appointments of the first five ordinary members* are to be made by the Secretary of State.

(2) *Subsequent appointments of ordinary members* are to be made by the Board, subject to sub-paragraph (4).

(3) *In making any appointment* by virtue of sub-paragraph (2) the Board must act in accordance with any procedure for making such appointments that may be prescribed.

(4) If, at any time, there are less than five ordinary members, *the Secretary of State must appoint* such number of ordinary members as is required to bring the number of ordinary members to five. [. . .].[136]

– repeals and consequential amendments

SCHEDULE 20

CONSEQUENTIAL AMENDMENTS RELATING TO PART 7

[. . .]

2(1) Section 12 (notice of compulsory purchase by local and other authorities) *is amended as follows*.

(2) In the title, for "and occupiers" *insert* , "occupiers and others".

(3) In subsection (2)—

(a) *omit* the "or" at the end of paragraph (a), and
(b) at the end of paragraph (b) *insert* ", or
(c) the person is entitled to the benefit of an obligation under a conservation covenant (within the meaning of Part 7 of the Environment Act 2021) relating to the land." [. . .].[137]

136 Pensions Act 2004 (legislation.gov.uk).
137 Environment Act 2021 (legislation.gov.uk).

Looking at the extract reported above, the drafter repeals and amends explicitly in the form a list of affected provisions that are placed in a single section in the Final provisions. Repeals might take the form of a simple deletion (*in subsection 2 omit ... at the end of the paragraph b insert...*) where no further legislative action is required. In this case the verbs typically used are *repeal, omit, delete*, and *cancel*. Or a new provision combines elements of the existing provision leaving the law substantially unchanged (... the *person is entitled to the benefit of an obligation under a conservation covenant (within the meaning of Part 7 of the Environment Act 2021) relating to the land...*).

– tables setting out benefits and resources, or rates for taxes

Acts of the Northern Ireland Assembly 2021 c. 5

SCHEDULE 2

Amounts of resources authorised for use and amounts of accruing resources which may be used in the year ending 31 March 2022[138]

Purpose	Resources authorised (£)	Total Accruing Resources (£)
Department of Agriculture, Environment and Rural Affairs A. For use by the Department of Agriculture, Environment and Rural Affairs on the provision of agricultural, educational and knowledge transfer services, research and development and payments and grants to societies, associations, institutions and clubs for agri-food purposes, horticultural and rural development; [...]	371,937,000	99,102,000

138 Budget (No. 2) Act (Northern Ireland) 2021 (legislation.gov.uk).

Purpose	Resources authorised (£)	Total Accruing Resources (£)
Department for communities A. For use by the Department for Communities on social security administration; payment of social security benefits, other benefits, and National Insurance credits to people of working age, to pensioners and customers abroad and to people with disabilities and their carers, provision of grants, compensation, discretionary grants and loans and repayment of loans [. . .]	2,885,588,000	197,129,000

A general warning for legislative drafters is that they should identify which provisions need to be placed in the text and which can be safely inserted in the Schedule(s). Among the guiding rules that drafters can resort to, the subsidiary and consequential nature is one of the more suitable principles for identifying the provisions that can be safely transferred to a Schedule.

4.2.3.5 Explanatory notes

Since 1999 nearly all Acts of the UK Parliament have been accompanied by 'Explanatory notes'. Their purpose is to explain the Act without the need for legal or other specialized knowledge, bringing the reader – particularly laypeople – closer to an authentic interpretation and application of the Act:

> What these notes do
>
> These *Explanatory Notes* relate to the Agriculture Act 2020 (c. 21) which received Royal Assent on 11 November 2020.
>
> - *These Explanatory Notes have been prepared* by the Department for Environment, Food and Rural Affairs (Defra) *in order to assist the reader of the Act.* They do not form part of the Act and have not been endorsed by Parliament.
> - *These Explanatory Notes explain what each part of the Act will mean in practice; provide background information on the development of policy; and provide additional information on how the Act will affect existing legislation in this area.*

- *These Explanatory Notes might best be read alongside the Act.* They are not, and are not intended to be, a comprehensive description of the Act.[139]

Explanatory notes give details about the policy behind the Act and the law reform pursued, and explain the new terms eventually used. For this reason, 'explanatory notes may form the bridge above the chasm of minimalism in law expressions and possible maximalism of law reform' (Xanthaki 2014: 228):

> These notes refer to the Criminal Justice Act 2003 (c.44) which received Royal Assent on 20th November 2003
>
> CRIMINAL JUSTICE ACT 2003 EXPLANATORY NOTES
>
> INTRODUCTION 1.
>
> 1. These *explanatory notes* relate to the Criminal Justice Act 2003 which received Royal Assent on 20th November. They have been prepared by the Home Office to assist the reader in understanding the Act. They do not form part of the Act and have not been endorsed by Parliament.
> 2. The notes need to be read in conjunction with the Act. They are not, and are not meant to be, a comprehensive description of the Act. So, where a section or part of a section does not seem to require any explanation or comment, none is given.
>
> SUMMARY AND BACKGROUND
>
> 3. In July 2002 the Government published a White Paper outlining its plans for the criminal justice system, from crime prevention through to the punishment and rehabilitation of offenders. Justice for All (Cm 5563) focused particularly on reforms to court procedure and sentencing, to make trials faster and to deliver clear, consistent, and appropriate sentencing. On these issues, the White Paper built on the proposals in two consultation documents: Review of the Criminal Courts of England and Wales by Sir Robin Auld (2001) and Making Punishment Work: report of a review of the sentencing framework of England and Wales (2001) by John Halliday.
> 4. This Act is intended to introduce reforms in these two areas. With regard to court procedure, the Act aims to improve the management of cases through the courts by involving the Crown Prosecution Service in charging decisions, by reforming the system for allocating cases to court, and by increasing magistrates' sentencing powers so that fewer cases have to go to the Crown Court. It

139 https://www.legislation.gov.uk/ukpga/2020/21/notes/division/1/index.htm

will enable action to be taken to reduce breaches of bail by introducing a new presumption against bail in certain circumstances.

5. The Act is designed to ensure that criminal trials are run more efficiently and to reduce the scope for abuse of the system. It will reform the rules on advance disclosure of evidence and will allow for judge-alone trial in cases involving threats and intimidation of juries, and paves the way for judge-alone trial in exceptionally long, complex serious fraud cases. It will ensure the wider involvement of the community as a whole, by reforming rules on jury service. Rules on evidence will be changed to allow the use of previous convictions where relevant, and to allow the use of reported (hearsay) evidence where there is good reason why the original source cannot be present, or where the judge otherwise considers it would be appropriate. It will enable any witness to give evidence using live links. A right of appeal for the prosecution against judicial decisions to direct or order an acquittal before the jury has been asked to consider the evidence will be introduced to balance the defendant's right of appeal against both conviction and sentence. The Act will also make it possible in certain very serious cases for a retrial to take place despite an earlier acquittal if there is new and compelling evidence of an accused's guilt. These notes refer to the Criminal Justice Act 2003 (c.44) which received Royal Assent on 20th November 2003.

6. The Act aims to provide a sentencing framework which is clearer and more flexible than the current one. The purposes of sentencing of adults are identified in statute for the first time, as punishment, crime reduction, reform and rehabilitation, public protection, and reparation. The principles of sentencing are set out, including that of any previous convictions, where they are recent and relevant and should be regarded as an aggravating factor which will increase the severity of the sentence. A new Sentencing Guidelines Council will be established. Sentences will be reformed, so that the various kinds of community order for adults will be replaced by a single community order with a range of possible requirements; custodial sentences of less than 12 months will be replaced by a new sentence, (described in the Halliday report as "custody plus"), which will always involve a period of at least 26 weeks post-release supervision in the community; and sentences over 12 months will be served in full, half in custody, half in the community, with supervision extended to the end of the sentence rather than the ¾ point as now. Serious violent and sexual offenders will be given new sentences which will ensure that they are kept in prison or under supervision for longer periods than currently. At the other end of the custodial scale, several "intermediate" sanctions will be introduced. These include intermittent custody and a reformed suspended sentence in which offenders have to complete a range of requirements imposed by the court. The intention is for the court to be able to provide each offender with a sentence that best meets the needs of the particular case, at any level of seriousness, and for sentences to be more effectively managed by the correctional services who will need to work together closely in delivering the new sentences.

7. The Act also addresses a number of other areas. It contains a number of provisions on drug related offences, including extending to those aged 14 and above the provisions to test persons in police detention and at other points in the criminal justice system for specified Class A drugs. It establishes a new scheme under which the court, rather than the Home Secretary, will determine the minimum term to be served in prison by a person convicted of murder. It will establish a five-year mandatory minimum custodial sentence for unauthorised possession of a prohibited firearm. It will increase the maximum penalty for causing death by dangerous driving from 10 to 14 years and retain the power of arrest for the possession of cannabis or cannabis resin following their proposed reclassification from Class B to Class C drugs. Finally, in relation to juveniles, the Act extends the use of parenting orders by making them available at an earlier stage and introduces individual support orders, requiring young people with anti-social behaviour orders to undertake education-related activities.
8. In general, the Act extends only to England and Wales.
9. The Act is in fourteen parts. Part 1 contains provisions on the Police and Criminal Evidence Act. Part 2 contains provisions on bail. Part 3 contains provisions on conditional cautions. Part 4 contains provisions on charging. Part 5 contains provisions on disclosure. Part 6 contains provisions on allocation and sending of offences. Part 7 contains provisions on trials on indictment without a jury. Part 8 contains provisions on live links. Part 9 contains provisions on prosecution appeals. Part 10 contains provisions enabling retrial for serious offences following acquittal (double jeopardy). Part 11 contains provisions on evidence of bad character (Chapter 1) and provisions on hearsay evidence (Chapter 2). Part 12 contains provisions on sentencing and is split into a number of Chapters. Chapter 1 contains general provisions about sentencing. Chapter 2 contains provisions on community orders for offenders aged 16 or over. Chapter 3 contains provisions on prison sentences of less than 12 months. Chapter 4 contains further provisions on orders under Chapters 2 and 3. Chapter 5 contains provisions on dangerous offenders. Chapter 6 contains provisions on release of prisoners on licence. Chapter 7 deals with the effect of life sentences. Chapter 8 contains other provisions about sentencing. Chapter 9 contains supplementary provisions. Part 13 contains miscellaneous provisions and Part 14 contains general provisions.[140]

Within the 'Table of contents of the explanatory notes', the 'Overview' section summarizes the content, provides context for the reader, and helps navigation around the Act and any part(s) of it:

140 Explanatory Notes to Criminal Justice Act 2003 (legislation.gov.uk).

Enterprise Act 2002 *Explanatory Notes*

Explanatory Notes Table of Contents

INTRODUCTION

OVERVIEW OF THE ACT

SUMMARY

COMMENTARY ON SECTIONS

Part 1: the Office of Fair Trading [. . .].[141]

An 'Overview' is not intended to have legal effect. The extract reported below represents a clear example of an Overview section that gives a full picture of the Act (i.e., *Enterprise Act 2002*) and the main changes that are made to the law:

Overview of the Act

3. The Act is divided into eleven parts and has 281 sections and 26 Schedules.
4. Part 1: *establishes* the Office of Fair Trading (OFT), *sets out* its general functions, and *provides for* arrangements for making super-complaints to the OFT.
5. *Part 2: establishes and makes* provisions for proceedings before the Competition Appeal Tribunal (CAT).
6. Part 3: *provides for* a new merger regime, *covering* the definition of a qualifying merger, the duty of the OFT to make references to the Competition Commission (CC); how references are determined; the procedures that relate to certain public interest cases and other special cases; powers of enforcement; undertakings and orders; and various supplementary matters, such as information and publicity requirements and powers to require information.
7. Part 4: *makes* provision for new market investigations arrangements. It sets out the power of the OFT and the Secretary of State to make references to the CC, and how the CC should report on the references. It *provides for,* particular arrangements to apply in public interest cases, and also *covers* powers of enforcement and various supplementary matters.
8. Part 5: *deals with* the CC and *provides for* its rules of procedure.
9. Part 6: *deals with* the creation of a cartel offence.

141 Enterprise Act 2002 - Explanatory Notes (legislation.gov.uk).

10. Part 7: *deals with,* a number of miscellaneous competition provisions, including powers to disqualify directors who engage in serious competition breaches.
11. Part 8: *deals with* new procedures on enforcing certain consumer legislation, and miscellaneous related matters.
12. Part 9: *provides for* rules to govern the disclosure of specified information held by a public authority, setting out the circumstances in which the information may be disclosed, and various related matters.
13. Part 10: *changes* insolvency law by providing for a new regime for company administration and restricting the future use of administrative receivership; abolishing Crown preference; establishing a new regime for the insolvency of individuals; and making changes to the operation of the Insolvency Services Account.
14. Part 11: *contains* a number of supplementary provisions, such as commencement, short title and territorial extent.[142]

Generally speaking, verbs such as *deal with*, *cover* and *contain* are used in the 'Overview section' to summarize the content of the Act (i.e., 'Part 5: *deals with* the CC . . .; and also *covers* powers of enforcement . . .; Part 11: *contains* a number of supplementary provisions . . .'). Whereas, verbs like to *establish, set out, make*, and *provide for,* are used to explain the main changes to the law (i.e., 'Part 1: *establishes* the Office of Fair Trading (OFT), *sets out* its general functions . . .; Part 4: *makes* provision for new market investigations arrangements . . .; Part 9: *provides for* rules to govern the disclosure of specified information . . .').

4.3 Future perspectives

The analysis conducted in this Chapter demonstrates that the structure of legislative texts might represent an important step in the direction towards a more clear and effective legislation. Notwithstanding the innovations highlighted here, the overall structure of Acts remains

142 Enterprise Act 2002 - Explanatory Notes (legislation.gov.uk).

strongly influenced by the drafting tradition of the governmental institutions. Indeed, a certain degree of adherence to traditional drafting might be understandable because it confers on the text the level of formality required to remind the readers of the authoritative function of normative texts (Bowers 1989; Fung and Watson-Brown 1994; Butt 2013; Xanthaki 2014, 2022) and the long traditions of the political organization, constitution of the state and administrative structure. Due to their function of creating, modifying or ceasing the rights and duties of individuals and/or institutions, legislative statements perform conventionalized communicative purposes that are mutually shared by the practicing members of the specialist community (Bhatia 1994; Gotti 2011, 2014) via the construction of uncommon sentence structures, redundant phraseology, and lexical and syntactic discontinuity. Perhaps, Xanthaki (2014: 133) observes, due to the adherence to this drafting tradition, 'little debate is currently taking place on the placement of legislative provisions within the text: drafters simply use the traditional structure as the unquestionable format of each new legislative text'. However, if the normative sentences have to be constructed in such a way that people can be certain about the objective of the Act with regard to their rights and duties, these rights and obligations have to be expressed in a way that reduces the intricacies of textual structure, and the obscurity of lexical and syntactic features typical of traditional legislation (Mellinkoff 1963; Bhatia 1994; Gotti and Dossena 2001; Tiersma 1999; Bhatia 2010, 2014, 2021; Gotti 2011, 2014; Butt 2013; Xanthaki 2014, 2022).

Increasing demand for a more approachable legislation (for instance, the plain movement's concerns come into play), has certainly directed legislative drafters to consider carefully which parts of the Acts need to be linguistically simplified and textually structured in a way that departs from what has been traditionally prescribed. In this regard, the analysis developed in this Chapter reveals that the major revisions that have been recently done both at the level of textual organization of Acts and lexico-grammatical structure of legislative provisions, have been made on the basis of the most appropriate considerations about the prioritization of messages conveyed to the final reader.

5 Improving legal communication

5.1 Plain language

Historically speaking, legal English evolved over the three-century period between the 1470s (the setting up of the first printing press in England) and the 1770s (American Declaration of Independence). Inevitably, its terminology and style are still in the form they had reached by the early years of the 19th century. In modern times, important changes have been brought to the length and layout of legal documents. Despite these important transformations, the language has remained largely frozen in time.

Traditional legal language has been increasingly challenged and this questioning has been increasingly stimulated by the consumer movement of the latter decades of the 20th century. Particularly relevant was the rise in the 1960s of western consumer movements which were concerned with empowering laymen so they could defend their rights against private companies and government bodies. Isolated attempts had been made during the first half of the 20th century, for example in the United States, to introduce measures to make legal English less convoluted (Mellinkoff 1963).

Across the Atlantic, in Liverpool, the plain English campaign was born in 1979 and by the mid-1980s it was already possible to speak of a Plain Language Movement operating in all major English-speaking countries, including Canada, Australia, New Zealand and, by the early 1990s, South Africa (Williams 2004: 116). During the same period (late 1970s), the movement took root in the United States when the *Executive Order 12044*[143] imposed regulations issued by federal agencies to be

143 http://www.presidency.ucsb.edu/

written in plain English. Lately, the *Plain Writing Act of 2010* aims to improve the effectiveness and accountability of federal agencies to the public by promoting clear Government communication.[144] Several states in the United States require insurance contracts to be written in plain English; yet, there has in fact been relatively little innovation in the drafting of legislation in the United States.

The same is also true of the United Kingdom which introduced the *Unfair Terms in Consumer Contracts Regulations* 1999 implementing a directive of the European Commission and stating at *Regulation 7* that 'any seller or supplier shall ensure that any written contract is expressed in plain, intelligible language'.[145]

In Canada, Australia, New Zealand and South Africa, plain language principles and techniques have developed more deeply, and many new laws are drafted in plain English these days to the advantage of legal drafting generally, and not merely the field of securities documents (Hernández and Volker 2017). In this regard, we can mention the *Companion Policy to National Instrument 81–101*, on the topic of disclosure in mutual fund prospectuses in Canada and the *Queensland Industrial Relations Act 1999*, which requires the Queensland Industrial Relations Commission to ensure that its written decision are '(a) in plain English; and (b) structured in a way that makes a decision as easy to understand as the subject-matter allows'.[146]

Proposals for reforming legal English have been choral and among the specific causes generally mentioned there are sentences of undue length, overuse of archaic and Latin expressions, unnecessary and repetition of definitions and expressions, partiality of nominalizations, a labyrinth of sentences and clauses. Several commentators have cited similar problems while others have expressed more muted versions of the problem, saying simply that there is a 'need to improve understanding and access to the law' (Barnes 2006: 97). Much of the criticism by plain language advocates of legal language is clearly reasonable in that much of it is objectively difficult for the average layperson to understand. As Williams (2004: 123) observes,

144 *Plain Writing Act of 2010*, Sec. 2.

145 SI 1999 No 2083, revoking and replacing SI 1994 No 3129.

146 Division 5 <Industrial Relations Act 1999 (legislation.qld.gov.au)>.

> drafters should attempt to use expressions and a phraseology that can bring legal texts closer to ordinary citizens, but not at the expense of creating uncertainty or ambiguity, as this would ultimately be even more detrimental to those citizens in whose defence the text may have been written to start with.

There are inherent factors that make it difficult for the drafter to convey the intentions of the legislator and ensure there are no ambiguities and misunderstandings in the words and expressions that have been chosen (Xanthaki and Pennisi 2012, 2016). Not only do increasingly complex societies imply ever more complex legislation, but increasing political demands to produce legislation quickly and efficiently on the one hand, and the lack of effective consultations between policy makers and legislative drafters on the other, certainly affect the language used and the underlying function of the text. In this regard, eminent scholars in the field of Language for Specific Purposes (Robinson 1980; Swales 1985, 1990; Bright 1992; Hyland 2002) observe that legal language is made up of several genres (Charaudeau 2002; Fairclough 2003), each with its own specific characteristics, ranging from

> the spoken exchanges in a court between, say, lawyers and witnesses in a cross-examination, to the relatively standardized instructions given to jury members who are required to express a verdict in a court case, to the jargon employed by members of the legal profession in interpersonal communication, to the written language in case law, law reports and prescriptive legal texts (Williams 2004: 111).

Undeniably, certain types of written legal language may contain lexico-grammatical features that mark it as being so peculiar as to be at times incomprehensible to anyone except legal experts. Describing the peculiarities of legal English, Butt (2013: 1) defines it as mysterious in form and expression, often bordering on intricacies, and

> larded with law-Latin and Norman-French, heavily dependent on the past, and unashamedly archaic. Antiquated words flourish – words such as *aforementioned, herein, therein,* and *whereas*, which are rarely now heard in everyday language. Habitual jargon and stilted formalism conjure a spurious sense of precision – *the said, the aforesaid, the same*. Oddities abound: oath-swearers do not believe something, they *verily* believe it; parties do not wish something, they are *desirous* of it; the clearest photocopy only purports to be a copy; and so on.[147]

147 Emphasis of the author himself.

Legal writing originates from different sources that have influenced its style. Some of them still exert constant influence/power over it, such as the pressure to conform to professional forms, the need to avoid ambiguity, the combination of various languages from which legal writing derives its vocabulary, conservatism in the legal profession, familiarity that comes from adopting words and expressions that have been used for years and seen to be effective. The main lexico-grammatical features of written legal texts are usually listed as follows:

(a) inclusion of archaic, or rarely used, words or expressions;
(b) inclusion of foreign words and expressions, especially from Latin;
(c) long, complex sentences, with intricate patterns of coordination and subordination;
(d) tendency towards nominalization;[148]
(e) high frequency of passive constructions;
(f) impersonal writing style;
(g) repetition of words, expressions and syntactic structures.

Written legal texts do not necessarily contain all the features outlined above, though many of them do, and the compound effect often makes them extremely difficult to decipher without a specific training (Williams 2004: 115). It is clear, therefore, that a contrastive analysis of key instances (legal language and Plain Language Movement) and key subjects (i.e., legal drafters and linguists), supported by the investigation of practical cases taken from the contemporary international context, would serve as a valuable aid to the legislator, the lawyer and the drafters involved in a process of plain language reform.

In the recent past, the increasing questioning of the traditional legal language has brought significant improvement notably in statutes and commercial documents (Butt 2013). In this regard, Justice Michael Kirby proposed 'the ten commandments for plain language in law'. On

148 For example, *to settle* nominalized into *to enter into a settlement agreement*, or *to refer* nominalized into a *made referral* (Tiersma 1999; Garner 2001; Williams 2004; Butt 2013).

the occasion of the Plain Language Conference held in Sidney the 17th of October 2009, Kirby stated that

> at stake in the plain movement is not just the theoretical objective of improving the understanding of the law by lawyers. It is the noble objective of making the law speak with a clearer voice to the people who are bound by the law. This is an idea central to the notion of democratic governance.[149]

Starting from the idea that a clear legal language is a goal that needs to be reached by democratic institutions, Kirby believes that the simplicity of legal expression can be attained via the following rules or 'commandments' (2009: 8–9):

1) Complex statements of facts and law should begin with a summary to let the reader know where he or she will be travelling.
2) Short sentences and shorter words should replace long.
3) The passive voice should generally be banished and replaced with the active voice [. . .].
4) Words of connection should be at the beginning of sentences. Words of emphasis should generally be at the end.
5) Where there is a choice, the shorter word (ordinarily from a Germanic root) should be preferred to the longer word (ordinarily from the French language of the Norman Conquest).
6) Sexist and obviously ambiguous language should be removed.
7) Vagueness is sometimes necessary in legal drafting. However, ambiguity should generally be tackled head on.
8) Those old potboilers "whereas", "hereinunder", "cognisant", "requisite" should be deleted.
9) Layout is a technique of communication that matters. It can assist human understanding. As can headings and sub-headings; and
10) In legal texts that will cross borders, it will generally be necessary to be especially careful in the use of words. [. . .].

Some criticism and caution have been expressed by those who consider plain language a synonym for kindergarten style of language (Asprey

149 PLAIN CONCORD (michaelkirby.com.au).

2010; Cooney 2012; Butt 2013). In fact, they believe that writing legal texts in a plain style eventually produces texts whose language is shorn of beauty, stripped of vocabulary, shortened in form, and poor in style. With a clear intention to shed light on the meaning of plain style, *Part D – Section 22* of the South African *Consumer Protection Act 2008* not only lists the main features of plain language, but also requires certain types of written information to be provided to the consumers. As can be read,

> Part D
>
> Right to disclosure and information
>
> Right to information in plain and understandable language
>
> 22. (1) The producer of a notice, document or visual representation that is required, in terms of this Act or any other law, to be produced, provided or displayed to a consumer must produce, provide or display that notice, document or visual representation -
>
> (a) in the form prescribed in terms of this Act or any other legislation, if any, for that notice, document or visual representation; or
> (b) in plain language, if no form has been prescribed for that notice, document or visual representation.
>
> (2) For the purposes of this Act, a notice, document or visual representation is in plain language if it is reasonable to conclude that an ordinary consumer of the class of persons for whom the notice, document or visual representation is intended, with average literacy skills and minimal experience as a consumer of the relevant goods or services, could be expected to understand the content, significance and import of the notice, document or visual representation without undue effort, having regard to -
>
> (a) the context, comprehensiveness and consistency of the notice, document or visual representation;
> (b) the organisation, form and style of the notice, document or visual representation;
> (c) the vocabulary, usage and sentence structure of the notice, document or visual representation; and
> (d) the use of any illustrations, examples, headings or other aids to the reading and understanding.
>
> (3) The Commission may publish guidelines for methods of assessing whether a notice, document or visual representation satisfies the requirements of subsection (1)(b).

(4) Guidelines published in terms of subsection (3) may be published for public comment.[150]

This *Act* clearly makes the point that '"plain language" is concerned with more than mere words' (Butt 2013: 103). Here, the key point lies in the phrase:

> a notice, document or visual representation is in plain language if it is reasonable to conclude that an ordinary consumer of the class of persons for whom the notice, document or visual representation is intended (*Section 22(2)*),[151]

where the central assumption is that the 'final addressee / reader' (to whom the legislative document is addressed) is the parties to the document, and not just the legislative drafters / institutional bodies who have written it.

Eventually, plain language style requires more than facilitating communication. Beginning from the identification of the specific categories of final addressees / potential readers of the legislative text, the drafter needs to take into account the word meaning, sentence structure, textual organization and general layout of the final document. Undoubtedly, plain language has revolutionized legislative drafting by turning the attention of institutional bodies, and expressly legislative drafters, from the restricted legal audience (i.e., lawyers, governmental institutions, experts in law, etc.), to the much wider context of the intended addressees (mostly, laypeople), and/or potential readers of the legislative text.

5.2 Legislative provisions in context

Legislative provisions are required to be clear, precise and unambiguous, one the one hand, and all-inclusive, on the other (Bhatia 2010). The challenge in the construction of legislative discourse is the nature

150 Consumer Protection Act 68 of 2008 (ndrc.org.za).

151 *Ibid.*

and extent of specification of legal scope in the expression of legislative intentions. A clever balance between the two is the essence of the craftsmanship of legislative intent. Linguistics can certainly provide a method by which drafters can assess the effectiveness of their draft. In particular, the study of language demonstrates that drafters often miss the focus of the policy concepts that they wish to communicate, and aims to identify a method by which drafters may achieve their conceptual focus (De Benedetto 2018). For this reason, it might be useful to start from the concept of 'discourse' in linguistics and then, concentrate on legislative provisions.

Discourse is the construction and organization of the segments of language above as well as below the sentence. It is units of language which may be larger or smaller than a single sentence, but the meaning is always beyond the sentence. The elements of grammar, lexis and phonology still play a fundamental role, but they are reconsidered as a part of that multilayered cognitive and socio-cultural phenomenon linguists define discourse (Lemke 1990; Bhatia 1993; Wodak and Meyer 2001; Haspelmath et al. 2005; Gotti 2011).

As Bhatia (2010) observes, this is particularly true within the common law jurisdictions. Legislative drafters deal with a universe of human behaviour which is unlimited, in the sense that it is impossible to predict exactly what may happen within the human universe. Legislative drafting is a narrower concept to the civil law equivalent of law-making: law-making embraces the whole process of conceptualization of legislation until its very implementation and thus reflects the legislative process, whereas legislative drafting reflects the drafting process only. This does not mean to say that drafting is completely foreign to the legislative process. In fact, the drafting process is part of the legislative process, which in turn is part of the policy process (Stefanou 2011). Furthermore, the context of a legal document is often scrutinized to shed light upon the intent of an ambiguous or obscure provision so that it may be interpreted as its drafter intended.

The aim is to make provisions that are clear, precise, unambiguous and all-inclusive as possible whereas the nature and function of participant organizations unsurprisingly influence the legislative actions. The implementation of legislation may be significantly influenced by a range of filtering agents at whom legislation is directed and who may constrain, adapt and modify the intentions that form the basis of the approved legislation in the first place. As we have seen in Chapter 4, modern legislative drafting theory urges legislative drafters to bare the text from preliminary provisions and to start as early as possible with the regulatory message that the government is trying to convey to its citizens. And so, the pursuit of modern drafters is to share that message with the users of the legislation in a manner that allows them to be heard loud and clear (Stefanou and Xanthaki 2008). It therefore becomes crucial to explore how linguistics may be of some help for the legislative drafters who want to know how a piece of legislation is structured in terms of lexico-grammatical and discoursal features.

In the field of linguistics, scholars have extensively analyzed specialized discourse and the different communicative purposes of specialized texts that have public implications (Driedger 1982; Bhatia 1987, 1993, 1994, 2014; Bowers 1989; Campbell 1996; Mattila 2006; Galdia 2009; Goddard 2010; Gotti 2011, 2014; Engberg 2013a). In this case, two versions of the specialized text need to be produced: (i) one for specialists, and (ii) the other for ordinary citizens. The two version will have two different communicative purposes (one legislative, and the other informative), depth of specificity and level of reader accessibility. In the case of legislation, one communicative purpose will be strictly legislative and governmental, whereas the other communicative purpose will be informative and directed to the public at large.

In order to make the specialist versions easier for processing and interpretation, Bhatia (2010, 2021) suggests the 'easification' of legislative provisions, keeping them clear, precise, unambiguous, and all-inclusive, and as transparent as linguistic resources permit. The provision will still be equally authoritative, detailed, adequately specified, serving the same legislative function in the court of law (Table 8).

Table 8. Easification measures.

Easification	
legislative purpose	necessarily
	• all-inclusive • informative • authoritative • authentic • complete in all respect • serving the same function in the court of law
depth of specificity	still relatively more accessible to the intended readers
specialists	

According to Bhatia (2010, 2021), greater accessibility can be achieved by using a number of 'easification measures'. However, 'easification measures' does not mean 'simplified versions'. In fact, they are by no means synonyms. To be more specific, a simplified version is meant to be a simple account of an authoritative version to inform citizens about the main legislative intentions and their implication for their personal and public activities.

Table 9. Simplification measures.

Simplification	
informative purpose	not necessarily
	• all-inclusive • informative • authoritative • authentic • complete in all respect
public awareness	easily accessible to a larger body of unintended readers
non-specialists	

As Table 9 above shows, a simplified version is not necessarily all-inclusive, informative, authoritative, authentic, complete in all respects, and easily accessible to larger non-specialist readers. At this point, it becomes interesting to consider both the simplification and the 'easification' strategies, their own characteristics and peculiarities, and the circumstances in which they can be successfully used in order to make legislative provisions more accessible.

5.2.1 Simplification strategies

Simplification in legislative texts can be achieved via introducing Purpose clause, Explanatory notes, subheadings, etc. However, this added information cannot be placed in all legislative texts. In some cases, their use might oversimplify and distort the content and intended meaning of the original text (Langton 2005).

A simplified version is not intended to replace the original, and simplification strategies may be successfully applied where an original text needs to be explained to or summarized for non-specialist readers. This is true of the International Advisory Commission of the Commonwealth Human Rights Initiative which felt the need to explain the legislation relating to disability to the citizens of Ghana. As the then chair of the CHRI's International Advisory Commission, Sam Okudzeto, explains in the last paragraph of the foreword to *The Simplified Version of Disability Rights in Ghana*

> [. . .] This book aims to simplify the legislation so that more people may understand it. It is hoped that by improving the general public's understanding of the law and by increasing awareness, more people will begin to demand the rights to which they are legally entitled.[152]

Approximately 10% of Ghana's twenty million citizens are persons with disability. Although their rights are guaranteed both by Ghana's Constitution and by international conventions, in reality, these provisions have offered them very little actual protection against discrimination. For example, in 2000, 80.2% of the general population in Ghana was employed. However, only 69% of persons with disability had a job. Therefore, The Simplified Version of Disability Rights in Ghana is

152 Microsoft Word – PWD final.doc (humanrightsinitiative.org).

a timely and welcome publication. At this point, a lexico-grammatical and textual analysis of both texts, that is, the original legislative text *The Persons with Disabilities Act 2006 – Act 175* and its simplified version reveals interesting insights.

The original legislative text, *The Persons with Disabilities Act 2006*, consists of a short preamble, eight sections and sixty Articles. It displays a rather clear structure, with no lengthy initial case description. In Section 2 'Employment of persons with disability', for instance, the case description is placed after the main provisionary clause, textually mapped in the form of two subsubsections listed rather unclearly, in subsection (1) as 1, 2, 3, as shown below:

> Appropriate training for the unemployed person with disability
>
> 13. (1) Where the name of a person with disability remains on a job search list for more than two years, the Ministry shall take the name of that person off the list, and where applicable
>
> 1. give that person appropriate training,
> 2. Provide that person with necessary working tools and materials, and
> 3. Assist that person to access loan capital for that person to start a business
>
> 2. A person with disability who sells the tools or materials received under subsection (1) and a person who buys the tools or materials given to a person with disability under subsection (1) commits an offence and each person is liable on summary conviction to a fine not exceeding two hundred and fifty penalty units or to a term of imprisonment not exceeding one year or to both.[153]

Overall, the text is characterized by an excessive use of textual-mapping devices breaking down each section into different subsections and sub-subsections (ranging from two to eight subsections), as can be seen in the two extracts reported below, both taken from *The Persons with Disabilities Act 2006*. The first is taken from Section 4 'Transportation' – Art. 24 and contains five subsections that, with the exception of subsection (1), ('A person with disability may import a vehicle adapted or

153 https://lawsghana.com/post-1992-legislation/table-of-content/Acts%20of%20Parliament/PERSONS%20WITH%20DISABILITY%20ACT,%202006%20(ACT%20715)/164

modified for use by persons with disability'), are all listed with the same number, i.e., number '2':

> Importation of non-conventional vehicles
>
> 24. (1) A person with disability may import a vehicle adapted or modified for use by persons with disability.
>
> 2. A person without disability shall not import a vehicle adapted or modified for use by persons with disability except with the express approval of the Minister.
>
> 2. A vehicle imported under subsection (1) shall upon the recommendations of the Minister and with approval of the Minister for Finance be exempt from the payment of import duty and any other tax relating to the importation.
>
> 2. A vehicle imported under subsection (1) shall not be re-exported.
>
> 2. A person who contravenes subsection (4) commits an offence and is liable on summary conviction to a fine not exceeding two hundred and fifty penalty units or to a term of imprisonment not exceeding twelve months or to both.[154]

The second extract is taken from – Art. 45 and is divided into 8 subsections that, as well as observed in the previous extract, do not follow a numerical order. With the exception of subsection 1, 'The Board shall meet at least once every three months for the despatch of business at the times and in the places determined by the chairperson', the following seven subsections are all listed with number '2':

> Meetings of the Board
>
> 45. (1) The Board shall meet at least once every three months for the despatch of business at the times and in the places determined by the chairperson.
>
> 2. The chairperson shall at the request in writing of at least one-third of the members of the Board convene an extraordinary meeting of the Board at the place and time determined by the chairperson.
>
> 2. The quorum at the meeting of the Board is nine members of the Board or a greater number determined by the Board in respect of an important matter.

154 https://lawsghana.com/post-1992-legislation/table-of-content/Acts%20of%20 Parliament/PERSONS%20WITH%20DISABILITY%20ACT,%202006%20 (ACT%20715)/164

2. The chairperson shall preside at meetings of the Board and in the absence of the chairperson; a member of the Board elected by the members present from among their number shall preside.

2. Matters before the Board shall be decided by a majority of the members present and voting and in the event of an equality of votes, the person presiding shall have a casting vote.

2. The Board may co-opt any person to act as an adviser at its meetings but a co-opted member shall not vote any matter for decision by the Board.

2. The proceedings of the Board shall not be invalidated by reason of a vacancy among the members or a defect in the appointment or qualification of a member.

then

2. Subject this Section, the Board shall determine and regulate the procedure for its meeting.[155]

The *Simplified Version of Disabilities Rights in Ghana 2006* (hereafter, *Simplified Disabilities Rights*) on the other hand, renders the original legislative text more accessible and easier to read due to a strategic use of linguistic and textual devices.

Such simplified versions should be meant for public awareness, which may include legal intentions, explanations, and typical examples. It is a common practice in sciences, where we have the original reports on experiments, and also, a popular version for non-specialist readers (Langton 2005; Bhatia 2010). The *Simplified Disabilities Rights* consists of two parts. In Part 1 'Simplified Version of the Persons with Disability Act 2006', there is an indication of the main topics regulated by the Act and consists of sixteen Provisions (which are listed below). In the second part there is the 'Simplified Version of the International Legal Framework' relating to persons with disability.

As the linguistic and textual analysis reveals, there is no loss of intended meaning although the format is quite unusual. This is achieved by using a subheading in the form of a question to reveal legislative intent, and mostly used in Part 1 as shown below:

155 https://lawsghana.com/post-1992-legislation/table-of-content/Acts%20of%20Parliament/PERSONS%20WITH%20DISABILITY%20ACT,%202006%20(ACT%20715)/164

Part 1

Simplified Version of the Persons with Disability Act, 2006

1. What are the Contents of the Act?
2. What is the purpose of the Act?
3. What rights of a person with disability are protected under the Act?
4. Do other people have responsibilities?
5. Can persons with disability be employed? Under what circumstances?
6. What are Rehabilitation Centers?
7. What are the legal provisions on Education for persons with disability?
8. What are the other responsibilities?
9. How are the transportation needs for persons with disability addressed?
10. Can a person with disability own a driver's license?
11. What are the legal provisions on healthcare and facilities for persons with disability?
12. Law enforcement and disability
13. What other matters does the Act address?
14. What structures will be set up to implement and enforce the Law? What will the objectives of these new structures be?
15. How much time do the public have to make the changes implemented by this Act?
16. Who is a person with disability in Ghana?[156]

The *Simplified Disabilities Rights* also explains what 'a disabled person' means:

16. Who is a person with disability in Ghana?

A person with a physical, mental, or sensory impairment including a visual, hearing or speech functional disability, which gives rise to physical, cultural or social barriers that substantially, limits one or more of the major life activities of that individual.

156 https://www.humanrightsinitiative.org/publications/ghana/disability_rights_in_ghana.pdf

It also provides clear and straightforward examples to illustrate the rules via a strategic use of *if* and *then* clauses, as shown below:

> 6. Can persons with disability be employed? Under what circumstances?
>
> [...]
>
> *If* the name of a person with disability remains on the job search list for more than two years, the Ministry shall give the person appropriate training, provide that person with necessary working tools, and assist the person to access loan capital to start a business.
>
> *If* the person who has been given the tools sells them *then* he/she is guilty of a criminal offence. [...]
>
> *If* a person suffers a disability as a result of employment, the employer is under an obligation to re-train or deploy the person to another section of the workplace which is more suited to the person's disability and should give that person any relief that he/she is entitled to under the Workmen's Compensation Law, 1987 (PNDCL 187) [...]
>
> 7. What are the legal provisions on Education for persons with disability?
>
> It is mandatory for parents or guardians of children with disability to send them to school. *If* a parent does not send such a child to school, he/she is guilty of a criminal offence. [...]
>
> 9. How are the transportation needs for persons with disability addressed?
>
> *If* a person without disability would like to import a vehicle which is adapted for persons with disability, she/he may only do so with the approval of the Minister.
>
> 10. Can a person with disability own a driver's license?
>
> The law is not very clear on who can apply for a driving license. It says that persons who have a hearing disability may own a driving license *if* they pass a driving test and satisfy VELD conditions. [...]
>
> At least two seats shall be reserved for persons with disability on commercial buses. However, *if the* bus gets full and the reserved seats are not occupied by persons with disability, the bookman or loading driver can fill the seats with other passengers.[157]

157 https://www.humanrightsinitiative.org/publications/ghana/disability_rights_in_ghana.pdf

The *Simplified Disabilities Rights* makes use of cautious textual-mapping. Unnecessary cross-referencing, overused textual-mapping and multiple negative phrasing are eventually removed.

In the case of UK legislation, in 2010 the Department for Business, Innovation and Skills[158] of the UK Government commissioned a Report on the *Consolidation and Simplification of UK Consumer Law*.[159] In the 'Introduction' to the 'Executive Summary' to the Report (reported below), the main reason for assigning this task is explained:

> 1. EXECUTIVE SUMMARY Introduction 1.1
>
> This Report was commissioned because there was a belief that consumer contract law could be simplified, streamlined by separating out into a coherent package the legal provisions affecting consumers, and rationalised by adopting more appropriate terminology. (2010: 1.1)

As clarified in the Report, the Research Team[160] worked on three parts, that is,

(i) simplifying the substance of the law;
(ii) reorganizing and reordering the structure, and separating the provisions;
(iii) rationalizing and simplifying the terminology.

For each section, the format was to begin from the current position, then to analyze the problems, before providing the options for change aimed at ameliorating the present system, and finally making comments and recommendations. In this regard, they consider that in a foreseeable future an omnibus consumer contract law would be generally advisable.

---

158 The Department for Business, Innovation and Skills (BIS) and the Department of Energy and Climate Change (DECC) have merged to form the Department for Business, Energy and Industrial Strategy (BEIS) <https://www.gov.uk/government/organisations/department-for-business-innovation-skills>.

159 Simplifying consumer law – GOV.UK (www.gov.uk).

160 Members of the Research Team are listed in the Report as follows: Andrew Bell, Rick Canavan, Annette Nordhausen Scholes, Deborah Parry, Professor Chris Willett <https://www.gov.uk/government/organisations/department-for-business-innovation-skills>.

In fact, they plainly admit that 'This is an opportunity to simplify the law by only having the consumer provisions in the statute' (2010: 1.6).

Among the practical techniques proposed in the Report for structuring the new law, are:

- to include a series of underpinning principles at the beginning of the legislation. In fact, the content of these might well depend upon the precise scope of the legislation;
- to express in non-legalistic language or plain language the fundamental rules found in the consecutive paragraphs.

A general conclusion reached by the Research Team was that consumer contract law would be improved if many of the provisions were brought together in a single consumer contract law. In particular, the Team suggested that the rules should be informed by general principles reflecting the need for the contract to fulfil reasonable consumer expectations. In this regard, simpler modern terminology should be used that is appropriate for the consumer context and understandable to laypeople at large. As they further explain, 'this is intended to make the law accessible to consumers, their lay advisers and lawyers who may not be specialists in consumer law' (2010: 1.7). The overall approach is to simplify the rules both in content and concept to promote transparency and accessibility.

The final recommendation the Research Team provides is that there may be additional scope for using innovative drafting techniques, such as examples, guidance notes, glossaries, etc. to make the law more comprehensible to consumers and traders.

5.2.2 'Easification' strategies

To understand why legal rules are written the way they are (Bhatia 2010), it is important to recognize first the nature of legal reasoning, that is, communicative purposes, intended audiences, and linguistic features of the text itself (Coode 1848; Gunnarsson 1984). Then, how the legal reasoning affects traditional legal drafting methods (Bhatia 1983, 1987).

According to traditional legal drafting, most legal sentences in traditional common law legislative texts take a direct or indirect form of the legal reasoning formula '*if A* (case) *then B* (legal subject) *shall be / shall do C* (legal action)' (Crystal and Davy 1969; Searle 1979; Driedger 1982). Scholars working in this field suggest that when analyzing any complex legislation or legal text, the true structure of a rule should, whenever possible, be 'case + condition + sub-condition + legal subject + legal action' (Fung and Watson-Brown 1994). If this is so,

- (pre-)conditions and case descriptors might precede the action rule;
- passive voice main clauses (usually phrased using nouns and qualifying phrases or clauses) might be turned into the active voice;
- legal subjects should be highlighted making the verb in the first principal clause active voice;
- everything that comes after this main verb constitutes the legal action of the section/subsection;
- where and how legal subject(s) or action(s) are qualified by cases, pre-conditions, or conditions.

Then, in terms of the nature of legal rules a typical classification (Langton 2005) is made as follows (Table 10):

Table 10. Classification of legal rules.

definition rules	give special meanings that apply to whole or part of the legislative text in which they are placed
action rules	define duties, obligations and rights, such as prohibitions, powers and penalties
stipulation rules	state how and when rules apply
qualification rules	further classified in preparatory (i.e., case descriptors as to when the rule applies), operational (i.e., how the rule applies), and referential (i.e., what other sections of the legislative texts or other Acts need to be read as well)

Taking this tradition into account, Bhatia (2010: 11) observes that within common law jurisdictions

> it is considered advantageous to condense all the necessary information into a single sentence so as not to allow interpretation of any part of the provision out of the context.

Nevertheless, the construction of single sentences that carry such an information load has the effect of making them complex in their meaning and less accessible for the intended audience. Such syntactic complexity eventually makes cognitive processing beyond untrained and non-specialist readers. In this regard, 'cognitive structuring' is a term that linguists (Leech et al. 1994; Langton 2005; Bhatia 2010, 2014) use to indicate a practical tool for revealing potential confusion or misinterpretation present in the legislative provisions. Cognitive structures are the basic mental processes people use to make sense of information.[161] Clarifying cognitive structure is one of the most efficient 'easification' strategies. In other words, it might ease the cognitive and syntactic processing of long sentences with multiple qualifications that have the negative effect of adding excessive information load in the syntactic construction of legislative provisions (Bhatia 1983). More precisely, by means of 'easification' strategies it might possible to:

- easily recognize the legislative intentions;
- clarify legislative issues;
- reduce information load of sentences;
- decrease the occurrence of syntactic discontinuities;
- avoid unnecessary nominalizations;
- choose referential links wherever it is strictly necessary.

At this point it would be interesting to consider how the 'easification' strategies might be applied. The extracts reported below are some examples of these 'easification' techniques:

Human Rights Act 1998

Art 13 (1)

If a Court's determination of any questions arising under this Act affect the exercise by a religious organisation (itself or its members collectively) of the

161 Other names for cognitive structures include 'mental structures', 'mental tools', and 'patterns of thought' (Gardner 2004).

> Convention right to freedom of thought, conscience and religion, it must have particular regard to the importance of that right.[162]

It is a relatively simpler provision but serves well as a typical example of legislative provision bearing in mind a number of difficulties. In order to make it easier for the readers to process, some of the difficulties can be removed from the following alternative version by adapting what Bhatia (1983, 2010) calls vertical diagramming (Table 11) to our purposes:

Table 11. Cognitive structuring of *Human Rights Act 1998*.

Cognitive mapping Human Rights Act 1998 – Art 13 (1)			
main provision			subsidiary provision/ qualification
stipulation rule	If a Court's determination	of any question arising under this Act	preparatory
//	affects the exercise		
//		by a religious organization	referential
//		(itself or its members collectively)	preparatory
	of the Convention right to freedom of thought,	conscience and religion,	preparatory
action rule	*it* must have particular regard to the importance of that right.		
			stipulation + referential

162 http://www.legislation.gov.uk/ukpga/1998/42/data.pdf

Therefore, thanks to the 'easification' strategies the main provision reported above (i.e., *Human Rights Act 1998* Art 13 (1)) will be as follows:

> If a Court's determination *affects the exercise of the Convention right to freedom of thought* (stipulation rule + qualification: preparatory), it must pay particular regard to the importance of that right (action rule).[163]

And the subsidiary provisions/qualifications will be those following:

> of any question arising under this Act / by a religious organization / (itself or its members collectively) / conscience and religion.[164]

Indeed, there is a potential ambiguity as to whether the phrase 'it must have particular regard to the importance of that right (action rule)' refers to the 'Court's determination' or 'religious organization' or 'its members collectively' or 'the Convention right'. The way the clauses are structured seems to suggest that *it* refers to the intended accused 'Court's determination'.

As a matter of fact, 'easification' strategies do not modify or rewrite content but clarify and make content more accessible. 'Easification' strategies aim to make the text clearer, not simpler, as is shown below:

> *Human Rights Act 1998*
>
> Art 13 (1)
>
> If a Court's determination of any question arising under this Act affect the exercise of the Convention right to freedom of thought, conscience and religion,
>
> (i) by a religious organization
>
> (ii) (itself or its members collectively),
>
> Then, *Court's determination* must pay particular regard to the importance of that right.[165]

By regrouping ideas and using bullet points to create one legal subject and one case descriptor, and substituting *it* with 'Court's determination',

---

163 http://www.legislation.gov.uk/ukpga/1998/42/data.pdf

164 *Ibid.*

165 *Ibid.*

the problem with the confusing use of *it* is removed without significantly changing the scope or content of the original text. By using some direct repetition 'Court's determination' and inserting a 'Then' clause to reflect the underlying legal reasoning and nature of the legal rules, the problem of the interpretation of *it* is removed.

Nevertheless, there might be other problems related to language or textual structure of the legislative text. Let us consider this other example taken from *Health Services Act 1980* – Chapter 53. In particular, the following Section 28A, which according to Art. 4 of the Health Services Act (1980) has to be inserted 'After section 28 of the Act of 1977...', is one of a few of the most complex sections, whereas others are generally easier to process and understand:

> *Health Service Act 1980*
>
> 4. Power to make grants towards expenditure on services of common concern to health authorities etc. and local authorities
>
> (1) After section 28 of the Act of 1977 there shall be inserted the following section -
>
> Power to make grants towards expenditure on services of common concern to health authorities and local authorities.
>
> 28A
>
> (1) *An Area Health Authority or District Health Authority may*, if they think fit, *make grants* subject to and in accordance with the provisions of this section to the following local authorities towards expenditure to be incurred by them in connection with the performance of the following functions, that is to say -
>
> (a) *to any local social services authority, in respect of expenditure in connection with the performance of any function* which, by virtue of section 2(1) or (2) of the Local Authority Social Services Act 1970, *is to be performed through the social services committee of the authority*
>
> (b) *to any district council in respect of expenditure in connection with the performance by the council of any function of their*s under section 8 of the Residential Homes Act1980 or the corresponding enactment repealed by that Act (meals and recreation for old people). [166]

At first glance, the 141-word sentence (i.e., Section 28A) appears to be a classic example of conventional legislative discourse with its

166 http://www.legislation.gov.uk/ukpga/1980/53/pdfs/ukpga_19800053_en.pdf

quite standard opening case description, which accounts for 63 words of the legislative sentence. Then, we have what in legal terminology is known as *legal action* that 'An Area Health Authority or District Health Authority may make grants to the local authorities'.

This sentence has a few linguistic characteristics, one of which is the use of binomial or multinomial expressions, such as 'subject to and in accordance with the provisions of . . . by them in connection with. . ./ by virtue of section 2(1) or (2) of the Local Authority Social Services Act 1970 / of any function of theirs under section . . .or the corresponding enactment repealed by. . . / (meals and recreation for old people)'.[167]

In terms of the cognitive structuring of Section 28A, another interesting device commonly used in legislative sentence is what linguists often call 'syntactic discontinuities', of which a good example is the use of 'towards expenditure to be incurred by them in connection with. . .,' and 'that is to say / in respect of expenditure in connection with the performance of any function which, by virtue of section 2(1) or (2) of the Local Authority Social Services Act 1970, is to be. . .' or 'in connection with the performance by the council of any function of theirs under section 8 of the Residential Homes Act 1980 or the corresponding enactment' that limit 'the performance of any function' in the case the addressee towards which the performance is addressed is 'any local social services authority' (28A, 1(a)), or 'any district council' (28A, 1(b)).

This is a typical instance of the use of multinomials to make the legislative provision all-inclusive in terms of adequate specification of complex contingencies. These multinomials have been highlighted in the extracts reported below:

Health Service Act 1980

[. . .]

28A

(1) An Area Health Authority or District Health Authority may, if they think fit, make grants *subject to and in accordance with the provisions of this section to*

167 In this regard, Le Cheng and Wagner (2014: 218) observe that 'while binomials consist of pairs of words or pairs of syntactic sequence connected by a lexical link – usually "and" or "or" – multinomials are extended nominal binomials with "an enumerative sequence [which] may contain several members" of the same category' (Gustafsson 1975:17)'.

> *the following local authorities towards expenditure to be incurred by them in connection with the performance of the following functions, that is to say -*
>
> (a) to any local social services authority, in respect of expenditure in connection with the performance of any function which, *by virtue of section 2(1) or (2) of the Local Authority Social Services Act 1970,* is to be performed through the social services committee of the authority.
> (b) to any district council in respect of expenditure in connection with the performance by the council of any function of theirs *under section 8 of the Residential Homes Act1980 or the corresponding enactment repealed by that Act (meals and recreation for old people).* [168]

If we remove all the multinomials, the 'easified' version of Section 28A (i.e., Art. 4 of the *Health Services Act 1980*) should be the following:

> *Health Service Act 1980*
>
> [. . .]
>
> 28A
>
> (1) An Area Health Authority or District Health Authority may, if they think fit, make grants [. . .] to the following local authorities [. . .] -
>
> (a) to any local social services authority, in respect of expenditure in connection with the performance of any function which [. . .] is to be performed through the social services committee of the authority.
> (b) to any district council in respect of expenditure in connection with the performance by the council of any function of theirs [. . .].[169]

As is shown above, the legislative provision (i.e., Art. 4 of the *Health Services Act 1980* – Section 28A), though quite thin in the specification of legal scope, will become even simpler and more accessible.

Overall, drafting legislative provisions is a very complex and difficult task, which involves both legal knowledge and linguistic awareness. The construction of legal norms is greatly conditioned by specific factors that strictly depend on the context, such as the numerous cultural, linguistic, and legal environments in which it takes place.

The analysis of simplification and 'easification' strategies certainly provides interesting insights into how legislative provisions can be

168 http://www.legislation.gov.uk/ukpga/1980/53/pdfs/ukpga_19800053_en.pdf
169 *Ibid.*

linguistically and textually improved depending on the communicative purposes which have originated them and the context in which they will eventually be applied. Thanks to the linguistic research methodology, it becomes possible to:

(i) investigate how meaning and text functions evolve in the process of text production;
(ii) discover what the functions of the produced legislative texts are;
(iii) asses if the texts' functions match with the original intensions of the drafters;
(iv) make legislative drafters known about the linguistic strategies that can be applied to match the law's functions with the intention of drafters, thus developing techniques that can lead to the desired result.

So far, the analysis of the lexico-grammatical and textual elements that are essential to give an account of how legislative provisions are structured, demonstrates that legal texts, and particularly legislative provisions, cannot be considered in isolation from their communicative context(s). By considering legislative provisions from a linguistic point of view, tests of language can surely be conducted in a number of texts and documents belonging to the common law drafting practice to assess the effectiveness of their draft, and eventually to ascertain a loss of conceptual focus by legislative drafters.

5.3 Gender neutrality in legislative drafting

Gender-neutral drafting has been the norm for some years in many jurisdictions which use the English language to draft legislation. Given the prevalence of English as lingua franca, an increasing number of English language jurisdictions and international organizations have recently shown some instances of a drafting style which is much more inclined to gender neutrality.

Overall, gender-specificity in legislation started being questioned from the late 20th century, and the need to reform the way in which laws have been written for more than one-hundred years has been particularly evident in English-language jurisdictions. In this regard, the legislative drafting policy conventionally known as the 'masculine rule', whereby 'he includes she', raised opposition in the 1970s under the pressure of feminist movements in the United States and Europe. In the 1990s and 2000s, the adoption of a plain English style forced legislative drafters to basically avoid sentences of undue length, superfluous definitions, repeated words, and gender specificity with the aim of achieving clarity and minimize ambiguity.

In order to avoid gender specificity, experts in the legal field have suggested reorganizing sentences avoiding male pronouns, repeating the noun in place of the pronoun, replacing a nominalization with a verb form, resorting to 'the singular they' (Xanthaki 2022). At this point it would be interesting to considers the use of the 'singular they' in the English language, focusing on the legislative drafting guidance issued in English-language jurisdictions and, in particular, in the UK.

Given the environment of legislative drafting techniques where considerable reliance on precedent is inevitable, any proposal to change legislative language may produce interesting results in different jurisdictions.

5.3.1 Language and gender

Languages vary widely in terms of gender systems showing differences in the number of classes, underlying assignment rules, and how and where gender is marked. According to Audring (2016: 1),

> gender is a grammatical feature, in a family with person, number, and case. In the languages that have grammatical gender—according to a representative typological sample, almost half of the languages in the world—it is a property that separates nouns into classes. These classes are often meaningful and often linked to biological sex, which is why many languages are said to have a 'masculine' and a 'feminine' gender. In this regard, a typical example is Italian, which has masculine words for male persons (il bambino 'the M. little boy') and feminine words for female persons (la bambina 'the F. little girl').

In everyday speech, the word gender is usually associated with the biological and social differences between men and women. In addition, people might know that languages, such as Spanish and Italian, can have masculine and feminine words. So, at first glance, it may seem that grammatical gender is a reflection of natural gender in grammar (Audring 2016: 2).

The view that grammatical gender mirrors natural gender has been widespread since antiquity and is still evident in the terms, masculine, feminine, and neuter, which are used to label individual gender distinctions, especially in Indo-European languages (Corbett 2013). However, not all languages function like this. Indeed, many languages do not have grammatical gender at all. In this regard, Audring (2016: 2–3) recognizes that

> of those [languages] that do, some disregard the difference between male and female and assign all words for humans or for living beings to the same class. Yet other languages have a special 'vegetable' gender for plants, a gender for foodstuffs, a gender for large or important things, a gender for liquids or abstracts, and many more. Such patterns remind us that the word gender (Greek: γένος) originally meant 'kind' rather than 'sex'. While the split into male and female is the most common semantic base of gender systems, it is by no means the only option.

Research on gender and language has demonstrated that there exist two categories of languages: 'gender languages',[170] and 'languages without grammatical gender'(Corbett 1991, 2007; Holmes 1991; Helliger and Bußmann 2001). In the case of the English language, while Old English (750-1100/1150 AD) had three gender classes, feminine, masculine, and neuter, and all inanimate nouns belonged to one of the three classes, the category of 'grammatical gender' was lost by the end of the 14th century due to the decay of inflectional endings and the disintegration of declensional classes (Curzan 2003).

In their seminal work on *Gender Across Languages*, Hellinger and Bußmann (2001: 11) observe that word-formation represents 'a particularly sensitive area in which gender may be communicated'. Languages with or without grammatical gender have historical generated processes

170 Such as Arabic, Czech, Danish, Dutch, French, German, Greek, Hebrew, Hindi, Icelandic, Italian, Norwegian, Polish, Romanian, Russian, Serbian/Croatian/Bosnian, Spanish, Swedish, and Welsh.

of derivation and compounding having an important function in the formation of gendered personal nouns, particularly in the use of existing terms and the creation of new feminine/female equivalent terms, as in the case of the area of occupational terms (English feminine/female *steward-ess* from masculine/male *steward* or feminine/female *chairwoman* from masculine/male *chairman*). This is evident in the case of the Italian language, with the recent formation of the feminine/female term *ministra* which derives from masculine/male *ministro* (En. *minister*), and the feminine/female *sindaca* which derives from masculine/male *sindaco* (En. *mayor*). It usually has the suffix which carries the lexical gender formation in agreement.

Gender systems may rely on other semantic distinctions or may be related to formal properties of the noun. For this reason, an important defining property is 'agreement', that is, the behaviour of associated words. For instance, in Italian

> the masculine gender of the noun *bambino* matches its meaning as well as its form—the noun ends in *-o* and inflects like a regular –-o class noun—but the true indicator of gender is the form of the article. This can be seen in words like *la mano* 'the F. hand', which is feminine despite its final *-o*, and *il soprano* 'the M. soprano', which is masculine, although it usually refers to a woman. For the same reasons, we speak of grammatical gender only if the distinction is reflected in syntax; a language that has words for male and female persons or animals does not necessarily have a gender system (Audring 2016: 1).

Despite a long-standing debate over the cross-linguistic analysis of gender, scholars working in the field of gender and language have generally agreed on the identification of four categories of gender, namely, 'grammatical', 'lexical', 'referential', and 'social gender' (Kramarae et al. 1984; Tannen 1990; Corbett 1991; Bergvall et al. 1996; Unterbeck et al. 2000; Sunderland 2006; Prewitt-Freilino et al. 2012; Sato et al. 2017). Before looking at each of them, it might be said that 'social gender' plays a crucial role in English since it refers to the semantic bias of an otherwise unspecified noun towards one or the other gender, such as *nurse* and *teacher* denoting stereotypically female persons, and *surgeon* and *professor* male ones. In this regard, traditional practice in English has prescribed the choice of *he* in neutral contexts even for general human nouns such as *employee* or *consumer*, the so-called 'masculine rule' (Stefanou and Xanthaki 2008; Williams 2011).

5.3.2 The English language and gender

In the case of the English language, while Old English had three gender classes (feminine, masculine, neuter), the category of grammatical gender was lost by the end of the 14th century due to the decay of inflectional endings and the disintegration of declensional classes. Unlike Spanish and Italian, which have several elements inside and outside the noun phrase (determiners, adjectives, pronouns) that vary according to the noun's grammatical gender, Modern English shows no such morphological agreement. Table 12 below shows the categories of gender in English.

Table 12. Gender in English.

gender		
grammatical	lost by the 14th century	
lexical	*mother / father*	
referential	non-linguistic reality	
social	semantic bias	*nurse* (female) *surgeon* (male)
social	general nouns	*consumer / pedestrian*

In English, for instance, family relationship nouns are lexically specified as carrying semantic property, female or male, that relate to the sex of referent. For this reason, those personal nouns may be described as gender-specific, either female-specific or male-specific.

In the case of terms without lexical gender, i.e., gender-indefinite nouns such as *consumer*, pronominal choice is usually, but not always, determined by the grammatical gender of the antecedent noun or subject to which they are related. Referential gender, therefore, identifies a referent as female, male, or gender-indefinite by linking linguistic terms to the non-linguistic realities. In referential gender, when reference is made to a particular subject, the choice of anaphoric pronouns may be referentially motivated and may prevail over the grammatical gender of nouns (Hellinger and Bußmann 2001). Most English personal nouns, however, are unspecified for gender, and can be used to refer to both female and male referents, e.g., *person, consumer, employee.*

Social gender refers to the semantic bias of an otherwise unspecified noun towards one or the other gender, as in the case of *babysitter(s)* denoting stereotypically female persons, and *electrician(s)* male ones. Social gender has to do with stereotypical assumptions about what the appropriate social roles for women and men are, including expectations about who will be a typical member of the class of, say, *surgeon* or *nurse*. Deviations from such assumptions will often require formal markings, for example by adjectival modification: *female surgeon* or *male nurse*. Even for general human nouns such as *pedestrian* or *patient*, traditional practice prescribes the choice of *he* in neutral contexts.

Languages have generated processes of derivation and compounding which have an important function in the formation of gendered personal nouns, particularly in the use of existing terms and the creation of new feminine (f.) equivalent terms, as in the case of the area of occupational terms, for instance, f. *actress* from m. *actor* and f. *chairwoman* from m. *chairman*.

Then, the agreement establishes a syntactic relationship between a noun's satellite element, e.g., an article, adjective, pronominal or verbal form, and the noun's gender class. Traditionally, agreement has favoured the masculine in coordination and, generally, masculine agreement has predominated. On the contrary, feminine agreement is female-specific and, in many contexts, non-obligatory and irregular, depending on the extralinguistic factors such as tradition, prescription or speaker attitude (Audring 2016). In this regard, pronominalization has been 'a powerful strategy of communicating gender both in languages with and without grammatical gender' (Hellinger and Bußmann 2001: 14) as well. Pronouns may emphasize traditional and/or reformed practices, as when a speaker chooses between a false generic (i.e., *he*) or a more gender-neutral choice (i.e., singular *they*).

The interpretation of pronominalization as one type of agreement remains controversial. English exemplifies a type of relation between noun and pronoun which is not syntactically motivated. Only reflexes of the original grammatical gender system remain in the third person singular pronouns (*he, she, it*), and the choice of anaphoric pronouns is controlled by lexical-semantic properties of the antecedent, by referential gender (including intended reference), or social gender. Eventually, this classification is semantically based, and English is no longer a gender language.

5.3.3 He/his/him and the 'masculine rule'

For more than 150 years English-language jurisdictions had drafted legislative texts based on the rule that the norm of humanity is male.

By the 1970s the 'masculine rule' started to be contested in the United States and Europe and calls were made to change such a 'sexist language' (Ehrlich and King 1992). By the 1990s other social groups, such as the gay community, became aware of the need for gender-neutral drafting. It is evident that in itself the instruction by which words importing the masculine gender shall be deemed and taken to include females, the so-called 'masculine rule' (Petersson 1999), establishes a convention that is merely linguistic. For many years the UK drafting of Primary legislation has relied on Section 6 of the *Interpretation Act 1978*:

> Interpretation and construction
>
> Section 6 Gender and number
>
> In any Act, unless the contrary intention appears,
>
> (a) words importing the masculine gender include the feminine.
>
> (b) words importing the feminine gender include the masculine.
>
> (c) words in the singular include the plural and words in the plural include the singular.[171]

From a purely linguistic point of view, it does not necessarily involve a form of gender bias and/or sexual discrimination. However, one should consider the historical reasons that contributed to the establishment of this rule and determined the choice of the masculine to be used as an epicene for masculine and feminine. As Williams observes (2004, 2022), with the burgeoning of the feminist movement in the western world during the latter half of the 20th century, the question of drafting

171 https://www.legislation.gov.uk/ukpga/1978/30/contents/enacted

legislative texts according to principles of gender neutrality emerged as part of a more general policy which aimed at removing the socio-economic differences resulting from long-stinging discrimination against women.

Gender-neutral language, also called non-sexist, gender-inclusive, or non-gender-specific language,[172] refers to language which includes words or expressions that cannot be taken to refer to one gender only. Non-sexist language campaigns have been under way for a few decades now, especially focusing on gender-specific terms (but also pronouns), which in turn are parallel to women's liberation movements, to the increasing attention given to LGBTQ[173] rights, and relevant societal changes.

However, it should be noted that gender-neutral drafting does not necessarily produce legislation that is an effective tool against gender-inequality. As Mclean (2013) observes, ways of doing relations (i.e., at work, personal sphere, etc.) are embedded with ways of 'doing gender'. In other words, the apparent differences between sexes not only entail distinct expectations of what women and men should do and behave like in social situations, but are also used to legitimize a gender hierarchy that subordinates women, any other gender belonging to the a LGBTQ community, and what they do (Connell 2010).

Doing gender is a social, interactive act, done relationally to the specific historical and socio-cultural context, and embedded with the language which represents and recreates that context itself (Ehrlich and King 1992). Gender-neutral drafting can set the stage for, and might favour, the effectiveness of legislation in combating gender-inequality. Eventually, the adoption of non-sexist language in legislation may help reinforce or consolidate such changes.

5.3.4 Reforming gender language

The traditional assumption that 'he includes she' had been the norm in many jurisdictions and obviously reflected women's status in society,

172 *UNESCO – Priority Gender Equality Guidelines*, 2011.

173 The Oxford English Dictionary defines LGBTQ an abbreviation for lesbian, gay, bisexual, transgender, and queer (or questioning), viz. the LGBTQ community.

prejudices against them in an essentially male-centred society and the generally shared expectations of sexual roles. Many alternatives have been suggested to replace asymmetric or sexist usage in English.

One form such protest has taken, is the development of numerous guidelines for gender-neutral language.[174] In reformed usage, the principle of neutralization has the highest priority in English, in contrast to German (as well as in Italy), where female visibility is the basic characteristic of gender-fair usage. Neutralization means the avoidance of false generics, especially usages of generic *man*, as in *mankind*, *salesman* or *chairman*. Gender-inclusive wording can also be achieved by avoiding gender-marked terms for female referents, especially derivations ending with the suffix *-ess* or *-ette*, as in the case of *authoress* and *majorette*.

In this regard, it is interesting to acknowledge that in English the suffix *-ess* has been used since the Middle Ages to form nouns denoting female persons, using a neutral or a male form as the base (as *hostess* and *actress* from *host* and *actor*, for example). Despite the apparent equivalence between the male and female pairs of forms, they are rarely equivalent in terms of actual use and connotation in modern English (one might consider the differences in meaning and use between *manager* and *manageress*, or *poet* and *poetess*).

In the late 20th century, as the role of women in society changed, some of these feminine forms became problematic and were seen as old-fashioned, sexist, and patronizing (e.g. *authoress, editress*). The male form is increasingly being used as the 'neutral' form, where the gender of the person concerned is simply unspecified.[175]

Then, the use of *-ette* as a feminine suffix for forming new words is relatively recent. It was first recorded in the word *suffragette* at the beginning of the 20th century and has since been used to form only a handful of well-established words, including *usherette* and *drum majorette*, for example. In the modern context, where the tendency is to use words which are neutral in gender, the suffix *-ette* is not very productive and new words formed using it tend to be restricted to the deliberately dismissive or humorous, as, for example, *ladette* and *punkette*.[176]

174 From the McGraw-Hill guidelines of 1972 to the UNESCO guidelines of 1999.

175 http://www.lexico.com/en/definition/-ess

176 https://www.lexico.com/en/definition/-ette

Another way towards a more gender-neutral language is the avoidance of stereotyping when talking about men and women. In this regard, Frankson (2000: 33) provides some guidelines for 'gender-sensitive language', and suggests

> to avoid stereotyped assumptions about the roles of men and women. For example, the sentence 'Research scientists often neglect their wives and children', assumes that women are not research scientists, whereas a simple change – 'Research scientists often neglect their families', acknowledges that women as well as men are research scientists; similarly, 'Transport will be provided for delegates and their wives', assumes all delegates are men whereas, 'Transport will be provided for delegates and their spouses', correctly recognises women as well as men in the role of delegate.

The avoidance of marked forms (i.e., *female doctors*) where no parallel male forms would be used, might be seen as a subordinate strategy of neutralization including the visibility of potential female referents, when the strategy of pronominal splitting *he or she / she or he* is employed, as in *patient*. At the same time, this example illustrates symmetric usage, which should be observed whenever specification of referential gender is required, as in *female* and *male athletes* (Miller and Swift 1980; Wattman Frank and Treichler 1989; Pauwels 1998). In this regard, a gender-neutral alternative might be the use of 'singular they' as in 'a lawyer must listen to their clients'.

'Singular they' becomes the pronoun to replace *he and she* in cases where the gender of the antecedent (the word the pronoun refers to) is unknown, irrelevant, or nonbinary. As the Oxford English Dictionary[177] acknowledges us, this usage has an eminent origin tracing 'singular they' back to 1375, where it appears in the medieval romance *William and the Werewolf.* In the 18th century, grammarians began warning that the singular *they* was an error because a plural pronoun can't take a singular antecedent (Fens-De Zeeuw 2018). They clearly forgot that the singular *you* was a plural pronoun that had become singular as well. *You* functioned as a polite singular for centuries, but in the 17th century the singular *you* replaced *thou, thee*, and *thy*, except for some dialect use. That change met with some resistance. In 1660, George Fox,

177 public.oed.com/blog/a-brief-history-of-singular-they/acknowledges us

the founder of Quakerism, wrote a whole book labeling anyone who used singular *you* an idiot or a fool. And 18th-century grammarians like Robert Lowth and Lindley Murray regularly tested students on *thou* as singular, *you* as plural, despite the fact that students used singular *you* when their teachers weren't looking, and teachers used singular *you* when their students weren't looking. Anyone who said *thou* and *thee* was seen as a fool and an idiot, or a Quaker, or at least hopelessly out of date.[178]

In the 18th century, grammarians began warning that 'singular they' was an error because a plural pronoun can't take a singular antecedent.[179]

Toward the end of the 20th century, language authorities began to approve the form of the 'singular they'. Not only does the *New Oxford Dictionary of English* (1998) accept the form and use 'singular they' in their definitions, the *New Oxford American Dictionary* (2010) but also calls 'singular they' generally accepted with indefinites, and now common but less widely accepted with definite nouns, particularly in formal contexts'.

However, it is no surprise that 'singular they' has found some resistance. *Fowler's Dictionary of Modern English Usage* openly considers it an error (1926/2000: 648) and the *Chicago Manual of Style* still rejects 'singular they' for formal writing. Yet, Burchfield, in the 2015 edition of the *New Fowler's Dictionary of Modern English Usage* points out that 'such constructions are hardly noticed any more or are not felt to lie in a prohibited zone', although he defines them non-grammatical seeing their rise as a response to linguistic needs that could not otherwise be met. As Burchfield writes (2009: 779),

> All such 'non-grammatical' constructions arise either because the notion of plurality resides in many of the indefinite pronouns or because of the absence in English of a common-gender third person singular pronoun (as distinct from his used to mean 'his or her' or the clumsy use of his or her itself).

178 public.oed.com/blog/a-brief-history-of-singular-they/acknowledges us
179 *Ibid.*

Garner (2009: 736–737) considers 'singular they' a form of noun-pronoun disagreement, justified by the fact that indefinite pronouns, although singular, 'carry an idea of plurality'. To the question why this usage is becoming so popular, he replies saying that 'it is the most convenient solution to the single biggest problem in sexist language – the generic masculine pronoun' (Garner 2009: 736). Then, he suggests that

> where noun-pronoun disagreement can be avoided, avoid it. Where it can't be avoided, resort to it cautiously because some people may doubt your literacy (Garner 2009: 737).

Despite some fierce opposition, 'they' used as a gender-neutral singular pronoun was appointed '2015 word of the year' by the *American Dialect Society*. The society recognized 'singular they'

> for its emerging use as a pronoun to refer to a known person, often as a conscious choice by a person rejecting the traditional gender binary of he and she.[180]

And, in 2017 'singular they' made its way into two of the main stylebooks in academia and journalism (Perlman 2017) and has been acknowledged by the *American Psychological Association* (APA) stylebook.[181]

5.3.5 English-language jurisdictions and gender-neutral drafting

Among the English-language jurisdictions, Australia and New Zealand were the first to introduce legislative drafting guidance for gender-neutral language in 1980s, followed by Canada which adopted the first official policy adopting gender-neutral language in the early 1990s. The government of the United States intervened in 2009, whereas Acts of the Westminster Parliament continued relying on the interpretation provision and used *he, him* and *his* with the intention of including reference to males and females until 2007.

Overall, the legislative drafting manuals issued in the abovementioned English-language jurisdictions suggest the following as the standard techniques to avoid gender-specificity:

---

180 https://www.americandialect.org/2015-word-of-the-year-is-singular-they
181 https://store.apstylebook.com/2017-ap-stylebook-print-edition.html

- omission (mostly, pronouns, possessives, etc.);
- repetition;
- reorganization (rephrasing sentences to avoid the need of pronouns, etc., passive voice, relative pronouns; dividing propositions into a number of shorter sentences; avoiding subordinate clauses; using impersonal/plural nouns, etc.);
- 'alternative pronouns'
  - *he or she, s/he, she or he*
  - *they* singular
  - *they* plural;
- avoiding nouns that might appear to assume a man rather than a woman will do a particular job or perform a particular role (*chair* is now used in Primary legislation as a substitute for *chairman*);
- avoiding the feminine form of a particular occupation (*author/ authoress*);
- using gender-specific nouns and pronouns where provisions can only apply to persons of a particular gender (where a provision only applies to men or women, such as maternity pay for women);
- references to specific individuals (*Her Majesty*).

Among gender-neutral drafting indications, repetition, omission, rephrasing, and alternative pronouns are the standard techniques proposed to avoid gender-specificity. Let us consider these techniques in detail:

- manuals often indicate 'omission' as a standard way to have gender-neutral drafting. The following are typical examples of omission

  The chief executive may resign office [. . .]

  and

  [. . .] circumstances which justify *him* doing so.

  might be substituted by

  [. . .] circumstances which justify doing so.

In these examples, the pronoun is omitted without substituting it. Omitting the pronoun relies on the reader using the context to supply the word omitted, and care has to be used to ensure certainty. Indeed, words and expressions may be omitted whenever they appear to add anything to the meaning of the sentence. The omission of words such as *due for him* and if *he thinks fit*, which are quite common in English-speaking legislation, is strongly suggested not only for gender-neutral reasons (the personal pronoun would require the repetition of the noun), but also for reason of simplicity and clarity in legislation.

– 'Repetition' is the gender-neutral drafting technique proposed as an alternative to omission, as shown in the extracts below:

  The *President* may exercise *his* power if [. . .]

  that can be substituted by

  The *President* may exercise *Vice-president*'s power if [. . .].

  Here is another example where repletion can be safely used:

  [. . .] may give a youth conditional caution to *a child or young person* ("*the offender*") if *the offender* [. . .].

In this regard, Greenberg observes (2008: 67) that "it is of course the most obvious way of avoiding 'he'[. . .]. And it is a reasonably familiar technique for drafters and leaders alike". However, this technique may be open to the objection of inelegance and fails to conform to the ideals of plain language sentences. Furthermore, constant repetition of a noun in a way which is not used in speech can jar and detract from readability and requires the reader to substitute the actual wording required for the defined term. Repetition may be useful to distinguish between two or more people, but unlikely to be used solely for the purpose of achieving gender-neutral drafting.

– Another drafting technique consists in rephrasing the sentence to avoid the use of gender-specific personal pronouns, or repetition of words and expressions. More specifically,

a) the 'reorganization' of sentences can be done changing the active voice into the passive voice, as in the case of the following sentence:

  The Secretary of State must submit a memorandum explaining *why he has not laid the order*.

  which could be changed into

  The Secretary of State must submit a memorandum explaining *why the order has not been laid*.

Agentless passive construction may avoid the need for the use of gender-specific pronouns (e.g., *he*). The advantage of the active voice is that the subject of the sentence names the performer of the action stated in the verb. Furthermore, the passive form either omits, or reduces the emphasis on the person performing the action. Nevertheless, passive constructions may be less clear than their active counterparts and may give rise to ambiguities as in the case of 'When a person makes an application, *the following information must be supplied*' (who must supply 'the following information'?);

b) 'rephrasing' can be done using relative pronouns as in the extract below:

> A person commits an offence *if he* [. . .]
>
> that can be rephrased in
>
> A person *who* [. . .] commits an offence.

Active words are postponed to the end. It works very well in a short proposition, but much less in a long proposition with subordinate clauses, as in the following example taken from the *UK Fine Act 2010* where the repetition of *a person who commits an offence* cannot be avoided without affecting the overall meaning of the sentence:

> Subject to subsection (3), where an enactment enacted during a period specified in column (2) of the Table opposite a particular reference number specified in column (1) of the Table provides that a *person who commits an offence* under the enactment shall be liable, upon summary conviction, to a fine not exceeding an amount that falls within the range of amounts specified in column (3) of the Table opposite the same reference number, *a person who commits that offence* after the commencement date shall, upon summary conviction, not be liable to that fine, but shall instead be liable to a class A fine [...];

c) rephrasing propositions by dividing them into a number of shorter sentences can be another technique to avoid personal pronouns or the inelegant repetition of words and expressions. The extract reported here is a clear example of this technique:

> 853H Duty to deliver information about exemption from Part 21A
>
> (1) This section applies where a company —
>
> (a) which is not a DTR5 issuer, and
> (b) to which Part 21A does not apply (information about people with significant control, see section 790B), makes a confirmation statement.
>
> (2) The company must deliver to the registrar a statement of the fact that it is a company to which Part 21A does not apply at the same time as it delivers the confirmation statement.

(3) Subsection (2) does not apply if the last statement delivered to the registrar under this section applies equally to the confirmation period concerned.

It is a popular and quite attractive technique. However, its efficacy will vary from time to time, because,

> a series of short sentences can be longer and less pleasing than a single sentence which develops a single story intuitively, and through which the subordinate clauses flow so naturally as to aid rather than impede rapid comprehension (Greenberg 2008: 71).

d) the re-organization of propositions can be done using impersonal constructions, as shown here:

[. . .] the reasonableness or otherwise of *his conviction*

[. . .] the reasonableness or otherwise of *that conviction*

In terms of the message conveyed, impersonal constructions can produce unnatural dislocation between the person and the thing or event being spoken of. Furthermore, the use of *the/that* may lose the link between the noun and the person being spoken of.

– Legislative drafters might consider the possibility of using 'alternative pronouns' that are acceptably gender-neutral

  • *he or she* might be considered an appropriate solution to gender-neutral drafting, as shown in the following extracts:

A member of the Tribunal may resign *his or her* office.

She or he may do so with immediate effects [. . .].

Most Legislative Drafting Guidance considers this a 'natural solution' (Petersson 1999). However, some English-speaking jurisdictions are beginning to question the use of *he or she* because it does include neither 'a body of persons incorporated or unincorporate' (*UK Interpretation Act 1987*),[182] nor individuals who do not identify with a specific gender. It is not really gender-neutral and is especially objectionable where gender, in addition to masculine and feminine, includes LGBTQ. *He or*

---

182 Greenberg (2011) warns about the drafters' habit of using the masculine personal pronoun *he* in relation to a *person* despite the fact that Schedule 1 to the *Interpretation Act 1978* defines a *person* 'a body of persons corporate or unincorporate'. Indeed, *he or she* can be used only in the case of provisions directed exclusively to individuals.

she introduces complexity into the sentence as frequent repetition can be awkward, and concerns are expressed about the order of the personal pronouns (i.e., *he or she/she or he*);

- it is both possible to make greater use of the *plural pronoun* if one makes greater use of plural nouns:

Persons may submit applications only if *they* think [. . .].

[. . .] paying grants for amounts consistent with the aim of *people* enjoying the benefit of equivalent protection from air, water, or soil pollution and from noise, wherever *they* live in Australia [. . .].

Legislative Drafting Guidance often suggests the plural as a means of avoiding male terms in legal language in general. However, the plural is generally not regarded as a practical option for legislative drafting, accepting it when there is no other convenient way to avoid male terms. In this regard, the New Zealand Law Commission cautions that 'The general rule is to use the singular form unless the plural form avoids sexist singular pronouns' (New Zealand Law Commission, *Legislation Manual Structure and Style-Report* No. 35). If it is an easy option turning the noun into a plural noun and then use '*they*', it might happen that there is no coupling of plural pronouns with references to a single person;

- another alternative pronoun that has been proposed by legislative drafters to avoid gender-specific pronouns is *singular they*:

The Commission may resign *their* office.

A person may submit an application only if *they think* [. . .].

[. . .] in defending or resisting proceedings in which *the person is found* to have a liability for which *they could not* be indemnified under subsection (4) of this section [. . .].

Thus, though the third person plural avoids the problem of gender specificity, its potential for ambiguity makes it an 'unattractive approach to gender neutrality' (Petersson 1999);

- 'singular they'

Among the gender-neutral drafting indications recommended by English-speaking jurisdictions and analyzed in the present study, 'singular they' is one standard technique proposed to avoid gender-specificity even though with some variations. It is, therefore, interesting to briefly look at the indications provided by each of the selected English-language jurisdictions concerning the use of 'singular they'.

The Department of Justice of the Government of Canada provides a webpage in the Legistics section of its website[183] to introduce 'singular they', and to give some background information about it ('In Practice', 'Examples'), its meaning in 'Dictionaries', and other useful info, though brief, about 'Other Jurisdictions' ('Ontario' and 'Australia'). As we read in the 'Introduction':

> The use of the singular 'they' is becoming more common not only in spoken but in written English and can prove to be useful to legislative counsel in a legislative context to eliminate gender-specific language and heavy or awkward repetition of nouns.[184]

Following immediately after are some warnings inserted in the 'Recommendations':

> 1. Consider using the third-person pronouns 'they', 'their', 'them', 'themselves' or 'theirs' to refer to a singular indefinite noun, to avoid the unnatural language that results from repeating the noun.
> 2. Do not use 'they' to refer to a definite singular noun.
> 3. Ensure that the pronoun's antecedent is clear.[185]

Then, under the 'Background' caption, some indefinite and definite nouns are listed to describe when 'singular they' has to be used, or when it would be better to avoid it:

> Consider using the third-person pronouns 'they', 'their', 'them', 'themselves' or 'theirs' to refer to a singular indefinite noun, to avoid the unnatural language that results from repeating the noun. Examples of singular indefinite nouns are:
>
> anyone/anybody
>
> no one/nobody
>
> everyone/everybody

183 https://www.justice.gc.ca/eng/rp-pr/csj-sjc/legis-redact/legistics/toc-tdm.asp
184 *Ibid.*
185 *Ibid.*

> person
>
> every applicant
>
> any officer
>
> every judge
>
> manufacturer
>
> officer
>
> taxpayer
>
> Do not use 'they' to refer to a definite singular noun. Examples of definite nouns are:
>
> Minister
>
> Commissioner
>
> Solicitor General
>
> Chief Electoral Officer
>
> Receiver General
>
> Attorney General.[186]

Then, it is specified that when the use of 'singular they' in a sentence is ambiguous, the use of the pronoun is not advised and it would be advisable to repeat the noun, to replace it with *he or she*, or rewrite the sentence to avoid the use of the pronouns altogether, as in the example provided below:

> When an applicant notifies the other residents, *they* must lodge a section 12 notice within 14 days' could safely be rewritten as 'When notifying the other residents, an applicant must lodge a section 12 notice within 14 days', and so avoid any ambiguity about who ('an applicant' or 'other residents') must lodge a section within the period of time allowed.[187]

In the case of New Zealand, Chapter 3 of the Parliamentary Counsel Office (PCO)'s in-house Drafting Manual sets out the principles of clear drafting. In the *Guidelines for clear drafting – Write: to communicate with your reader*, the caption 'Sentences' includes, under the heading 'Always use gender-neutral language', indications on 'singular they'.[188]

---

186 https://www.justice.gc.ca/eng/rp-pr/csj-sjc/legis-redact/legistics/toc-tdm.asp

187 *Ibid.*

188 Subsections 3.69–3.74 <http://www.pco.govt.nz/clear-drafting#dm3.70A>.

More specifically, subsection 3.70A and 3.70B respectively, indicate when to use the technique and the reason for using it:

> 3.70A. [. . .] If you are using this technique, be careful to avoid ambiguity – this is most likely if a clause refers to 2 or more persons and it is not immediately clear which person the 'their' is referring to or if the 'their' is requiring collective rather than individual action.
>
> 3.70B. Drafters should use the technique of 'he or she' sparingly. This technique still uses gender-specific expressions and so is not gender neutral as now understood. It is particularly important to be gender neutral if the legislation applies widely to individual members of the public. It is also important to avoid this technique if the 'person' could be a body corporate. This technique is still appropriate (and the most pragmatic option) if you are only doing targeted amendments to the existing legislation (so as to ensure consistency). The ongoing use of this technique will be reviewed in 2019.[189]

Interestingly enough, the New Zealand POC's Drafting Manual lists the exceptions to its use, with the eventual recommendation to first discuss the matter with the team manager since any change in legislation towards a gender-neutral language might have implications for all existing Acts:

> 3.72 If you are amending legislation that contains gender-specific language, draft amendments using gender-neutral language in the same way as if you were starting from scratch, except that -
>
> - if the legislation currently uses 'he or she' throughout, generally you should not use 'they' for the amendments unless you are also amending the existing specific pronoun references to make the legislation consistent.
> - generally do not amend the existing gender-specific language throughout the legislation unless it can be done within the confines of the amendment that you are instructed to do or it can be done easily (e.g., by amending 1 or 2 additional provisions), or unless you are expressly instructed to do so.[190]

In 1995, a Simplification Task Force set up by the Commonwealth Attorney-General's Department of the Commonwealth of Australia to examine various drafting issues as part of its Corporations Law Simplification Program, produced a paper entitled *A singular use of THEY*.[191] The proposed new subsection 242(5) in Schedule 6 of the First Bill, for instance, reads:

189 http:// www.pco.govt.nz/ clear- draft ing#dm3.70A
190 *Ibid.*
191 http://www.editorscanberra.org/a-singular-use-of-they/

> *A person* is entitled to have an alternative address included in notices under sub-sections (1), (2) and (8) if:
>
> (a) *their* name, but not their residential address, is on an electoral roll . . . [. . .].[192]

In the First and Second Corporate Law Simplification Bills,[193] 'singular they' has been used to refer to an indefinite noun, rather than the traditional legal *he* or *he or she* (Levy et al. 2017).

The US House of Representatives started going gender neutral in 2009 when the then Speaker of the House, Nancy Pelosi, introduced *HR5*, a resolution rewriting the standing rules of the 111th Congress to eliminate generic masculine pronouns and any other linguistic remnants of this former 'masculine rule'.[194] The House, which since then had operated under the old Rule XXIX, which stated that

> 'the masculine gender include[s] the feminine', will start operating under the new rule, and that phrase will be replaced by 'one gender include[s] the other' - which suggests that the feminine includes the masculine and the masculine, the feminine.[195]

Here are some examples of the House's new drafting rules:[196]

> *he* will be replaced by *he or she*, or by a neutral expression (i.e., *conduct himself* becomes *behave*)
>
> *his expenses* becomes *the expenses of such individual*
>
> *chairman* / *chairmanship* becomes *chair*
>
> *his designee* becomes *a designee.*
>
> *the President submits his budget* becomes *the submission of the budget by the President.*[197]

---

192 http://www.editorscanberra.org/a- singular-use-of-they/

193 https://www.legislation.gov.au/Details/C2004A04965

194 https://www.congress.gov/bill/111th-congress/house-bill/5/text and https://www.congress.gov/bill/111th-congress/house-resolution/5

195 *Ibid.*

196 For more details on this issue, visits Dennis Baron at <https://blogs.illinois.edu/view/25>.

197 As Dennis Baron interestingly comments on it, 'the House anticipates the day when the president will be a woman (an event which can also lead to a nominalized passive)' <https://blogs.illinois.edu/view/25>.

As a matter of fact, the *HR5* provides no indication on the use of 'singular they' as a technique to avoid gender-specific language.

In the UK, before the mid-19th century it was relatively common to find legislation drafted in gender-neutral terms. That changed in 1850, when Parliament passed 'an Act for shortening the Language used in Acts of Parliament'.[198] The Act states:

> IV. Be it enacted, That in all Acts Words importing the Masculine Gender shall be deemed and taken to include Females, and the Singular to include the Plural, and the Plural the Singular, unless the contrary as to Gender or Number is expressly provided; [. . .].[199]

Clearly, it enabled those writing legislation to use masculine pronouns (*he / his / him*) to refer to people whatever their gender.

An attempt to repeal the 1850 Act was made in 1851, most probably because of fears that it might be applied to legislation relating to the franchise and give women the right to vote. The then Attorney General rejected that suggestion as 'really a most unaccountable supposition', a view that was later confirmed by the courts in 1868.[200]

The drafting rule that 'male includes female' was repeated in the *Interpretation Act 1978*, which is still in force, and equivalent wording appears in many private law agreements.

From 1850 until 2007, Acts of the Westminster Parliament relied on the general interpretation provision and used *he*, *him* and *his* with the intention of including reference to males and females. In 2007, Jack Straw, the then Chair of Modernisation of the House of Commons Committee, Leader of the House of Commons and Lord Privy Seal, publicly stated:

> For many years the drafting of primary legislation has relied on section 6 of the Interpretation Act 1978, under which words referring to the masculine gender include the feminine. In practice this means that male pronouns are used on their own in contexts where a reference to women and men is intended, and also that

198 An Act for shortening the Language used in Acts of Parliament, UK, 1850 – PrimaryDocuments.ca.

199 *Ibid.*

200 Bailey Diggory at <https://civilservice.blog.gov.uk/2020/01/10/breaking-down-gender-stereotypes-in-legal-writing/>.

> words such as chairman are used for offices capable of being held by either gender. [. . .]
>
> From the beginning of next Session, Government Bills will take a form which achieves gender-neutral drafting so far as it is practicable, at no more than a reasonable cost to brevity or intelligibility [. . .].[201]

Section 2.1 of the *Office of Parliamentary Council's Drafting Guidance 2020* gives some recommendations on gender-neutral writing in Primary legislation:

> 2.1 GENDER NEUTRALITY
>
> Office practice
>
> 2.1.1 It is government policy that primary legislation should be drafted in a gender-neutral way, so far as it is practicable to do so.
>
> 2.1.2 Gender neutrality applies not only when drafting free-standing text in a Bill but also when inserting text into older Acts which are not gender-neutral. This is unlikely to cause difficulties. However, in very limited circumstances, exceptions may be made when amending an older Act where it might be confusing to be gender-neutral. If you think you need to make an exception, consult your team leader.
>
> What does gender-neutral drafting require?
>
> 2.1.3 In practice, gender-neutral drafting means two things:
>
> avoiding gender-specific pronouns (such as 'he') for a person who is not necessarily of that gender.
>
> avoiding nouns that might appear to assume that a person of a particular gender will do a particular job or perform a particular role (e.g. 'chairman').[202]

Incidentally, it is interesting to consider the indications given on the use of 'singular they':

> 2.1.16 They (singular). In common parlance, 'they' is often used in relation to a singular antecedent which could refer to a person of either sex.
>
> 2.1.17 Whether this popular usage is correct or not is perhaps a matter of dispute. OED (2nd ed, 1989) records the usage without comment; SOED (5th ed, 2002) notes considered an error by some. It is certainly well-precedented in

201 Hansard source (Citation: HC Deb, 8 March 2007, c146WS).
202 guidancebook.book (publishing.service.gov.uk).

respectable literature over several centuries. In the debate on gender-neutral drafting in the House of Lords in 2013 a number of peers expressed concern about the use of 'they' as a singular pronoun.

2.1.18 It may be that 'they' as a singular pronoun seems more natural in some contexts (for example, where the antecedent is 'any person' or 'a person') than in others.

2.1.19 They (plural). It may be possible to turn the noun into a plural noun and then to use 'they' (relying on section 6(c) of the Interpretation Act 1978). [. . .].[203]

Then, a final, yet significant, recommendation is provided:

2.1.20 Take care to ensure that the plural does not create an ambiguity that would be avoided if the singular were used. [204]

Given its usefulness for gender-neutrality, there are reasons to believe 'singular they' will eventually make its way into legislation in the English-speaking jurisdictions analyzed. Yet, there is still a dispute, particularly in the UK, about whether it is grammatically correct (Greenberg 2014).

5.3.6 UK 'Guide to Gender-Neutral Drafting (2019)'

In 2019, the OPC launched a practical 'Guide to Gender-Neutral Drafting' (hereafter, *G-N Guide2019*), declaring its intention to share the OPC's experience gained over the past years with the wider legal community outside of government.[205]

Since 2019, the OPC has started writing legislation in gender-neutral language. It took a bit of getting used to at first, but has since become second nature. The use of masculine words to address people regardless of gender or sex is now considered 'unnecessary, inaccurate and tends to reinforce historic gender stereotypes'.[206] Besides, the OPC considers gender-neutral writing strongly related to the issues of clarity, inclusion and equality.

203 guidancebook.book (publishing.service.gov.uk).

204 *Ibid.*

205 https://www.gov.uk/government/organisations/office-of-the-parliamentary-counsel

206 https://civilservice.blog.gov.uk/2020/01/10/breaking-down-gender-stereotypes-in-legal-writing/

G-N Guide2019 contains practical advice on how to use gender-neutral language and includes three fundamental ways to avoid gender-specific pronouns, that are illustrated with examples. Written by the OPC and the Office UK Government Legal Department, *G-N Guide2019* is supported by the Interlaw Diversity Forum[207] and Global Butterflies.[208]

In the 'Introduction from the Office of the Parliamentary Counsel and Government Legal Department' to the *G-N Guide2019*, Elizabeth Gardiner (CB First Parliamentary Counsel – OPC) and Jonathan Jones QC (Hon, Treasury Solicitor – Government Legal Department), state:

> The UK's Office of the Parliamentary Counsel and Government Legal Department have been promoting the use of gender-neutral drafting for UK statutes and statutory instruments for many years. Both organisations are at the heart of drafting legislation in the UK and are proud to have this opportunity to share our approach to gender-neutral drafting with the wider legal profession responsible for private law agreements and other products. There is no reason why gender-neutral drafting cannot become the norm across the profession.
>
> We are both committed to being outstanding legal organisations and brilliant places to work, where our people can thrive and fulfil their potential. We are also committed to being leading employers in relation to diversity and inclusion. We are most grateful to the InterLaw Diversity Forum for helping us reach out to their network of practitioners for this breakfast seminar, perhaps the first of its kind in London. We hope to exchange best practice with colleagues across the legal profession and demonstrate how it is easy to draft in a way that is legally effective and gender neutral. [209]

With the apparent objective of demonstrating how easy it is to draft in a way that is legally effective and gender neutral, the *G-N Guide2019* condenses years of work by both organizations to promote gender-neutral drafting in a wide range of UK government legal documents.

5.3.7 'Good law' and UK legislative drafting

In the 'Foreword' to the OPC Guidance on *Common legislative solutions: a guide to tackling recurring policy issues in legislation 2022*

---

207 https://www.interlawdiversityforum.org/

208 https://globalbutterflies.com/

209 https://www.interlawdiversityforum.org/guide-to-gender-neutral-drafting

(hereafter *Guide 2022*), Elizabeth Gardiner (First Parliamentary Counsel) makes this statement:

> As the legislative drafting office for the UK Government, the Office of the Parliamentary Counsel is committed to producing clear and effective legislation to the highest possible standards in the public interest. We lead the legislative drafting profession within Government and work to promote greater awareness of the principles underpinning good law.[210]

Above all, she asserts that:

> It [*Guide 2022*] represents an excellent example of civil service collaboration, exemplifying principles of mutual respect and cooperation in the carrying out of one of our most essential public functions, the creation of good law.[211]

In a talk given in 2014 at the Institute of Advanced Legal Studies on common law and statute law, Richard Heaton provided a definition of the expression of 'good law'. As we read in the transcript of the speech as it was delivered,

> You might find this a strange word [good law] to use in the context of law and law-making.[212] [...]
>
> In Lord Bingham's words, the rule of law requires that "the law must be accessible and so far as possible intelligible, clear and predictable". For legislative drafters, and for the government's online publishers, this is a fundamental part of our mission. [...].
>
> And we can hardly claim to respect the rule of law if the citizen's prevailing view of the law is that it is too difficult, too obscure, that it isn't really for them.

210 https://www.gov.uk/government/publications/common-legislative-solutions-a-guide-to-tackling-recurring-policy-issues-in-legislation/common-legislative-solutions-a-guide-to-tackling-recurring-policy-issues-in-legislation#foreword-by-elizabeth-gardiner-first-parliamentary-counsel

211 *Ibid.*

212 https://www.gov.uk/government/speeches/making-the-law-easier-for-users-the-role-of-statutes--2

Such a definition of ‘good law’ substantiates what we have previously discussed specifically in Chapter 2 (and more generally throughout the book) and represented in Diagram 9 below.

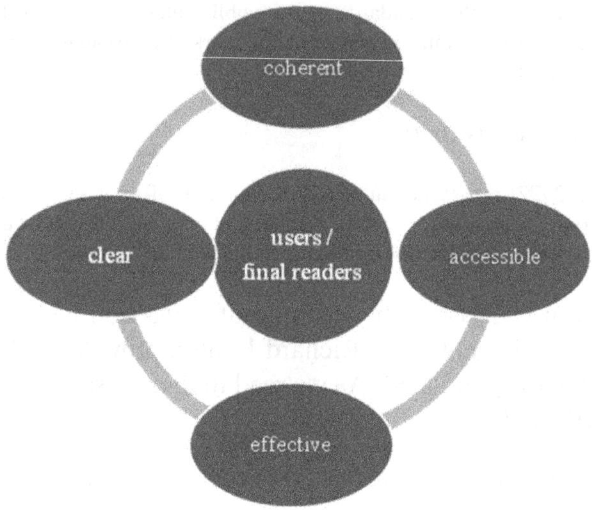

Diagram 9. ‘Good law’ principles.

Eventually, ‘good law’ becomes a demand for writing and making legislation that is clear, coherent, effective, and accessible, with a mutual objective of making legislation work well for the users (i.e., the citizens, final readers, etc.) of today and tomorrow.

Conclusions

The main assumption proposed in this book is that legislative drafting represents an example of professional discourse, where the propositions of specialized information, or knowledge of the actors participating in the legislative process, is translated into meanings, and such meanings are given as input to the rules and strategies of grammatical formulation. Discourse being the construction and organization of the segments of language above as well as below the sentence, the elements of grammar, lexis, and phonology still play a fundamental role, but they are reconsidered as a part of that multi-layered cognitive and socio-cultural phenomenon. Professional knowledge is acquired, shared, and used among members of various kinds of scholarly or other specialized communities. These specialized communities are defined not only by their specialized knowledge, but also by their specialized social practices, including their specialized discourse and communication, as well as by a complex network of organizations and institutions such as universities, professional groups, and associations, to name but a few.

A relevant question for our understanding of modern legislative process is related to the effects of 'context' at different levels, such as the situated communicative event, the environmental framework (i.e., the workplace, the organization, the discipline), and the societal framework (i.e., the legal-political, socio-cultural, and linguistic frameworks) within which legislative process takes place (Chapters 1 and 2). By looking at those levels, the analysis conducted in the book demonstrates that it becomes possible to: (i) reach a deeper understanding of the professional groups taking part in the process (Chapter 3); (ii) better assess the lexico-grammatical and textual features of its final product, i.e., normative texts (Chapter 4); (iii) suggest alternative linguistic and textual strategies aimed at making texts more accessible to potential readers and/or intended users (Chapter 5).

Within common law jurisdictions legislative drafters deal with a universe of human behaviour which is unlimited, in the sense that it is impossible to predict exactly what may happen within the human universe (Bhatia 2010; Gotti 2011, 2014). Legislative drafting is a narrower concept to the civil law equivalent of law-making: law-making embraces the whole process of conceptualization of legislation until its very implementation and thus reflects the legislative process, whereas legislative drafting reflects the drafting process only. This does not imply that drafting is completely foreign to the legislative process. In fact, the drafting process is part of the legislative process, which in turn is part of the policy process (Stefanou 2011).

The context of a legal document is often scrutinized to shed light upon the meaning of an ambiguous or obscure provision so that it may be interpreted as its government intended it initially to be. A common belief is that legal concepts and legal documents are often difficult to understand. In the case of legislative drafting the position is complicated by other factors, such as the addressees of the normative act, i.e., the legislative audience on the one hand, and the nature of legislation, i.e., the types of normative texts, on the other. A plurality of actors with specific abilities intervenes at different stages of the production of norms as the result of the legal expression of a public policy. Among them, one of the most challenging roles is that of the legislative drafter. Constrained by the legal-political framework at local, national and supranational levels, legislative drafting is deemed to be strongly influenced by government policy and the legislative traditions that are reflected in the laws and regulations which regulate professional discourse. Looking at the text-formation and its end result, i.e., the normative text, there is more than a mere linguistic product. In reality, the composition of the working team groups and the various contextual frameworks in which the text is constructed, make the text more or less readable, more or less comprehensible.

As was discussed throughout the book, normative texts cannot produce adequate regulatory results without the synergy from the other actors of the policy process. The government seeks to implement its agendas by use of the policy process, and the legislative process comes into play. It is within the legislative process that drafters go through each one of Thornton's (1996) five stages of drafting legislation. By taking this holistic picture of legislative process as a tool for regulation into account, one recognizes that the goal of both government and drafters is to achieve quality in legislation.

Incidentally, a salient feature of the legislative drafting is the expected capacity of drafters to choose the appropriate rule and convention that reaches the aimed results according to the specific and practical context at any given time. In order to perform this task, Xanthaki (2013) suggests that legislative drafters should be aware of existing sets of rules and conventions (particularly those disciplining similar cases), identify the most relevant set of circumstances applicable to the problem, and have the theoretical knowledge and practical experience to promote the rule or convention that best applies (under the specific characteristics of the case). Overall, the aim is to make provisions that are as clear, precise, unambiguous, and all-inclusive as possible, whereas the nature and function of participant organization unsurprisingly influence the legislative actions.

The implementation of legislation is significantly influenced by a range of filtering agents at whom legislation is directed and who may constrain, adapt, and (possibly) modify the intentions that form the basis of the legislation approved in the first place. Modern legislative drafting theory urges legislative drafters to bare the text from preliminary provisions and to start as early as possible with the regulatory message that the government is trying to convey to its citizens (Chapter 4). And, so, the pursuit of modern drafters is to share that message with the users of the legislation in a manner that allows them to be heard loud and clear (Stefanou and Xanthaki 2008). For this reason, the author has decided to show how linguistics may be of some help to the legislative drafters who want to know how a piece of legislation is structured (and may be alternatively structured) in terms of lexico-grammatical and discoursal features (Chapters 4 and 5).

This study is based on the assumption that legislative writing, like other types of text writing, is surrounded by a consistent variety of situational factors, such as: why a legislative text is produced, when a legislative text is produced, to whom the legislative text is addressed, and which form (i.e., formal, elaborate, etc.) a legislative text takes from its conception till its final production. Though more formal and elaborate, the writing process involved in normative texts might be assumed to be similar to those involved in writing a poem, an article, or a letter: thoughts must be generated, mentally organized, and translated into a text. Then, texts must be assessed and eventually revised. Being a consistent collective writing process, legislative drafting needs to be analyzed in its own social and societal contexts (Chapters 2 and 3). More specifically, the factors that the author has considered can be listed in:

- social variables at group level, i.e., the professional and social background of the members participating in the drafting and the formal and informal social order within the groups;
- contextual frameworks surrounding the legislative drafting, that represent the particular conditions under which normative texts are produced;
- the target readers of the normative texts.

When producing a text, there occurs a relatively conscious or unconscious adaptation to the norms and attitudes of the discourse community which the members are part of. In the case of a text produced in different steps by various groups of professionals, (i.e. collective writing, additional negotiations about the content structuring, wording, layout, etc.) these happen during the drafting process. This implies that not only does the final text reflect the aims, knowledge, norms and attitudes of the members of professional groups involved in the process, but also the interaction among them throughout the same process.

In the case of professional writing done collectively by various groups within the same discourse community, the drafting process consists in a continuous adaptation to the various groups and the public sphere of the discourse community. The drafting of normative texts becomes a collective process where the preparation of the draft text is done by one person, in most cases the secretary, who assumes the role of interpreter and combiner of different ideas. Then, the representation of the text is made collectively by the members of the drafting commission. The chairperson and the politicians have decisive roles, and the members of the commission contribute by reviewing the issue from their perspectives and possibly extending the content of the text (Gunnarsson 2009). Eventually, various groups of professionals crowd the discourse community governing the legislative process. Lawyers, politicians, representatives of different public organizations, and drafters play a role in this process, and they actively take part in the construction, editing and reviewing phases of the final text.

However, legislative drafters are those who are responsible for producing a text that is directed towards a specific group of people, the intended readers of the normative text. Looking more closely at professional documents, we have found that another key element is the comprehensibility problem that results in various comprehension levels depending on the properties of the text, such as (i) the superficial level represented by typography and syntax, (ii) an intermediate level represented by semantics, and (iii) a deeper level represented by pragmatic factors, such as perspective and function-orientation. Likewise, the analysis conducted in the book (Chapter 2) revealed that different reading purposes may direct the reading process towards different text levels, where the processing of more superficial levels is overtaken by deeper text levels, and different text levels are responsible for the diverse levels of comprehension. And, the more superficial text level the addressee focuses on, the less important reading purpose they aim at. This method of analysis becomes particularly useful when taking into account professional texts and, in particular, the comprehensibility of action-oriented texts such as legislative texts.

In the case of normative texts, we have seen that the comprehension of the text by the addressees entail a general legal knowledge, such as lexico-grammar and textual conventions (i.e., the structuring of law texts, legal terminology, etc.), and a specific knowledge for the law text in question. With regard to the background knowledge, a further distinction does exist among the readers of legislative texts; the one between lawyer (legal representatives, administrative staff, public officer, etc.) and laypeople. Overall, legislative texts can be read in order to obtain an overall picture of their content, to know how to act under specific circumstances, or to judge in specific situations. The setting in which the reading of legislative texts takes place (i.e. the situational context) can occur when one comes across a piece of legislation and wants to acquire knowledge about its content; for instance the cases it regulates, the categories of citizens it is aimed at, the rights and duties it assigns and imposes, etc., and eventually wants to use the information for subsequent actions. On the other hand, the situational context might be a concrete case which motivates the search for the normative text regulating it, reading the parts (Articles, Sections, etc.) in the text that discipline it, and operating in accordance with the provisions in the normative text that discipline the concrete case that have motivated the reading in the first place. Comprehension, therefore, is strongly linked to the situational contexts that orientate the reading to the entire text or some of its parts. Eventually, the comprehension of the text requires the potential reader to link up the sphere of application of the rules with their own situational context.

One of the main purposes of this book has been to demonstrate that accessibility and comprehensibility issues need to become part of the construction of legislative texts. In their pursuit of quality in legislation, drafters play a crucial role in the governing process, and legislation is one of the last and least choices at the government's disposal to implement regulation.

As has been discussed throughout the book, the main goal for legislation is efficacy. Often confused with effectiveness, it can be defined as the power of legislative provisions to achieve the regulatory aims that they are set to address (Xanthaki 2014). As efficacy is the final goal of the legislative process, legislative drafters can contribute by producing texts that are evaluated via the qualities of simplicity, clarity, precision, and unambiguity. In this regard, the use of plain language, the more recent linguistic transformation (i.e., 'singular they' and gender-neutral language) and a textual reorganization of normative texts (i.e., 'easification techniques'), which the author has explored in Chapter 5, represent some practical and useful techniques to achieve clarity, precision and unambiguity in legislation. Such recognition of the fact that comprehensibility and accessibility issues are a part of text content might represent the next step that ought to be taken in the work of making good law.

The author's hope is that the theoretical framework and the analyses presented in this book will shed some light on the dynamic value of professional discourse in the legislative context, and the decisive role played by linguistic analysis to aid drafters in their attempt to write more comprehensible and accessible pieces of legislation.

References

Asprey, Michele M. 2010. *Plain Language for Lawyers*. Sydney: Federation Press.

Audring, Jenny. 2016. *Gender. Oxford Research Encyclopedia of Linguistics* <Gender | Oxford Research Encyclopedia of Linguistics>.

Baffour Adjei, Stephen. 2013. Discourse Analysis: Examining Language Use in Context. *The Qualitative Report* 18(50), 1–10.

Baker, Mona. 2002. Corpus-based Studies within the Larger Context of Translation Studies. *Génesis: Revista Científica do ISAI* 2, 7–16.

Barnes, Jeffrey. 2006. The Continuing Debate about 'Plain Language' Legislation: A Law Reform Conundrum. *Statute Law Review* 27(2), 83–132.

Bergvall, Victoria L. / Bing, Janet M. / Freed, Alice F. (eds) 1996. *Rethinking Language and Gender Research: Theory and Practice*. London: Longman.

Bhatia, Vijay K. 1983. Simplification v. Easification. The Case of Legal Texts. *Applied Linguistics* 4(1), 42–54.

Bhatia, Vijay K. 1987. Textual-mapping in British Legislative Writing. *World Englishes* 1, 1–10.

Bhatia, Vijay K. 1993. *Analysing Genre – Language Use in Professional Settings*. London: Longman.

Bhatia, Vijay K. 1994. Cognitive Structuring in Legislative Provisions. In Gibbons, John (ed.) *Language and the Law*. London: Routledge, 136–55.

Bhatia, Vijay K. 2004. *Worlds of Written Discourse*. London: Continuum.

Bhatia, Vijay K. 2010. Drafting Legislative Provisions: Challenges and Opportunities. *Commonwealth Association of Legislative Counsel / The Loophole*, 5–15 <Loophole Journal – December 2010 (wordpress.com)>

Bhatia, Vijay K. 2014. Linguistic and Socio-pragmatic Considerations in Legislative Drafting. In Pennisi, Giulia A. (ed.) *Theory and Practice of Legislation. Special Issue on Legislative Drafting and Linguistics,* Taylor & Francis Online, Vol. 2(2), 169–183.

Bhatia, Vijay K. 2021. Legal Writing: Specificity. In Coulthard, Malcolm / Johnson, Alison (eds) *The Routledge Handbook of Forensic Linguistics*. London: Routledge, 37–50.

Biber, Douglas / Conrad, Susan. 2009. *Register, Genre, and Style*. Cambridge: Cambridge University Press.

Billig, Michael. 1997. The Dialogic Unconscious: Psychoanalysis, Discursive Psychology and the Nature of Repression. *British Journal of Social Psychology* 36(2), 139–159.

Blommaert, Jan. 2007. Sociolinguistcs and Discourse Analysis: Orders of Indexicality and Policentricity. *Journal of Multicultural Discourse* 2(2), 115–130.

Bowers, Frederick. 1989. *Linguistic Aspects of Legislative Expression*. Vancouver: University of British Columbia Press.

Bowman, Geoffrey. 2006. The Art of Legislative Drafting. *Amicus Curiae* 64, 2–9.

Bright, William. 1992. *International Encyclopaedia of Linguistics*. New York: Oxford University Press.

Burchfield, Robert W. 2009. *Fowler's Dictionary of Modern English Usage*. Oxford: Oxford University Press.

Butt, Peter. 2013. *Modern Legal Drafting. A Guide to Using Clearer Language*. Cambridge: Cambridge University Press.

Campbell, Lisbeth. 1996. Drafting Styles: Fuzzy or Fussy? *Murdoch University Electronic Journal of Law* 17(3) <http://www5.austlii.edu.au/au/journals/MurdochUeJlLaw/1996/17.html>.

Candlin, Christopher N. 1997. General Editor's Preface. In Gunnarsson, Britt-Louise / Linell, Per / Nordberg, Bengt (eds) *The Construction of Professional Discourse*. London: Longman, viii–vxiv.

Candlin, Christopher N. / Crichton, Jonathan / Moore, Stephen H. 2017. *Exploring Discourse in Context and in Action*. London: Palgrave Macmillan.

Chafe, Wallace. 2008. Aspects of Discourse Analysis. *Brno Studies in English* 34, 23–37.

Charaudeau, Patrick. 2002. A Communicative Conception of Discourse. *Discourse Studies* 4(3), 301–318.

Cheng, Patricia W. / Holoyoak, Keith J. 1985. Pragmatic Reasoning Schemas. *Cognitive Psychology* 17, 391–426.

Connell, Catherine 2010. Doing, Undoing, or Redoing Gender? Learning from the Workplace Experiences of Transpeople. *Gender and Society* 24(1), 31–55.

Coode, George 1848. *On the Legislative Expressions, or, the Language of Written Law*. Philadelphia: T. & J.W. Johnson.

Cooney, Mark 2012. Plain isn't Plain. *Michigan Bar Journal*, 52–53.

Corbett, Greville G. 1991. *Gender*. Cambridge: Cambridge University Press.

Corbett, Greville G. 2007. Gender and Noun Classes. In Shopen, Timothy (ed.) *Language Typology and Syntactic Description*. Cambridge: Cambridge University Press, 241–279.

Corbett, Greville G. 2013. Sex-Based and Non-Sex-Based Gender Systems. In Dryer, Matthew S. / Haspelmath, Martin (eds) *The World Atlas of Language Structures Online*. Leipzig: Max Planck Institute for Evolutionary Anthropology <WALS Online – Chapter Sex-based and Non-sex-based Gender Systems>.

Crystal, David / Davy, Derek. 1969. *Investigating English Style*. London: Routledge.

Curzan, Anne. 2003. *Gender Shifts in the History of English*. Cambridge: Cambridge University Press.

Davies, Bronwyn / Harré, Rom. 1990. Positioning: The Discursive Production of Selves. *Journal for the Theory of Social Behaviour* 20(1), 43–63.

De Benedetto, Maria. 2018. Effective Law from a Regulatory and Administrative Law Perspective. *European Journal of Risk Regulation* 9(3), 391–415.

De Benedetto, Maria / Martelli, Mario / Rangone, Nicoletta. 2011. *La Qualità delle Regole*. Bologna: Il Mulino.

Driedger, Elmer A. 1982. *A Manual of Instructions for Legislative and Legal Writing*. Ottawa: Minister of Supply and Services Canada.

Durant, Alan / Leung, Janny. 2016. *Language and Law*. London: Routledge.

Eagleson, Robert D. / Jones, Gloria / Hassal, Sue. 1997. *Writing in Plain English*. Australia: Australian Government Pub. Service.

Eckert, Penelope / McConnell-Ginet, Sally. 1992. Think Practically and Look Locally: Language and Gender as Community-Based Practice. *Annual Review of Anthropology* 21, 461–488.

Ehrlich, Susan / King, Ruth. 1992. Gender-Based Language Reform and the Social Construction of Meaning. *Discourse and Society* 3(2), 151–166.

Endicott, Timothy. 2022. Law and Language. In Zalta, Edward N. (ed.) *The Stanford Encyclopaedia of Philosophy* <https://plato.stanford.edu/archives/spr2022/entries/law-language/>.

Engberg, Jan. 2013a. Legal Linguistics as a Mutual Arena for Cooperation. Recent Developments in the Field of Applied Linguistics and Law. *AILA Review* 26, 24–41.

Engberg, Jan. 2013b. Comparative Law for Translation: The Key to Successful Mediation Between Legal Systems. In Borja Albi, Anabel / Prieto Ramos, Fernando (eds) *Legal Translation in Context: Professional Issues and Prospects*. Bern: Peter Lang, pp. 9–25.

Fairclough, Norman. 1989. *Language and Power*. Longman: Harlow.

Fairclough, Norman. 1995. *The Critical Study of Language*. London: Longman.

Fairclough, Norman. 2003. *Analysing Discourse: Textual Analysis for Social Research*. London: Routledge.

Fairclough, Norman / Wodak, Ruth. 1997. Critical Discourse Analysis. In van Dijk Teun (ed.) *Discourse Studies: A Multidisciplinary Introduction*. London: Sage, 258–284.

Fens-De Zeeuw, Lyda. 2018. The Huge Presence of Lindley Murray: An Illustration of the Scope of Lindley Murray's Authority on All Things Prescriptive. *English Today* 34(4), 45–61.

Fillmore, Charles J. / Baker, Collin F. 2009. A Frames Approach to Semantic Analysis. In Heine, Bernd / Narrog, Heiko (eds) *The Oxford Handbook of Linguistic Analysis*. Oxford: Oxford University, 313–340.

Fjeld, Ruth V. 2001. Interpretation of Indefinite Adjectives in Legislative Language. In Mayer, Felix (ed.) *Languages for Special Purposes: Perspectives for the New Millennium*. Tübingen: Narr, 643–650.

Flower, Lynda / Hayes, John. 1981. A Cognitive Process Theory of Writing. *College Composition and Communication* 32, 365–387.

Flower, Lynda / Hayes, John. 1984. Images, Plans, and Prose: The Representation of Meaning in Writing. *Written Communication* 1, 120–160.

Fowler, Roger / Hodge, Bob / Kress, Gunther / Trew, Tony. 1979. *Language and Control*. London: Routledge and Kegan Paul.

Frankson, Joan R. 2000. *Gender Management System Series. A Quick Guide to Gender Mainstreaming in Information and Communication*. London: Commonwealth Secretariat.

Fung, Spring Y. C. / Watson-Brown, Anthony. 1994. *The Template: A Guide for the Analysis of Complex Legislation*. London: University of London, Institute of Advanced Legal Studies.

Galdia, Marcus. 2009. *Legal Linguistics*. Frankfurt: Peter Lang.

Gardner, Howard. 2004. *Changing Minds: The Art and Science of Changing Our Own and Other People's Minds*. Cambridge (MA): Harvard University Press.

Garner, Bryan A. 2001. *Legal Writing in Plain English: A Text with Exercises*. Chicago: University of Chicago Press.

Garner, Bryan A. 2009. *Garner's Modern American Usage*. New York: Oxford University Press.

Garner, Bryan A. 2011. *Garner's Dictionary of Legal Usage*. Oxford: Oxford University Press.

Garner, Bryan A. 2013. *Legal Writing in Legal English*. Chicago: The University of Chicago Press.

Garner, Bryan A. 2014. *The Winning Brief: 100 Tips for Persuasive Briefing in Trial and Appellate Courts*. Oxford: Oxford University Press.

Garzone, Giuliana. 2013. Variation in the Use of Modality in Legislative Texts: Focus on Shall. *Journal of Pragmatics* 57, 68–81.

Geeraerts, Dirk. 1995. Cognitive Linguistics. In Verschueren, Jef / Östman, Jan-Ola / Blommaert, Jan (eds) *Handbook of Pragmatics*. Amsterdam: John Benjamins, 111–116.

Geeraerts, Dirk / Cuyckens, Hubert. 2010. *The Oxford Handbook of Cognitive Linguistics*. Oxford: Oxford Handbooks.

Gibbon, Dafydd / Griffiths, Sascha. 2017. Multilinear Grammar: Ranks and Interpretations. *Open Linguistics* 3(1), 265–307.

Goddard, Murray J. 2009. The Impact of Human Intuition in Psychology. *Review of General Psychology* 13(2), 167–174.

Goddard, Christopher. 2010. Legal Linguistics as an Academic and Professional Discipline: Identifying Clients, Customers, Stakeholders. In Heine, Carmen / Engberg, Jan (eds)

Reconceptualizing LSP: Online Proceedings of the XVII European LSP Symposium 2009. Aarhus School of Business, Aarhus: Aarhus University <https://www.asb.dk/fileadmin/www.asb.dk/isek/goddard.pdf>.

Gotti, Maurizio. 2011. *Investigating Specialized Discourse*. Bern: Peter Lang.

Gotti, Maurizio. 2014. Linguistic Insights into Leglislative Drafting. In Pennisi, Giulia A. (ed.) *The Theory and Practice of Legislation. Special Issue on Legislative Drafting and Linguistics*, Taylor & Francis Online, Vol. 2(2), 123–143.

Gotti, Maurizio / Dossena, Marina. 2001. *Modality in Specialized Texts*. Bern: Peter Lang.

Greenberg, Daniel. 2008. The Techniques of Gender-neutral Drafting. In Constantin, Stefanou / Xanthaki, Helen (eds) *Drafting Legislation: A Modern Approach*. Aldershot: Ashgate, 63–76.

Greenberg, Daniel. 2011. *Laying Down the Law: A Discussion of the People, Processes and Problems that Shape Acts of Parliament*. London: Sweet & Maxwell.

Greenberg, Daniel. 2014. Gender Neutrality in the House of Lords (and Ladies). *Statute Law Review*, 35(1), v–vii.

Gunnarsson, Britt-Louise. 1984. Functional Comprehensibility of Legislative Text: Experiments with a Swedish Act of Parliament. *Text & Talk* 4(1–3), 71–105.

Gunnarsson, Britt-Louise. 2009. *Professional Discourse*. London and New York: Continuum.

Gustafsson, Marita. 1975. *Some Syntactic Properties of English Law Language*. Turku: Publications of the Department of English, University of Turku.

Gustafsson, Marita. 1984. The Syntactic Features of Binomial Expressions in Legal English. *Interdisciplinary Journal for the Study of Discourse* 4, 123–142.

Haack, Susan. 2014. *Evidence Matters*. Cambridge: Cambridge University Press.

Harré, Rom / Moghaddam, Fathali M. 2003. *The Self and Others: Positioning Individuals and Groups in Personal, Political, and Cultural Contexts*. Westport (CT): Praeger Publishers.

Harvey, David J. 2015. *The Law Emprynted and Englysshed: The Printing Press as an Agent of Change in Law and Legal Culture 1475-1642*. Portland: Hart Publihing.

Haspelmath, Martin / Dryer, Matthew S. / Gil, David / Comrie, Bernard. 2005. *The World Atlas of Language Structures*. Oxford: Oxford University Press.

Helliger, Marlis / Bußmann, Hadumod. 2001. *Gender Across Languages*. Amsterdam and Philadelphia: John Benjamins.

Hernández, Mario H. / Volker, Heydt. 2017. Legislative Language and Style. In Ulrich, Karpen / Xanthaki, Helen (eds) *Legislation in Europe: A Comprehensive Guide for Scholars and Practitioners*. London: Bloomsbury Publishing, 129–144.

Holmes, Janet. 1991. Language and Gender. *Language Teaching* 24(4), 207–220.

Hudson, Richard A. 1996. *Sociolinguistics*. Cambridge: Cambridge University Press.

Hyland, Ken. 2002. Directives: Argument and Engagement in Academic Writing. *Applied Linguistics* 23(2), 215–239.

Jackson, Kevin T. 1985. Definition in Legal Reasoning. *Jurimetrics*, 25(4), 377-386.

Kenny, Anthony. 2010. *A New History of Western Philosophy*. Oxford: Oxford University Press.

Kong, Kenneth. 2014. *Professional Discourse*. Cambridge: Cambridge University Press.

Kramarae, Cherise / Schulz, Muriel / O'Barr, William M. 1984. *Language and Power*. London: Sage.

Kurzon, Dennis 1986. *It is Hereby Performed...Exploration in Legal Speech Acts*. Amsterdam: John Benjamins Publishing Company.

Lakoff, George / Johnson, Mark. 1998. *Philosophy in the Flesh. The Embodied Mind and Its Challenge to Western Thought*. New York: Basic Books.

Langacker, Ronald W. 1991. *Foundations of Cognitive Grammar Vol. 2: Descriptive Application*. Stanford: Stanford University Press.

Langton, Nicola. 2005. Cleaning Up the Act: Using Plain English in Legislation. *Clarity* 54, 28–32.

Le Cheng, King K. / Wagner, Anne. 2014. *The Ashgate Handbook of Legal Translation. Law, Language and Communication.* London: Routledge.

Leech, Geoffrey N. / Deuchar, Margaret / Hoogenraad, Robert. 1994. *English Grammar for Today*. London: Macmillan.

Lemke, Jay L. 1990. *Talking Science: Language, Learning, and Values*. New York: Ablex Publishing Corporation.

Levy, Ron / O'Brien, Molly / Rice, Simon / Ridge, Pauline / Thornton Margaret. 2017. *New Directions for Law in Australia: Essays in Contemporary Law Reform*. Australia: Australian National University Press.

Malyuga, Elena N. 2020. *Functional Approach to Professional Discourse Exploration in Linguistics*. Singapore: Springer.

Mattila, Heikki. 2006. *Comparative legal Linguistics*. Hampshire: Ashgate.

Mclean, Vanessa. 2013. Is Gender-Neutral Drafting an Effective Tool Against Gender Inequality Within the Legal System? *Common Law Bulletin* 39(3), 443–454.

Mellinkoff, David. 1963. The Language of the Law. *Michigan Law Review* 63(1), 180–186.

Mertz, Elizabeth. 2007. Semiotic Antropology. *Annual Review of Antropology* 36, 337–353.

Miller, Casey / Swift, Kate 1980. *The Handbook of Nonsexist Writing: for Writers, Editors and Speakers*. New York: Harper & Row Publishers.

Mousmouti, Maria. 2019. *Designing Effective Legislation*. Cheltenham and Northampton (MA): Edward Elgar Publishing.

Pauwels, Anne. 1998. *Women Changing Language*. London and New York: Longman.

Perlman, Merrill. 2017. Stylebooks Finally Embrace the Single 'They'. *Columbia Journalism Review* <https://www.cjr.org/language_corner/stylebooks-single-they-ap-chicago-gender-neutral.php>.

Petersson, Sandra. 1999. Gender-Neutral Drafting: Recent Commonwealth Developments. *Statute Law Review* 20(1), 1–55.

Potter, Jonathan. 2003. Discursive Psychology: Between Method and Paradigm. *Discourse & Society*, 14(6), 783–794.

Potter, Jonathan / Wetherell, Margaret. 1987. *Discourse and Social Psychology: Beyond Attitudes and Behaviour*. London: Sage.

Prewitt-Freilino, Jennifer L. / Caswell, Andrew T. / Laakso, Emmi K. 2012. The Gendering of Language: A Comparison of Gender Equality in Countries with Gendered, Natural Gender, and Genderless Languages. *Sex Roles: A Journal of Research* 66, 268–281.

Robinson, Pauline C. 1980. *ESP (English for Specific Purposes): The Present Position.* Cambridge (MA): Elsevier Science & Technology Books.

Sato, Sayaka / Öttl, Anton / Ute, Gabriel / Gygax, Pascal. 2017. Assessing the Impact of Gender Grammaticization on Thought: A Psychological and Psycholinguistic Perspective. *Osnabrücker Beiträge zur Sprachtheorie* 90, 117–135.

Scollon, Ron. 2001. Action and Text: Towards an Integrated Understanding of the Place of Text in Social (Inter)action, Mediated Discourse Analysis and the Problem of Social Action. In Ruth, Wodak / Meyer, Michael (eds) *Methods of Critical Discourse Analysis*. London: SAGE Publications, 139–195.

Searle, John R. 1979. *Expression and Meaning*. Cambridge: Cambridge University Press.

Seel, Norbert M. 2012. *Encyclopedia of the Sciences and Learning*. Boston (MA): Springer.

Solan, Lawrence M. 1993. *The Language of Judges*. Chicago: The University of Chicago Press.

Solan, Lawrence M. 2005. Private Language, Public Laws: The Central Role of Legislative Intent in Statutory Interpretation. *Georgetown Law Journal* 93(2), 427–486.

Solan, Lawrence M. / Tiersma, Peter 2012. *Oxford Handbook of Language and Law*. Oxford: Oxford University Press.

Stefanou, Constantin. 2011. Legislative Drafting as a Form of Communication. In Mader, Luzius / Travares de Almeida, Marta (eds) *Quality of Legislation Principles and Instruments*. Baden-Baden: Nomos, 308–320.

Stefanou, Constantin / Xanthaki, Helen 2008. *Drafting Legislation: A Modern Approach*. London: Routledge.

Sunderland, Jane. 2006. *Language and Gender: An Advanced Resource Book.* London and New York: Routledge.

Swales, John. 1985. English as the International Language of Research. *Regional Language Centre Journal* 16(1), 1–7.

Swales, John. 1990. *Genre Analysis. English in Academic and Research Settings*. Cambridge: Cambridge University Press.

Swales, John. 2016. Reflections on the Concept of Discourse Community. *Asp* 69, 7–19.

Swales, John / Rogers, Priscilla S. 1995. Discourse and the Projection of Corporate Culture: The Mission Statement. *Discourse and Society* 6(2), 223–242.

Talmy, Leonard. 2006. Cognitive Linguistics. In Brown, Keith (ed.) *Encyclopedia of Language & Linguistics*. Cambridge (MA): Elsevier, 542–546.

Talmy, Leonard. 2017. *The Targeting System of Language*. Cambridge (MA) and London: The MIT Press.

Tannen, Deborah. 1990. Gender Differences in Topical Coherence. *Discourse Processes* 13, 73–90.

Tannen, Deborah. 2005. Interactional Sociolinguistics. In Ammon, Ulrich / Dittmar, Norbert / Mattheier, Klaus J. (eds) *Sociolinguistics: An International Handbook of the Science of Language and Society*. Berlin: de Gruyter, 76–88.

Taylor, Edward. 2001. Transformative Learning Theory: A Neurobiological Perspective of the Role of Emotions and Unconscious Ways of Knowing. *International Journal of Lifelong Education* 20, 218–236.

Thompson, John B. 1982. Universal Pragmatics. In Thompson, John B. / Held, David (eds) *Contemporary Social Theory*. London: Palgrave, 116–133.

Thornton, Garth. 1996. *Legislative Drafting*. London: Butterworths.

Thring, Henry. 1902. *Practical Legislation. The Composition and Language of Acts of Parliament and Business Documents*. London: John Murray, Albemarle Street.

Tiersma, Peter. 1999. *Legal Language*. Chicago: Chicago University Press.

Tirado, Francisco / Galvez, Ana. 2008. Positioning Theory and Discourse Analysis: Some Tools for Social Interaction Analysis. *Historical Social Research* 33(1), 224–251.

Unterbeck, Barbara / Rissanen, Matti / Nevalainen, Terttu / Saari, Mirja. 2000. *Gender in Grammar and Cognition I. Approaches to Gender II. Manifestations of Gender*. Berlin and New York: Mouton de Gruyter.

van Dijk, Teun A. 1985. *Handbook of Discourse Analysis*. London: Academic Press.

van Dijk, Teun A. 1993. Principles of Critical Discourse Analysis. *Discourse & Society*, 4(2), 249–283.

van Dijk, Teun A. 1997. *Discourse Studies. A Multidisciplinary Introduction*. London: Sage.

van Dijk, Teun A. 2005. Contextual Knowledge Management in Discourse Production. A CDA Perspective. In Wodak, Ruth / Chilton, Paul (eds) *A New Agenda in (Critical) Discourse Analysis*. Amsterdam: Benjamins, 71–100.

van Dijk, Teun A. 2007. *Discourse Studies Vol. 2*. London: Sage.

Verschueren, Jef. 1999. *Understanding Pragmatics*. London: Arnold.

Wattman Frank, Francine / Treichler, Paula A. 1989. *Language, Gender, and Professional Writing: Theoretical Approaches and Guidelines for Nonsexist Usage*. New York: Modern Language Association.

Weatherill, Stephen. 2007. *Better Regulation*. Oxford and Portland (OR): Hart Publishing.

Wenger, Etienne. 1998. *Communities of Practice: Learning, Meaning, and Identity*. Cambridge: Cambridge University Press.

Williams, Christopher. 2004. Legal English and Plain language: An Introduction. *ESP Across Culture* 1, 111–124.

Williams, Christopher. 2011. Legal English and Plain Language. An Update. *ESP Across Cultures* 8, 139–151.

Williams, Christopher. 2022. *The Impact of Plain Language on Legal English in the United Kingdom*. London: Routledge.

Willig, Carla. 2013. *Introducing Qualitative Research in Psychology*. New York: McGraw-Hill Education.

Wodak, Ruth / Meyer, Michael. 2001. *Methods of Critical Discourse Analysis*. London: Sage.

Xanthaki, Helen. 2013. Legislative Drafting: A New Sub-discipline of Law is Born. *IALS Student Law Review* 1(1), 57–70.

Xanthaki, Helen. 2014. *Drafting Legislation. Art and Technology of Rules for Regulation*. Oxford / Portland (OR): Hart Publishing.

Xanthaki, Helen. 2022. *Thornton's Legislative Drafting,* 6th edn. London: Bloomsbury Publishing.

Xanthaki, Helen / Pennisi, Giulia A. 2012. Crossing the Borders between Legislative Drafting and Linguistics: Linguists to the Aid of Legislative Drafters. In Tessuto, Girolamo (ed.) *Explorations in Language and Law: Approaches and Perspectives.* Aprilia: Novalogos, 83–109.

Xanthaki, Helen / Pennisi, Giulia A. 2016. Legislative Drafting e Linguaggio: Ipotesi di Semplificazione del Testo Normativo. *Studi Parlamentari e di Politica Costituzionale* (185–186), 41–71.

Zamboni, Mauro. 2018. Legislative Policy and Effectiveness: A (Small) Contribution from Legal Theory. *European Journal of Risk Regulation* 9(3), 416–430.

Zapatero Gómez, Virgilio. 2019. *The Art of Legislating*. Cham (CH): Springer.

Appendix

Guide to Making
Legislation
2023[213]

The parts of the *Guide to Making Legislation* 2022 reported here are: 'Contents', 'Section A (1,3,4)', 'Section B (9)', 'Appendix A' and 'Appendix E'.

Contents

Section A: Introduction to the legislative process and bidding for legislation
1. How to use this guide and the role of the Parliamentary Business and Legislation (PBL) secretariat
2. The government's legislative programme and the work of the PBL Committee
3. Summary of stages in the legislative process
4. Key players in making legislation
5. Securing a slot in the legislative programme
6. The bill and bill team management
7. Collective agreement
Section B: Preparing the bill for introduction
8. Drafting the bill
9. Drafting the bill: Structure and content of instructions to OPC
10. Explanatory notes
11. The European Convention on Human Rights (ECHR)

213 Adapted from <https://www.nationalarchives.gov.uk/doc/open-government-licence/version/3/>.

12. Other legal issues
13. Impact assessments
14. Devolved legislatures and administrations
15. Delegated powers
16. Crown dependencies and overseas territories
17. Queen's and prince's consent
18. Tax and public expenditure
19. Handling strategies
20. PBL Committee approval for inclusion in the programme and introduction to parliament
21. Publication in draft and pre-legislative scrutiny

Section C: Essential guidance for bill teams

22. Amendments
23. Briefing ministers for bill work and the use of ministerial statements in construing statute

Section D: Commons stages

24. The commons: Overview of stages
25. Money resolution and ways and means resolution
26. Programming
27. Commons introduction and first reading
28. Commons second reading
29. Commons Committee stage
30. Commons remaining stages (report and third reading)
31. Carrying over legislation

Section E: Lords stages

32. The lords: Overview and differences from Commons' stages
33. Lords introduction and first reading
34. Lords second reading
35. Lords committee stage
36. Lords remaining stages (report and third reading)

Section F: Further action after completing commons and lords stages and after royal assent

37. Consideration of amendments and 'Ping-pong'
38. Royal assent and commencement
39. Further action after royal assent
40. Post-legislative scrutiny

Section G: Other types of government bill
41. Hybrid bills
42. Consolidation bills, law commission bills, statute law repeal and revision bills
Section H: Private members' bills
43. Private members' bills: Introduction
44. Private members' bills: Parliamentary procedure
45. Private members' bills: Responding to non-government bills
46. Private members' bills: Government 'Handout' bills
Appendix A: Glossary
Appendix B: Contact details
Appendix C: Other guides
Appendix D: Checklists for each stage
Appendix E: Codes of practice and legislation
Appendix F: Securing legislative consent motions in the devolved legislatures

Section A: Introduction to the legislative process and bidding for legislation

1. How to use this guide and the role of the PBL Secretariat

1.1 The Guide to Making Legislation was prepared by the Secretariat to the Parliamentary Business and Legislation (PBL) Cabinet Committee, a part of the Cabinet Secretariat at the Cabinet Office. It was produced together with the advice of Parliamentary Counsel and the Offices of the Commons Chief Whip, Lords Chief Whip, Leader of the House of Commons, Leader of the House of Lords, the Public Bill Offices of both Houses and officials in other government departments.

1.2 It covers the procedures to be followed in preparing primary legislation and taking it through Parliament, setting out what is required of bill teams at each stage of the process. It should answer the most commonly asked questions but should not be regarded as an authoritative statement of parliamentary practice. Parliamentary Counsel (who may in turn consult the House authorities), the Whips Offices or the Public Bill Offices should always be consulted on matters of procedure.

1.3 The Guide is written with the needs of departmental teams in mind, to help them manage their work effectively throughout the process of preparing legislation and taking it through Parliament. It describes the main features of the normal legislative process but cannot cover every possible circumstance: every bill is different.

1.4 The different stages are dealt with in chronological order. Bill teams starting out on the process of preparing legislation, particularly those new to bill work, would be well advised to read through the main sections to familiarise themselves with the tasks ahead and help plan their work effectively. However, it is also designed for officials to consult quickly during the legislative process to identify the key points and actions required at each stage. A summary of key points is provided at the start of each chapter and checklists for each stage are included in Appendix D.

1.5 The main part of the Guide deals with conventional government bills and will be the sections used by most bill teams. Section G deals with certain other types of government bill: hybrid bills and consolidation bills. Section H deals with private members' bills and will be of use to departmental parliamentary clerks and to policy officials and private secretaries advising and supporting ministers responsible for responding on behalf of the Government to private members' bills, particularly where the Government is supporting a private members bill.

1.6 This Guide does not cover:

- finance bills;
- consolidated fund bills;

- appropriation bills;
- codes of practice;
- bills relating exclusively to Scotland, Wales or Northern Ireland, although these are now increasingly rare;
- private bills (bills promoted by a body outside of Parliament and distinct from private members' bills, which are public bills) where the Government is normally represented by parliamentary agents. Guidance should be sought from departmental legal advisers in the first instance, or from the Private Bill Office clerks as far as parliamentary processes are concerned;
- secondary legislation. Departmental parliamentary branches or legal advisers
- should hold copies of the Statutory Instrument Practice, which provides guidance on
- the parliamentary process of secondary legislation. Departmental officials should
- contact their departmental SI lead, PBL Secretariat for information on the Statutory
- Instrument Capability Programme and internal guidance including on seeking
- collective agreement for secondary legislation; or
- legislative reform orders (LROs). See the Legislative Reform Order-making Powers guidance.

1.7 While the Secretariat will always endeavour to alert current bill teams to relevant changes in procedure, please note that the electronic version is the most up-to-date version and any queries on parliamentary procedure should be addressed to Parliamentary Counsel or the Whips Offices.

Role of the PBL Secretariat

1.8 The Parliamentary Business and Legislation (PBL) Secretariat is part of the Cabinet Secretariat. It provides the secretariat to the PBL Cabinet Committee, advice to the Leader of the House of Commons on clearance of legislative proposals (including amendments to bills) and advice to other ministers on the legislative programme. The full list of Cabinet committees can be found on GOV.UK.

1.9 Bill teams, secondary legislation teams or other officials working on legislation can contact the Secretariat (contact details at Appendix B) with any queries relating to their legislation or the legislative programme. The Secretariat should be notified as early as possible of all requests for clearance and prior to clearance being sought.

[. . .]

3. Summary of stages in the legislative process

Key points

- This chapter provides a summary of the key actions and issues to be considered at each stage in the preparation and passage of primary legislation through Parliament. It precedes more detailed guidance and checklists to support each stage throughout this guide.
- These will usually have been preceded by the normal stages in policy development: a green paper discussion or consultation document, a white paper (major policy proposals set out in more detail) and one or more rounds of public consultation.
- This chapter is intended to give an at-a-glance overview of all stages, but it is not definitive. Officials involved in work on a bill should read individual chapters for guidance on procedure at each stage (and consult Parliamentary Counsel and the Whips Offices for guidance on parliamentary procedure).

Before introduction

3.1 *Securing a slot in the legislative programme*: departments must bid for a slot in the legislative programme for any bills they wish to introduce. Normally this will be through a bidding round when the Leader of the House of Commons, as chair of the PBL Committee, invites Cabinet colleagues to submit bids for bills for the following session of Parliament.

3.2 Bids must be by letter to the chair of the PBL Committee and accompanied by a bid template (which will be available from the Secretariat). The PBL Committee will assess bids on their priority and state of readiness and advise Cabinet on the contents of the programme. The programme will be reviewed in preparation for the Queen's speech, in the light of any emerging bids and progress in preparing those bills already provisionally in the programme. Late bids must have a very strong case, as other bills are likely to have to be removed to accommodate them.

3.3 *Public commitment to legislate*: ministers should not make a public commitment to legislate in the forthcoming session of Parliament unless or until PBL Committee has agreed the inclusion of a bill. The Government's announcement of its intention to legislate on a particular issue will normally be made as part of the Queen's speech. Prior to this, ministers should use the standard wording that they intend to legislate 'when parliamentary time allows' (and then only if the policy content has already been collectively agreed).

3.4 *Setting up the bill team*: A well-resourced bill team is critical. A dedicated bill manager and team should be appointed as soon as the department secures a slot in the forthcoming legislative programme, and appropriately trained. The bill manager will need to produce and monitor progress against a delivery plan, coordinate all work on the bill and provide regular updates to ministers, officials involved in work on the bill, departmental lawyers, the departmental parliamentary branch and the PBL Secretariat. A senior project board should be established to monitor progress on the bill, in most cases reporting in to a strategic legislation board overseeing the department's wider legislative programme.

3.5 *Collective agreement*: The relevant policy Cabinet committee must agree the policy content of the bill before drafting instructions can be sent to Parliamentary Counsel and must also agree any amendments to the bill that represent a significant change in policy. Collective agreement from the PBL Committee is required at the following stages:

- bidding for a slot in the programme;
- publishing a bill or clauses in draft;
- announcing the intention to legislate to a specific timetable, or in a specific bill;
- before introduction, to approve the final text of the bill; and
- for any amendments to the bill after introduction.

3.6 *Drafting instructions to Parliamentary Counsel*: Parliamentary Counsel draft bills on the basis of instructions from departments. Drafting work can begin when the bill has been allocated a slot in the programme and its policy content has collective agreement. Bill team and departmental lawyers should meet Parliamentary Counsel at an early stage to discuss a timetable for sending instructions to them, and this should also be agreed with PBL Secretariat. Parliamentary Counsel will produce draft clauses on the basis of these instructions, which the department will consider and comment on. Re-drafting will continue until a final version of the bill is agreed.

3.7 *Publication in draft*: PBL Committee agreement is needed to the principle of publication in draft, usually as part of the annual bidding round for bills. Once drafting reaches an advanced stage, Business Managers will seek agreement through the usual channels to a plan for pre-legislative scrutiny and then make the necessary arrangements with the House authorities. When the bill is ready for publication in draft, it must be circulated to the PBL Committee for clearance, along with a covering memorandum which should include parliamentary handling, explanatory notes, impact assessment, legal issues memorandum, and delegated powers memorandum. Draft bills should be presented to Parliament and published as command papers, with the delegated powers memorandum sent to the DPRRC. Your departmental parliamentary clerk can advise on publishing command papers.

3.8 *Explanatory notes*: Explanatory notes must be published alongside every government bill and are drafted by the bill team in consultation with departmental lawyers. They must be ready by the time the bill comes to the PBL Committee for approval for introduction and should be published at the same time as the bill. They must be approved for publication by the Clerk of Legislation in both Houses, and so the final draft needs to be ready sent to the Public Bill Office no later than two days before the text of a bill is handed in by Counsel (the 'Notice of Presentation') to allow time for feedback from the Public Bill Office and necessary revisions. The final explanatory notes need to be sent to the Clerk of Legislation, the Clerk of Publishing, and the Public Bill Office before introduction. Explanatory notes are updated by the department at various points during the passage of a Bill, with a final version published alongside the Act after Royal Assent.

3.9 *European Convention on Human Rights*: Departmental legal advisers will need to prepare a legal issues memorandum for the PBL Committee before the bill is introduced, setting out, among other things, the bill's compatibility with the European Convention on Human Rights (ECHR). The minister in charge of the bill in each House must also sign a statement as to the bill's compatibility with the ECHR. This appears on the front page of a bill as introduced, and as reprinted for the second House. As part of this, the department should provide analysis of why the Bill is considered ECHR compliant and whether the Bill's provisions engage Convention rights and if so, what those issues are. This is either done through the explanatory notes (if not too lengthy an analysis) or a separate human rights memorandum (often called a JCHR or ECHR memorandum). The Secretariat can provide further advice on a case by case basis.

3.10 *Other legal issues*: The department must also consider other legal issues, and produce an internal legal issues memorandum for consideration by the Law Officers. Specific consent must be obtained from the Law Officers to any retrospective provisions or early commencement of provisions. You should contact the Data Protection Policy Team in DCMS for more advice if needed. New legislative proposals which relate to the processing of personal data should be compatible with data protection legislation. To ensure that the proposals are read as being subject to the data protection legislation, specific wording should be used to make this clear[214] . The Data Protection Policy Team in DCMS can provide further advice and support if required. Parliamentary Counsel should be able to advise on suitable wording. There are also legal requirements for government departments to consult the Information Commissioner's Office on the development of such proposals, as set out in Article 36(4) of the UK General Data Protection Regulation (UK GDPR).

3.11 *Environmental provision*: Departments must consider whether the bill contains environmental law under section 20 of the Environment Act 2021. If a bill contains environmental law, the Minister in charge of the bill must state that this is so, and also state either that the provision will not lower the current level of environmental protection provided for in existing environmental law or that they are unable to make a statement to such effect, but that the Government nevertheless wishes the House to proceed with the Bill. Ministers will need to sign a statement which appears on the front page of the bill.

3.12 *Impact assessments*: Impact assessments are generally required for all UK government interventions of a regulatory nature that affect the private sector, civil society organisations and public services (full details available in the impact assessment guidance). The final impact assessment must be circulated to the PBL Committee alongside the bill and other papers when it is considered for approval for introduction. It is published alongside the bill and the

214 Sometimes this is referred to as the 'statutory override' because it makes it clear that the provisions should be read as being subject to the data protection legislation. For example, see section 49(2) and (3) of the Agriculture Act 2020.

final document should be shared with the Public Bill Office together with the explanatory notes and Delegated Powers Memorandum.

3.13 *Impact on the devolved administrations*: Departments must identify from an early stage whether or not their legislation will legislate in devolved or transferred areas of competence, or will impact the executive or legislative powers of the devolved institutions; in these circumstances, legislative consent (LCM) will be required from the devolved legislatures. Officials in the Union and Constitution Group, along with officials in the Scotland, Wales and Northern Ireland Offices should be engaged from the outset if departments believe that their legislation will engage the LCM process and will have implications for the devolved administrations. Before a bill's introduction, the PBL Committee will also expect the devolved administrations to have been consulted on the bill's devolved provisions, with all devolution-related issues substantively resolved (unless there are exceptional circumstances). Departments should also remember that the devolution settlements in Scotland, Wales and Northern Ireland are unique and asymmetrical, and so departmental policy and legal officials will need to consider carefully the implications the provisions within their bill will have under each of the devolution settlements.

3.14 *Delegated powers*: Departments must consider what degree of parliamentary scrutiny is considered appropriate for any delegated powers in the bill, and produce a delegated powers memorandum for the PBL Committee, justifying the inclusion of powers and addressing any concerns that might be raised. Particular attention should be given to 'Henry VIII' powers (powers to amend primary legislation through secondary legislation) that the bill seeks to confer. The memorandum must be published on introduction in the first House and should be shared with the Public Bill Office together with the explanatory notes and the Impact Assessment. It should also be formally submitted to the Lords Delegated Powers and Regulatory Reform Committee (DPRRC) on the day of introduction. If the House of Commons is the first House and amendments are made in the first House, the memorandum should be updated on introduction to the second House of Lords and formally re-submitted to the Lords DPRRC. Where a bill is published in draft before introduction, a completed delegated powers memorandum should be published alongside and a copy sent to the DPRRC.

3.15 If the Bill will change the regulation of digital technologies, such as adding a new regulatory burden, departments should contact the Digital Regulation Team in the Department for Digital, Culture, Media & Sport to ensure the measures are in line with collectively-agreed digital regulation principles.

3.16 *National Security*: New policy, powers and legislation may impact the UK's National Security capabilities, even where there is not an immediately obvious link to national security. Departments should therefore consider any read across to national security carefully and can contact colleagues in the National Security community to discuss any proposed measures. The key stakeholders in this area are the United Kingdom Intelligence Community (known as UKIC and consisting of MI5, SIS (MI6) and GCHQ), the Home Office, Foreign, Commonwealth and Development Office and Cabinet Office. The Cabinet Office can provide contact details if needed. You should adhere to departmental security advice when discussing sensitive matters.

3.17 It is important to consider what can and cannot be discussed in public and parliamentary handling may seem challenging. However, there are many options that can be considered, such as briefing individuals on Privy Council terms. Departments should seek advice from the National Security community on options and advice on what information can be disclosed.

3.18 The work of the intelligence Agencies and various other parts of Government's national security machinery is overseen by the Intelligence and Security Committee (ISC) of Parliament, which has members from the House of Commons and the House of Lords. The ISC has special arrangements and facilities to handle highly classified material. Proactive briefing is often helpful and support from Committee members can be very useful. The Cabinet Office coordinates the relationship across the Agencies and departments within the ISC's remit.

3.19 *Impact on Overseas Territories*: Departments must identify the implications, if any, of their legislation for the Overseas Territories (Anguilla; Bermuda; the British Indian Ocean Territory; the British Antarctic Territory; the Cayman Islands; Gibraltar; the Falkland Islands; Montserrat; Pitcairn, Henderson, Ducie and Oeno Islands; South Georgia and the South Sandwich Islands; the Sovereign Base Areas of Akrotiri and Dhekelia (on the island of Cyprus); St Helena, Ascension Island and Tristan da Cunha; the Turks and Caicos Islands; and the Virgin Islands (commonly known as the British Virgin Islands). It is for departments to ensure they consult the Overseas Territories on proposals with implications for them.

3.20 *Application to the Crown*: Departments should decide early on whether the obligations or restraints that the proposed legislation will impose are to apply to the Crown, to servants or agent of the Crown or in relation to Crown property. The policy as regards Crown application will be something that will need to be considered carefully with departmental lawyers and the decisions taken will need to be set out in the instructions to Parliamentary Counsel.

3.21 *Queen's and Prince of Wales' consent*: Departments should identify at an early stage whether Queen's or Prince of Wales' consent are required. Advice should be sought from Parliamentary Counsel as these may be required in some unexpected cases and the agreement of the House authorities will be required. The department must then seek these consents, which are signified at Third Reading. If there is any doubt as to whether these consents are required or when they should be signified, Parliamentary Counsel will consult the two Public Bill Offices.

3.22 *Tax and public expenditure implications*: The agreement of the relevant HM Treasury minister must be obtained to any tax proposal, or to tax implications of new activities or bodies proposed. HM Treasury agreement must also be obtained to the bill's public expenditure and public service manpower implications. Bilateral agreement with HM Treasury should have been reached before the policy comes for collective agreement. Departments must also ensure they observe the guidance on expenditure propriety in the Managing Public Money guidance. Departments cannot normally incur expenditure in advance of both Royal Assent of the enabling legislation and any necessary parliamentary authority through the Appropriation Act.

3.23 *Application in relation to Parliament*: Departments must identify the implications, if any, of their legislation for Parliament and the Parliamentary estate. The areas of law where issues of this kind might arise include employment, health and safety, enforcement regimes, rights of entry, licensing, advertising, contracting, planning and public order aspects of criminal law. If there are implications, Departments are expected to give the House Authorities an opportunity to comment on the proposals at an early stage.

3.24 *Handling strategies*: bill teams will need to prepare a parliamentary handling strategy and a wider stakeholder/media handling strategy in consultation with the Government Whips' Offices in the Commons and Lords and with the departmental press office respectively (see Appendix B for contact details for the Commons/Lords Whips' Offices).

3.25 *PBL Committee approval for introduction*: When a bill is ready for publication or introduction it must be circulated to the PBL Committee, accompanied by a covering memorandum and the supporting documents mentioned above, including: explanatory notes, impact assessment, legal issues memorandum, parliamentary handling strategy and delegated powers memorandum. The Committee will usually meet to agree to a bill's introduction.

Summary of parliamentary stages

3.26 The bill will start in either the Commons or the Lords. The House and date of introduction will be agreed by the PBL Committee on advice from the Business Managers. Bills starting in the Lords must complete the same stages. There are five key stages in each House (summarised below).

Summary of a bill's stages:
1. First Reading – formal presentation of the bill (no debate)
2. Second Reading – debate on general principles of the bill
3. Committee Stage – detailed line-by-line examination of the bill, consideration of amendments, oral evidence heard and written evidence published (if necessary)
4. Report Stage – Further opportunity to consider amendments made in Committee and to amend the bill
5. Third Reading – Final consideration of the bill

Detail of each stage

3.27 Introduction into the Commons and First Reading: the Clerk at the Table will read out the short title of the bill, a minister nods, after which the bill is deemed to have been read the first time. There is no debate. Introduction is supported by the provision and publication of various documents:

- The final text of the bill is supplied by Parliamentary Counsel to the Public Bill Office the day before introduction and ahead of publication.
- The department is responsible for supplying the final text of the explanatory notes to the Public Bill Office the day before introduction (having cleared the draft version with them in advance).
- The department should also ensure that the minister who will be in charge of the bill has signed the ECHR statement and that confirmation that this has been signed has been sent to Parliamentary Counsel. If a separate ECHR

memorandum has been prepared (setting out the ECHR impacts separately to the explanatory notes) this should be published on GOV.UK but also shared with the Public Bill Office alongside the explanatory notes.

- The department is also responsible for the publication of an impact assessment, which should also be shared with the Commons' Public Bill Office, and for ensuring the appropriate availability of relevant older papers and revised editions of Acts.
- The department must also formally submit their delegated powers memorandum to the Delegated Powers and Regulatory Reform Committee, and to the Public Bill Office to be published.
- Supporting papers must be delivered to the Vote Office (who will be able to advise on how many copies are required); it is not sufficient to refer members to a website.

3.28 *Commons Second Reading*: There is a convention that the debate will not usually take place until two weekends have passed following the publication of the bill. Speaking notes and briefing need to be prepared for both the minister opening (usually the relevant Secretary of State) and the minister (usually the lead bill minister) winding up the debate. Programme motions are normally taken immediately after Second Reading without debate, followed by money resolutions, ways and means resolutions and, if necessary, carry-over motions. Their preparation is a matter for Parliamentary Counsel.

3.29 *Commons Committee Stage*: This is the principal stage for detailed scrutiny and amendment of the bill and can usually begin the week after Second Reading. Scrutiny normally takes place in a public bill committee (formerly known as a 'standing committee'), which in most cases will take evidence from experts and interest groups, including from the minister and officials before beginning clause-by-clause scrutiny of the bill according to the programme resolution.

3.30 For bills that have been subject to pre-legislative scrutiny, the committee may decide that oral evidence sessions will not be held. Oral evidence is not heard for bills that started in the Lords. The Committee Stage can also take place in 'Committee of the whole House', which is usually for bills of a financial or constitutional nature or for 'emergency' legislation that is being taken forward under the fast-track procedure. The Government, the opposition or backbenchers can table amendments. Clearance to table government amendments must be obtained from the PBL Committee and from the relevant policy Cabinet committee if the amendments represent a change in policy. For both a public bill committee and a committee of the whole House, briefing and speaking notes must be produced for ministers on each clause (clause stand part) and on any amendments tabled.

3.31 *Commons Report Stage*: A further chance to consider amendments to the bill, this happens on the floor of the House and can take place anytime from a week after Committee Stage (or sometimes even earlier). Debate is confined to amendments selected for debate, rather than a clause-by-clause examination of the bill. This is usually the final amending stage in the Commons.

3.32 *Commons Third Reading*: Normally takes place immediately after Report Stage. It is a further chance for the House to consider whether it wishes the bill as a whole to proceed, in the light of amendments at Committee and Report Stages. No amendments (other than 'purely verbal' amendments, which are extremely rare) are permitted at Third Reading.

3.33 *Transmission to the Lords and First Reading* (or introduction in the Lords, for those bills starting life in the Lords): When a bill is passed by the Commons, it is taken to the Lords by a Commons Clerk. The First Reading is moved immediately without debate and the bill is printed. If the bill comes from the Commons, the explanatory notes and impact assessment should be revised to take into account changes in the first House and a further ECHR statement must be signed by the minister who is in charge of the bill in the second House. The explanatory notes should be sent to the Lords Public Bill Office for publication (having first cleared the draft with them) and the impact assessment should be published on GOV.UK and also shared with the Commons Public Bill Office to be uploaded on the bill's page on the Parliament website. The minister must also formally submit the delegated powers memorandum to the Lords' Delegated Powers and Regulatory Reform Committee, having updated it to reflect any changes made to the bill in the Commons and this should be shared with the Public Bill Office for publication. Where a bill starts its passage in the Lords, the bill minister reads out the long title of the bill at First Reading.

3.34 *Lords Second Reading*: This can take place once two weekends have elapsed since introduction. The procedure is similar to in the Commons, with some minor differences including that the House of Lords does not vote on Second Reading. There is also no programme motion in the Lords.

3.35 *Lords Committee Stage*: Either takes place on the floor of the House ('committee of the whole House'), or in a committee room ('grand committee') and can begin once fourteen calendar days have elapsed since Second Reading. The requirement for producing speaking notes and background for ministers on clauses and amendments is the same as in the Commons. As in the Commons, PBL Committee clearance must be sought to table government amendments to the bill, and policy clearance is also necessary if the amendments would effect a change in government policy.

3.36 Note: A supplementary delegated powers memorandum should be submitted to the Delegated Powers and Regulatory Reform Committee in relation to any government amendments which include provision relating to delegated powers. The amendments and the supplementary memorandum should be made available to the committee in sufficient time in advance of the day on which they are to be considered by the House to enable the committee to report on them. This also applies to government amendments tabled at Lords' Report Stage and Third

Reading and for those considered at Lords' consideration of Commons amendments.

3.37 *Lords Report Stage*: For all bills of considerable length and complexity, Lords Report Stage takes place at least fourteen calendar days after Committee Stage. Debate is limited to amendments before the House, so there is no need to debate each clause.

3.38 *Lords Third Reading*: At least three clear sitting days after Report Stage. The scope for amendments is limited at this stage, unlike in the House of Commons, amendments at Third Reading in the House of Lords can only be made if the issue has not been fully considered and voted on during either Committee or Report Stage. It is often used to 'tidy up' a bill such as clarifying specific parts of the bill.

3.39 *'Ping-pong'*: If the bill has been amended in the second House, it goes back to the House of introduction for consideration of the amendments in question ('Commons consideration of Lords' amendments' or 'Lords consideration of Commons' amendments'). The first House can accept, reject, amend or suggest an alternative to the amendments (amendment in lieu), which the second House will then consider. The matter goes back and forward between the two Houses ('ping pong') until agreement has been reached, or until there is 'double insistence'[215] and the bill falls.

3.40 A final set of explanatory notes are required when a bill returns to the first House with amendments from the which explains the amendments made by the second House. These explanatory notes are to be published by the first House and a draft is to be checked by that House's Public Bill Office in advance of publication (the same with other explanatory notes). A supplementary delegated powers memorandum addressing any amendments which include provision

215 The term 'double insistence' is used to describe a situation where one House insists on an amendment to which the other has disagreed, and the other House insists on its disagreement without any alternative proposal. If this point is reached, and neither House has offered alternatives, the bill is lost.

relating to delegated powers made during Commons' consideration of Lords' amendments should be submitted to the Delegated Powers and Regulatory Reform Committee in advance of Lords' consideration of Commons' amendments.

On completion of parliamentary stages

3.41 *Royal Assent*: Takes place throughout the session by notification from the Speaker of each House or at prorogation. Requests for particular dates should be made through the Government Whips' Office in the Lords before the bill is introduced. Bill teams must make known to PBL Committee any requirements for Royal Assent by a particular date and the reasons for this requirement.

3.42 *Commencement*: Commencement dates should be specified in the Act where possible and appropriate. No substantive provision of an Act should be brought into operation earlier than two months after Royal Assent, although some sections of the Act can be brought into force on Royal Assent, typically sections setting out how the Act is to be cited and what the procedure is for making regulations or commencing the Act. In exceptional circumstances, approval for early commencement should be sought from the Law Officers and the chair of the PBL Committee. Retrospective provisions also need to be agreed by the Law Officers (contact details for the Attorney General's Office and the Legal Secretariat to the Advocate General for Scotland can be found at Appendix B).

3.43 *Printing*: Departments should let Parliamentary Counsel and the Legislation Services Team in the National Archives know if an Act is expected to come into operation immediately. This is so that arrangements can be made for early clearance of the approved text, expedited printing and immediate publication of the Act on the www.legislation.gov.uk website.

3.44 *Guidance and publicity*: Where new legislation affects business or civil society, guidance should be published as early as possible before the act comes into effect and the changes in the law should be publicised. Departments should not leave preparation of guidance to the last minute. Departments should consider which other groups should be informed of the new legislation and how this can be achieved most effectively.

[. . .]

4. Key players in making legislation

The following people are a bill team's key contacts:

4.1 Preparation and passage of legislation requires strong cross-departmental and government working. This section provides an overview of the different players across government and their role in the process.

4.2 The PBL Secretariat supports the PBL Cabinet Committee in the overall management of the Government's programme of legislation and provides advice to ministers on legislative issues. The Secretariat to the relevant policy sub-committee of Cabinet will coordinate the collective agreement process for the policy in the bill or piece of secondary legislation.

4.3 The Office of the Parliamentary Counsel is responsible for drafting the bill.

4.4 The Public and Private Bill Offices of the two Houses support the legislative process in Parliament and advise government and opposition members, and the chair in the House and in Committee Stage. The Clerk of Legislation in the Commons and the Clerk of Legislation in the Lords clear bills for introduction as conforming with the rules of each House.

4.5 The Government Whips' Office in the Commons supports the government whips in liaising through the usual channels on programme motions and supporting ministers at all stages of the bill. It can also provide advice on the programming and timing of legislation and on parliamentary procedures for bills.

4.6 The Government Whips' Office in the Lords negotiates to secure time for bills in the Lords (where there is no programming) and negotiates the grouping of amendments. It offers advice and assistance with all aspects of parliamentary procedure and handling, including delegated powers, and will support the Lords minister in the chamber.

4.7 The Attorney General's Office and the Legal Secretariat to the Advocate General for Scotland advise the Law Officers where bills raise issues of particular legal difficulty, disagreement or importance. They also advise on retrospectivity, early commencement, Crown immunity, devolution or ECHR compatibility and will work with departments and relevant centres of excellence when considering such legal issues. They advise on legal issues memorandum and will consider draft memorandums before consideration by PBL Committee ahead of introduction.

4.8 Your departmental Better Regulation Unit advise on impact assessments, guidance for business and the third sector, applicability of legislation to small firms and any other regulatory issues, including obligations in free trade agreements. They should agree the approach taken with the impact assessment and will want to be satisfied that the bill does not impose disproportionate burdens on business or the third sector. They should also be able to advise on the process for submitting impact assessments to the Regulatory Policy Committee. The Digital Regulation Team in the Department for Digital, Culture, Media & Sport can help advise on best practice when legislation to regulate digital technologies. The Digital Regulation Team in the Department for Digital, Culture, Media & Sport can help advise on best practice when legislation to regulate digital technologies.

4.9 If your bill proposes to establish, disestablish, re-classify, or merge an arm's-length body (ALB), you must seek Cabinet Office and HM Treasury ministerial approval before taking steps to deliver the proposed change. Guidance is available in The Approvals Process for the Creation of New Arm's-Length Bodies: Guidance for Departments. Your departmental ALB partnership team will be able to assist you in navigating this approval process in the first instance. They may then connect you with the Cabinet Office's Public Bodies Team (publicbodiesreform@cabinetoffice.gov.uk) and HM Treasury.

4.10 If your bill impacts the United Kingdom Intelligence Agencies (MI5, SIS (MI6) and GCHQ), departments should contact colleagues to discuss the legislative proposals. The Foreign, Commonwealth & Development Office should be contacted in relation to SIS and GCHQ, and the Home Office for MI5. You should adhere to departmental security advice when discussing sensitive matters.

4.11 For proposals that may affect competition (for example, by raising barriers to entry or privileging one business model over another), Departments should discuss with the Competition and Markets Authority (CMA) and consider CMA's 'competition assessment checklist' to assess the likelihood of impacts on competition and consider mitigations or alternative options, including those which could promote competition, supplementing the analysis in the Regulatory Impact Assessment. Guidance on how to complete the checklist can be found in the Competition impact assessment: guidelines for policymakers. Departments who are undertaking a competition assessment with complex issues should speak to the CMA for further guidance (advocacy@cma.gov.uk). The Competition Policy team at BEIS can also provide advice (competition@beis.gov.uk).

4.12 Your department's equality and diversity lead can advise on how to ensure that you properly consider the impact of your proposed policies on different groups – such as in regard to race, gender, disability, etc. Note that it is a statutory requirement to do this when developing new policies. Detailed guidance is available from the Equality and Human Rights Commission. The Government Equalities Office can also assist, in the case of more complex enquiries.

4.13 The Scotland Office is the first port of call for discussing any provisions that may affect Scotland, including identifying where a legislative consent motion may be required if the bill touches on matters that are devolved to Scotland. It can also support departments in any negotiations with the Scottish Government.

4.14 The Office of the Advocate General for Scotland is part of the UK Government and provides legal advice on Scots law and associated devolution.

4.15 The Wales Office is the first port of call for discussing any provisions that may affect Wales, including identifying where a legislative consent motion may be required if the bill touches on matters that are devolved to Wales or where Welsh ministers should be consulted on provisions in the bill that extend to Wales. It can also support departments in any negotiations with the Welsh Government.

4.16 The Northern Ireland Office is the first port of call for discussing any provisions that may affect Northern Ireland, including identifying where a legislative consent motion may be required if the bill touches on matters that are transferred to Northern Ireland. It can also support departments in any negotiations with the Northern Ireland Executive.

4.17 The parliamentary private secretary to the bill minister or secretary of state will sit on the public bill committee and advise the minister on handling. Contact can be made through the bill minister's Private Office.

4.18 Departments should consult The National Archives and the legal team at the Department for Digital, Culture, Media & Sport at an early stage on any proposals to amend the Public Records Act 1958.

[...]

Section B: Preparing the bill for introduction

9. Drafting the bill: Structure and content of instructions to OPC

Key points

- This chapter has been produced by the Office of the Parliamentary Counsel (OPC) to help with the task of writing instructions for OPC to draft a bill. It needs to be read in conjunction with the preceding chapter, which gives an overview of the bill preparation process.
- This Chapter should also be read in conjunction with Common Legislative Solutions: a guide to tackling recurring policy issues in legislation. This guide identifies issues that may need to be addressed when working up and instructing on the proposed solution to certain commonly occurring policy issues.
- The task of writing instructions to OPC is not an easy one. The quality of the instructions will have a direct effect on the quality of the bill and the time it takes to prepare. Any person preparing instructions for OPC is therefore encouraged to look at this chapter on each occasion they are asked to work on a bill.
- Policy officials who are not directly instructing OPC may also find this chapter of use. It will help them anticipate the sorts of information the person instructing OPC will need to be able to complete their instructions to OPC.

General observations and guidance

9.1 Some general observations and guidance can be offered at the outset. First, it helps when it comes to writing instructions to OPC to stand back and try to imagine what it will be like for the drafter starting on the subject from scratch. A person who has been immersed in a subject for some time often needs to take pains to get it across to someone just coming to it.

9.2 Secondly, the departmental lawyer should structure the instructions and decide their contents on the basis of what seems likely to be most useful to the drafter. The guidance in this chapter should help in deciding what will be most useful but the departmental lawyer should feel free to depart from the guidance if there appears to be a better way of dealing with things. The departmental lawyer should also feel free to discuss how best to structure the instructions with the appropriate Team Leader or drafter in OPC.

9.3 Thirdly, the departmental lawyer should try to ensure that the policy is fully thought through and analysed before the instructions to OPC are finalised. Nonetheless, OPC do appreciate that the conditions for preparing instructions are seldom ideal and that it is not unusual for compromises to have to be made to cope with the pressures of the timetable or a delay in decision making. Where this is the case it will help to discuss these difficulties with the drafter and agree the best way to deal with them.

9.4 Fourthly, when writing instructions it is important to think of the drafter as a part of the bill team. This means that the instructions should be candid about any known difficulties with what is being proposed. For example, it may be that there is a gap in the policy or a logical wrinkle in the department's thinking that has not been ironed out. By airing these sorts of difficulties in the instructions you will save the drafter the trouble of discovering them. It may be that the drafter is able to offer a solution or a way forward that has not previously been considered by the department.

9.5 Finally, when writing instructions it is important to keep in mind the general rule that a bill should only contain legislative propositions. These are propositions that change the law: they bring about a legal state of affairs that would not exist apart from the bill. It can sometimes be tempting to ask the drafter to prepare a provision that is not intended to change the law but is instead designed to serve some political purpose or to explain or emphasise an existing law. However, non-legislative provisions of this sort are likely to go wrong because the courts will be inclined to attribute legal effect to them on the grounds that Parliament does not legislate unnecessarily and the legal effect attributed may be one the Government could not have predicted. Instead of asking for non-legislative provisions to be included in the bill, consider whether the point the department wishes to make can be made in another way, such as in a ministerial statement to Parliament, in the explanatory notes to the bill or in guidance.

Form of the instructions

9.6 OPC is sometimes asked how to format the instructions. Here is some guidance about what most drafters find helpful:

- it is helpful if both the pages and paragraphs of the instructions are numbered or lettered as these are easier to refer to than unnumbered or bulleted paragraphs;
- if the instructions are lengthy, headings and a table of contents are helpful;
- instructions are easier to read if they are typed in 1.5 or double spacing, in a legible 12-point font and with margins wide enough to allow the noting of comments and questions; and
- if it is necessary to provide the drafter with supplementary documents, it is preferable for the documents to be attached to the email sending the instructions rather than for a link to the document on the Department's server to be embedded in the instructions.

Structure and content of the instructions

9.7 As has already been said, instructions should be structured in whatever way the author thinks will be most useful to the drafter.

9.8 Nevertheless, a good way to structure the instructions will often be to divide them into five parts, as follows:

- introduction;
- existing law;
- detailed proposals;
- supplemental and incidental matters; and
- parliamentary and other handling matters.

9.9 The remainder of this chapter describes what each of these parts should deal with.

Part 1 – Introduction

9.10 The main purpose of this part of the instructions is to provide the drafter with a brief summary of the policy that the department wishes to pursue. The summary need not be detailed. The aim is simply to provide the drafter with an indication of where the instructions are headed. For example, the summary of the policy may say something like this:

> The Government wishes to regulate the activities of people who sell fireworks. For this purpose, the Government wishes to prevent anyone selling fireworks without a licence issued by the Secretary of State. The bill will need to make provision about the making of applications for licences and the criteria that must be satisfied for an application to be successful. The Government want the Secretary of State to be able to impose conditions on licence-holders and to be able to inspect the activities of licence-holders. The Government want it to be possible for people to appeal to the First-tier tribunal against certain decisions made by the Secretary of State in connection with the licensing regime.

9.11 In addition, this part of the instructions should briefly set out the factual and political background to the proposal to legislate. So to continue the example above, the instructions might briefly mention the recent problems that have arisen in connection with the sale of fireworks. The instructions might mention the results of any consultation carried out into the establishment of the proposed licensing regime and any ministerial commitments to establish it. If the proposal to legislate is a response to recent case law this fact should be mentioned.

9.12 If the instructions are likely to give rise to particularly difficult devolution or ECHR issues a warning about this should appear in the introductory part of the instructions (although a detailed explanation of these issues should be left until later on).

9.13 This part of the instructions should mention if there is any particular reason to think the department's proposals may change. For example, it should mention if any of the proposals have not yet been approved by the minister, do not yet have collective agreement or are the subject of an on-going consultation.

9.14 This part of the instructions can be used to set out any other information that the author thinks it is helpful for the drafter to know from the outset. For instance, it may be helpful to mention any acronyms or abbreviations used in the instructions. It might be a good idea to provide a web link to any consultation documents or other relevant publications.

Part 2: Existing law

9.15 This part of the instructions should identify and explain the existing law which is relevant to the department's proposals.

9.16 Drafters in OPC tend not to specialise in particular areas of law. So the drafter may need to rely on this part of the instructions to get to grips with the legal landscape in which they are being asked to operate. Even if the drafter happens to have some experience of the area of law concerned, a statement of the law by someone who is familiar with it can be very valuable.

9.17 The author of the instructions will, of course, need to exercise judgement in deciding which existing laws should be covered and how much detail to go into. What is appropriate in any given case will depend upon the nature of the department's proposals and what it is that the drafter is going to be asked to do.

9.18 For example, if the nature of the department's proposals mean that the drafter is going to be asked to prepare a wide range of amendments to an existing statutory regime it will be necessary to provide a thorough explanation of the regime which focuses, in particular, on the aspects of it that will need amending. By contrast, if the nature of the department's proposals will involve repealing an existing statutory regime altogether it may be that all the drafter needs to be given is an indication of where the existing regime can be found and a brief explanation of what the regime is concerned with.

9.19 The author of the instructions should seek to explain the existing law rather than simply copy out or paraphrase every statutory provision that is thought to be relevant. What the drafter will find helpful is something that, in particular, does the following sorts of things:

- identifies the salient features of the existing law and facilitates a rapid understanding of its structure and effect;
- identifies subtleties or nuances in the existing law which might easily be missed;
- draws attention to any conflicting decisions or opinions affecting the interpretation of the existing law; and
- highlights features of the existing law which are of particular importance in the context of the department's proposals.

9.20 It is often helpful for the explanation of the existing law to say something about its practical operation. This is particularly important if, as is sometimes the case, the existing law is in practice operated by the department in a way that might come as a surprise to the drafter.

9.21 The author of the instructions should consider if it would be helpful to provide some history of the existing law. For instance, if the existing legislation was the result of a consolidation exercise it may be helpful for the drafter to be told this and to be told where to find the original legislation from which the existing legislation was derived. It may be helpful to let the drafter know if the purpose of the existing legislation was to give effect to proposals contained in a Law Commission report. Sometimes the drafter may be assisted by an explanation of why a previous amendment to the existing legislation was made (e.g. to reverse the effect of an unwelcome court decision or to implement an international obligation).

9.22 It is particularly important that the instructions mention any relevant changes to the existing law that are in the pipeline. For example, the drafter should be told if the existing law is going to be changed by another bill or by a statutory instrument that the department is working on.

9.23 If the author of the instructions is aware of any relevant Law Officer's advice about the effect of the existing law this should be brought to the drafter's attention.

9.24 While it is important that the drafter is given a good grounding in the area they are going to be operating in, it is not necessary to provide a treatise on the existing law. Care needs to be taken to avoid the trap of including material in this part of the instructions which is of no relevance to the department's proposals just for the sake of being comprehensive.

9.25 The initial resources meeting between OPC and the department will provide an opportunity for discussion of how much detail will be appropriate in any given set of instructions.

Part 3 – Detailed proposals

9.26 *Introduction*: This part of the instructions should explain in detail (a) the policy objective that the department wishes to achieve and (b) the changes in law that the department wants to make in order to achieve that objective.

9.27 *Policy objective*: It is sometimes tempting to skip the first element and go straight on to describing the changes in law that the department wants. But there are two reasons why it is important to include a detailed explanation of the policy objective. The first is that the explanation will enable the drafter to assess whether the requested changes in law will achieve the objective. The second reason is that the explanation may enable the drafter to suggest an alternative change in law in the event that the drafter identifies a difficulty with the change suggested in the instructions.

Changes in law

9.28 When it comes to describing the changes in law that the department wants, the key is to concentrate on the substance of the proposed changes. In other words, the key is to concentrate on what legal effect the department wants the bill to produce (e.g. 'the bill should make it a criminal offence to do A, B or C' / 'the bill should confer a power on the Secretary of State to do A, B, and C' / 'the bill should abolish body A').

9.29 However, once the author of the instructions has set out the substance of the proposed changes there is no reason not to go on to mention any views they happen to have about the form that the changes should take. For example, if the author thinks the proposed changes should take the form of a freestanding provision rather than an amendment to an existing act then the author should feel free to say so. If the author thinks the proposed changes should take a similar form to an existing statutory provision then they should refer the drafter to the provision concerned. If the author has in mind a particular form of words which might capture the essence of a proposed test or rule they should not feel any hesitation in setting out the words in the instructions. The drafter will be more than happy to consider these sorts of drafting suggestions, if the author of the instructions chooses to make them.

9.30 It is important to remember though that providing drafting suggestions of this sort is not a substitute for clearly explaining the substance of the proposed change that is wanted. The drafter will be unable to produce draft provisions, or assess the merits of any drafting suggestions made by the author of the instructions, unless the drafter has been given a clear explanation of what substantive change in the law the department is trying to achieve.

9.31 In describing the substantive changes in law that the department wants it is necessary to spell out the details in full. If there are any gaps in the details provided the drafter may need to revert to the department for the gaps to be filled before being able to proceed with drafting. Alternatively, the drafter may continue drafting on the basis of their best guess as to what the department will want but there will then be a risk that their guess will be incorrect and the draft will need to be revised.

9.32 When describing the proposed changes in law the author of the instructions will, of course, need to exercise judgement to determine how much detail is enough but a good starting point is for the author to think about what they would want to know if asked to draft provisions to give effect to the change. The next four paragraphs illustrate the level of detail that is needed, by reference to particular types of legal changes that are commonly sought by instructing departments.

New criminal offence

9.33 If the department wants to create a new criminal offence the instructions will need to spell out the acts or omissions that are to be forbidden, the mental element of the offence, the mode of trial for the offence (i.e. summary only, triable either way or indictable only), the proposed penalty for the offence and whether the consent of any person is needed for a prosecution to be brought. If defences are wanted, the circumstances in which the defences should be available will need to be set out. It will also be necessary to set out, in relation to both the offence and any defences, where the burden of proof should fall and the standard of proof that is to apply. The instructions should also say if special provisions are wanted to deal with vicarious liability or the liability of company directors.

New power to make subordinate legislation

9.34 If the department wants to create a new power to make subordinate legislation the instructions will need to spell out the intended scope of the power, how it is thought that the power will be used, the person on whom the power should be conferred and whether that person should be able to delegate the power to someone else, the parliamentary scrutiny to which the power is to be subject and whether the power is to be exercised by statutory instrument (so that the Statutory Instruments Act 1946 applies). If the power is to be subject to the affirmative resolution procedure and it is possible that the power may be used to make legislation that would (if included in a bill) make a bill hybrid, the instructions should indicate whether provision is wanted in the bill to disapply the special House of Lords procedure that applies to hybrid instruments. It will be important to ensure that all delegated powers can be appropriately justified to Parliament.

New duties

9.35 If the department wants to create a new duty of any kind the instructions will need to set out the circumstances in which the duty is to arise, the precise nature of the duty and the person on whom the duty is to be imposed. But it will also be necessary for the instructions to explain how the duty is to be enforced. The department may wish the duty to be enforced by a criminal penalty or a civil sanction. It may want to enforce the duty by making compliance with it a pre-condition to the accrual of some right or benefit. If the duty is a public law duty, the department may want to rely on judicial review for enforcement. If the duty is a duty to comply with a court order the department may wish to rely on the law governing contempt of court. Even where the means of enforcement chosen will not need to be expressed in the bill an explanation of the means of enforcement should still be set out in the instructions so that the drafter is clear about what is intended.

New decision-making powers

9.36 If the department wants the bill to confer a decision-making power on someone it will be necessary, among other things, for the instructions to set out the details of any procedural requirements that the bill should impose as a pre-condition to the exercise of the power. It will be necessary for the instructions to say if the decision-making power should be capable of being delegated. It will also be necessary for the instructions to set out the details of any appeal or review mechanism that needs to be provided for in the bill.

Use of examples

9.37 In describing the parameters of a proposed change in the law it is sometimes helpful to set out examples of the sort of case that the change in law is to affect and of the sort of case that should not be affected. When requesting the creation of a criminal offence it may be helpful to give examples of the sort of conduct that should and should not be criminalised. When this approach is taken the instructions should also contain analysis of what it is that distinguishes the two sorts of case.

Alternatives

9.38 Sometimes there will be several ways in which the law could be changed in order to meet the department's policy objective. In this situation the author of the instructions should briefly explain why the chosen option has been preferred to the others. This is particularly useful if one of the alternative options might appear at first sight to be more attractive or straightforward than the chosen option.

Part 4 – Supplemental and incidental matters

9.39 The author of the instructions should consider whether anything needs to be said about any of the supplemental and incidental matters listed below.

9.40 If the bill is being instructed on in instalments it may be that some of the supplemental and incidental matters can be addressed in a general instalment that applies to the whole bill so that they do not need to be addressed separately in each of the remaining instalments.

9.41 In relation to some of the supplemental and incidental matters, such as territorial extent and commencement, something will always need to be said in the instructions (unless those matters have already been covered in a general instalment). But some of the matters will only occasionally need to be addressed.

9.42 The supplemental and incidental matters are as follows:

- ECHR compatibility;
- the territorial extent of the proposals (including whether the proposals should extend to the Channel Islands, the Isle of Man or the British Overseas Territories);
- the territorial application of the proposals (including application to the territorial sea);
- devolution issues;
- application to the Crown;
- application in relation to Parliament;

- consequential amendments and repeals;
- transitional, transitory and saving provisions;
- commencement; and
- retrospection (see Chapter 12 of this Guide).

9.43 Many of the matters listed above speak for themselves or are the subject of detailed guidance elsewhere. But a number of the matters require some additional commentary.

9.44 ECHR compatibility: The instructions should explain the department's analysis as to whether its proposals engage any of the rights under the ECHR and, if so, whether its proposals are compatible with those rights. It is not part of the drafter's role to confirm whether the department's analysis is correct. However, a short explanation of the department's analysis is needed so as to let the drafter know that the necessary issues have been considered.

9.45 *Application to the Crown*: The instructions should state whether or not the obligations or restraints that the proposed legislation will impose should apply to the Crown, to servants or agents of the Crown or in relation to Crown property. The drafter will then be in a position to consider with the departmental lawyer what, if anything, needs to be said in the bill to ensure that the government's policy as regards Crown application is achieved. In considering this question the drafter and departmental lawyer will take account of the general rule of statutory construction that legislation does not apply to the Crown or in relation to Crown property unless it does so expressly or by necessary implication.

9.46 *Application in relation to Parliament*: If the department's proposals are intended to apply to Parliament or the Parliamentary estate the department is expected to approach the House authorities to give them an opportunity to comment on the proposals. The instructions should confirm that this has been done or is in hand.

9.47 *Consequential amendments and repeals*: The department's proposals will often give rise to the need for consequential amendments or repeals of existing statutory provisions.

9.48 Wherever possible the consequential amendments and repeals that are needed should be included in the bill itself. (If there is a concern that a need for additional consequential amendments or repeals may be identified after Royal Assent then it may also be appropriate for the bill to include a power to make additional consequential amendments and repeals by regulations).

9.49 The other option is for the bill to confer a power enabling all the necessary consequential amendments and repeals to be made by regulations. This option may seem attractive to the department where there is a limited amount of time for instructions to be prepared. However, it is important to remember that if the drafting of consequential amendments and repeals is left until after Royal Assent the department (rather than OPC) will be responsible for preparing the drafting. Also, it is sometimes the case that the process of drafting the consequential amendments and repeals reveals problems with or omissions from the main provisions of the bill – if the drafting of the consequential amendments and repeals is left until after Royal Assent it will be too late to sort these problems or omissions out. Finally, it should be remembered that if the drafting of consequential amendments and repeals is left until after Royal Assent this can cause a delay in implementation. It is important that delegated powers should not be wider than needed to deliver the policy. The full width of all delegated powers needs to be justified to the Delegated Powers and Regulatory Reform Committee. Whilst precedents can be helpful to provide background and context, they are not in themselves sufficient justification for a delegated power or the parliamentary procedure attached to it.

9.50 The instructions should tell the drafter which option the department wishes to pursue. If the department wants the consequential amendments and repeals to be included in the bill it may be sufficient for the instructions to simply provide a list of all the existing provisions that need to be amended or repealed. (For example, if the department's proposal is to abolish an existing statutory body and transfer its functions to a new body it may be sufficient for the instructions to simply provide a list of all the existing statutory provisions which refer to the old body on the basis that it will be obvious to the drafter that the listed provisions need to be amended to refer to the new body.) However, on some occasions it will not be immediately obvious how the listed provisions should be amended and so it will be necessary for the instructions to go on to explain precisely what effect the department wishes to achieve.

9.51 *Transitional, transitory and saving provisions*: the instructions should say if the department's proposals give rise to the need for transitional, transitory or saving provisions.

9.52 A transitional provision is a provision that deals with how a case that begins under the existing law is to be treated when the new law in the bill is commenced. For example, suppose that the department wants the bill to replace an existing licensing regime with a new licensing regime, a transitional provision may be necessary to ensure that an application for a licence under the existing regime which has not been determined is treated as an application for a licence under the new regime.

9.53 A transitory provision is a provision that states that a provision in the bill will have effect with modifications for a limited period (perhaps until the coming into force of some other enactment). An example of a transitory provision would be a provision that says that until the coming into force of a general increase in penalties effected by some other act, the reference in a provision of the bill to a maximum of twelve months' imprisonment will have effect as a reference to six months.

9.54 A saving provision is a provision that keeps an enactment which is repealed by the bill alive for certain limited purposes. An example of a saving provision is a provision which says that the repeal by the bill of an existing enactment does not affect any right (such as a right to a payment) which accrued under the enactment prior to the commencement of the repeal.

9.55 As with consequential amendments and repeals, the transitional, transitory and saving provisions that are needed should be included in the bill itself wherever possible (perhaps with a regulation-making power if there is a concern that a need for additional transitional etc. provisions may be identified after Royal Assent).

9.56 The other option is for the bill to confer a power enabling all the necessary transitional etc. provisions to be made later by regulations. Again, this option may seem attractive where there is a limited amount of time for instructions to be prepared. It is important to remember that if the drafting of transitional etc. provisions is left until after Royal Assent this can result in a delay in implementation. In addition, it is necessary to bear in mind that the transitional provisions needed are often very complex and if the drafting is put off until after Royal Assent the department (rather than OPC) will be expected to do the drafting.

9.57 The instructions should tell the drafter which option the department wish to pursue.

9.58 *Commencement*: The instructions should tell the drafter what is wanted as regards commencement of the requested provisions. There are a range of options here but usually departments ask that their provisions be commenced:

- on a day appointed by regulations made by the Secretary of State;
- on a calendar date specified in the bill;
- on Royal Assent of the bill; or
- at the end of a specified period beginning with Royal Assent.

9.59 Where possible the day when the requested provisions come into force should be determined by the bill itself (rather than by regulations made under the bill). This provides greater certainty to those who are going to be affected by the provisions and also saves putting the reader to the trouble of looking up regulations. However, it is recognised that the department will frequently need the flexibility to be able to determine the date of commencement in regulations.

9.60 The author of the instructions should remember the convention concerning the early commencement of provisions in bills/acts. The convention is that, subject to certain exceptions, provisions in bills/acts should not be commenced before the end of the period of two months following Royal Assent, unless the Law Officers consent. In the case of provisions in a consolidation bill the relevant period is three months following Royal Assent. Further information on this convention can be obtained from the Attorney General's Office and the Legal Secretariat to the Advocate General for Scotland and the Law Officers' pages on LION.

9.61 If the department proposes that the provisions requested in the instructions be commenced (whether by the bill itself or by regulations made under it) before the end of the two-month period the instructions should say whether the author considers that one of the exceptions to the convention applies. If none of the exceptions apply the instructions should tell the drafter what stage the department has reached in seeking the Law Officers' consent to early commencement.

9.62 The author of the instructions should also remember that if the requested provisions will have a bearing on business it is likely that the provisions will have to be commenced on one of the 'common commencement dates' (i.e. 6 April or 1 October). The Department for Business, Energy & Industrial Strategy has issued detailed guidance on common commencement dates which can be accessed from its website or from the LION intranet site.

Part 4 – Parliamentary and other handling matters

9.63 This part of the instructions should set out anything the author thinks the drafter should know about the proposed handling of the bill. For example, it should set out the following sorts of things (in so far as they are known to the author):

- any plans for the bill to be published in draft for consultation or pre-legislative scrutiny and the timetable for this;
- the timetable for the PBL Committee and introduction to Parliament;
- any matters on which the department expects to have to make concessions in Parliament; and
- any pressing need for the bill to reach Royal Assent by a particular date.

9.64 This part of the instructions may also be a good place to raise any questions the department has about Parliamentary procedure. The drafter will, in particular, be able to answer questions on the following sorts of things (after consultation with the House authorities):

- the likely scope of the bill;
- whether the bill will require Queen's or Prince's consent;
- whether there is a risk that the bill will be treated as a hybrid bill; and
- whether the bill will require a money resolution or a ways and means resolution.

9.65 If the bill is being instructed on in instalments it may be that the matters mentioned in the preceding two paragraphs can be addressed in a general instalment that applies to the whole bill so that they do not need to be addressed separately in each of the remaining instalments.

[. . .]

Appendix A: Glossary

Affirmative instrument – delegated legislation that the parent act requires Parliament to explicitly approve before it is able to come into effect (through 'the affirmative procedure').

Amendment – a proposal to alter the text of a bill, motion or draft select committee report.

Bill – draft primary legislation.

CCLA – Commons consideration of Lords' amendments.

Clause – the basic unit of a bill, divided into subsections, then paragraphs, then sub-paragraphs. When the bill becomes an act, 'clauses' become 'sections' but the names of the other subdivisions stay the same.

Command paper – a document presented to Parliament by Command of Her Majesty but in practice by a Government Minister. Command papers are produced to a particular standard and are part of numbered series managed by The National Archives.

Commencement – the coming into effect of legislation. In the absence of a commencement provision, the act comes into force from the beginning of the day on which Royal Assent was given (at midnight).

Committee of the whole House – A Committee Stage that takes place in the House itself, rather than in a 'standing committee'. Any MP may take part in proceedings.

Delegated legislation – legislation made by a minister, or occasionally by a public body, under powers conferred by an act of Parliament. Different types of delegated legislation may be called orders, rules, regulations, schemes or codes, depending on what the 'parent act' calls them. Also known as 'secondary legislation'.

Dissolution – the formal conclusion of a Parliament ahead of a general election.

Draft bill – a bill that is published for pre-legislative scrutiny by a select or joint committee. A draft bill has not been formally introduced into either House.

Explanatory notes – a document accompanying a government bill that sets out the bill's intention and background. It explains the clauses in language that a lay person could understand.

Explanatory statements – a simple statement to explain what an amendment does. They are mandatory for government bills with the exception of Finance Bills.

First Reading – the formal first stage of a bill's passage through Parliament.

Grand committee – A Committee Stage in the House of Lords that takes place off the floor of the House.

Grouping – a set of related amendments for debate.

Guillotine – an order that imposes time limits on the remainder of its progress. Can be made at any stage in a bill's passage through the House of Commons. Also known as an 'allocation of time motion' or a 'Business of the House motion'.

Handout bill – a bill that is drafted by Parliamentary Counsel and offered to a back bencher to take forward as a private member's bill, usually with the continuing support and briefing of the government department concerned.

Introduction – the formal start of a bill's passage through Parliament. Also known as First Reading.

Knives – the deadlines within a programme motion. When a knife falls, only specified decisions may be taken. It may not be possible to debate or decide on certain clauses or amendments.

Law Officers – the collective term for the Attorney General, the Solicitor General and the Advocate General for Scotland. The Attorney General for England and Wales is also the ex-officio Advocate General for Northern Ireland. The core function of the Law Officers is to advise on legal matters, helping ministers to act lawfully and in accordance with the rule of law.

LCCA – Lords consideration of Commons' amendments.

Long title – the passage at the start of a bill that begins 'a Bill to…' and then lists its purposes. The content of the bill must be covered by the long title.

Money bill – a bill whose only purpose is to authorise expenditure or taxation.

Money resolution – a motion to authorise government expenditure in relation to a bill. When the motion is approved it becomes a resolution.

Negative instrument – delegated legislation that, under the parent act, may be made and come into effect unless one or other House decides otherwise ('the negative procedure').

Parliamentary Business Managers – the Leaders and Chief Whips of both Houses. Also known as the BMs or 4BMs.

Parliamentary Counsel – a group of government lawyers who are expert in drafting legislation. They draft all government bills.

PBL Committee – the Cabinet committee on parliamentary business and legislation chaired by the Leader of the House of Commons. Other members include the Leader of the House of Lords, the Chief Whips of both House, the Law Officers and the Secretaries of State of the territorial offices.

Ping-pong – the to and fro of bills and amendments between the two Houses towards the end of a bill's passage.

Prince of Wales' consent – agreement by the Prince of Wales that Parliament may proceed to consider legislation that would affect his interests.

Private bill – a bill that would only have a local or personal effect, rather than a general effect.

Private member's bill – a public bill introduced by a 'private member' of Parliament (not a minister) i.e. a backbencher in the Lords or Commons.

Prorogation – the formal end of a parliamentary session, bringing almost all parliamentary business to an end.

Public bill – a bill that, if passed, will have general effect in some or all of the constituent parts of the UK.

Queen's consent – agreement by The Queen that Parliament may proceed to consider legislation that would affect her interests.

Queen's speech – the Speech written by the Government and delivered by The Queen at the State Opening of Parliament. It outlines the

Government's plans for the new session, especially its legislative programme, and sets out the events for the coming year (including state visits).

Report Stage – the consideration of a bill in the form in which it left Committee, and an opportunity for any member to propose amendments (not just those who were on the committee).

Royal Assent – the sovereign's agreement to a bill.

Second Reading – approval of a bill in principle. The second stage of the passage of a bill through each House of Parliament.

Session – the main subdivision of time during a parliament. The period from State Opening to prorogation.

Short title – the title by which a bill is known during its passage through Parliament for example 'Civil Aviation Bill'.

Standing committee – In the Commons, a committee to which most bills are referred for their Committee Stage.

Sunset clause – a provision in legislation that makes it time-limited.

Table – to deposit formally before the House or committee, as 'to table an amendment'.

Third Reading – the final stage of the passage of a bill through each House of Parliament.

Usual channels – the informal and private contacts between the whips and Business Managers on both sides of each House.

[...]

Appendix E: Codes of practice and legislation

- Bill teams should read this section if there is a proposal to adopt, use, or otherwise refer to a code of practice or similar document in implementing the legislation. Where it is proposed to introduce a code of practice in a way or for a purpose which departs from the guidance below, Ministers should be aware that this is likely to be controversial, particularly in the House of Lords.

- Where use of a code of practice is contemplated as part of, or as an adjunct to, the scheme of an Act, the drafting of the code ought to begin early enough to enable a decision as to whether statutory provision is required, and if so what kind of provision is appropriate, to be made with a clear idea of the proposed contents of the code. Equally, if Parliament is to be asked to enact statutory provisions relating to a code, a draft of the proposed code should if at all possible be made available so that the appropriateness of the statutory provisions can be properly considered.
- Failure to do this can hinder the passage of the enabling legislation. While this chapter offers a general guide only and the paramount consideration in every case must be the framing of a legislative scheme which is appropriate for the particular purpose in hand, departure from the general rules in this guidance should rarely be necessary and will require justification. In particular, departments should bear in mind that any unusual or novel provision will be closely scrutinised in Parliament.

Meaning of 'code of practice'

- A 'code of practice' is an authoritative statement of practice to be followed in some field. It typically differs from legislation in that it offers guidance rather than imposing requirements: its prescriptions are not hard and fast rules but guidelines which may allow considerable latitude in their practical application and may be departed from in appropriate circumstances. The provisions of a code are not directly enforceable by legal proceedings, which is not to say that they may not have significant legal effects. A code of practice, unlike a legislative text, may also contain explanatory material and argument.
- A number of different kinds of document may be described by statute as a 'code of practice'. They may contain general principles or minute technical details, they may describe existing practice or practice

which is recommended for the future and they may contain explanation and information of various kinds. Conversely, other terms may be used to describe essentially the same kind of document. This guidance refers to 'codes of practice' but its comments apply equally to similar documents under other names.

- It will usually be undesirable for an Act to refer to some other kind of document as a 'code of practice'. This is apt to mislead as to the status or intention of the document. Some more accurate descriptive title should be used.
- Different kinds of provisions may be found within a single document. Accordingly, where this guidance refers to a type of code the comment should be read as applicable to particular provisions of that description in a code of practice.

Is statutory provision necessary?

- This guidance is concerned with legislation and is therefore not concerned with non-statutory codes. However, a preliminary question which must always be considered is whether statutory provision is necessary.
- There are many things departments can properly do without express statutory authority. It has been the practice for many years for departments to issue information, advice or exhortation of various kinds, for the guidance of the public or of the authorities or officers charged with administering some branch of Government. These documents may be described as 'codes' and may be of considerable practical importance. It does not follow that statutory provision is necessary.
- A provision which merely confers on a Minister power to issue a code of practice consisting of information, advice or exhortation which is not intended to have any particular legal effect is unnecessary.
- Statutory provision is justifiable if the code is intended to have a particular legal effect (the various types of which are described below). It is also justifiable if it is intended to impose a legal duty to issue a code of practice or to impose legal requirements as to the procedure to be followed in connection with its issue. Either of those courses indicates that importance is attached to the code of practice

and careful consideration should be given to the question of its legal effect.

- Statutory provision may also be justifiable when setting up a statutory body to make clear that the body has power to issue codes of practice. Express provision is not necessary where, as will usually be the case, the issuing of codes is merely incidental to the body's general functions.
- If statutory provision is necessary but the code is not intended to have any particular legal effect of the descriptions below, there should be appropriate words indicating that the code is issued only for purposes of advice or information.
- Codes of practice are not to be used to define specific legal obligations. Where specific legal obligations are to be imposed, breach of which leads directly to civil or criminal liability, their content should be spelled out in primary or secondary legislation. A code of practice is not appropriate for this purpose, either to delineate the main obligation or to provide for exceptions or defences.
- A code of practice may be appropriate to explain or supplement the provisions of primary or secondary legislation. It should not be regarded as a substitute for legislation. It is the function of legislation to set minimum standards of conduct and it is usual to provide for penalties for those who fall below the minimum standard and for legal remedies for the protection or compensation of those who suffer injury or loss as a result. It is usual to set legal minimum standards notwithstanding that the overall policy objective is to raise standards generally above the minimum - an objective towards which a code of practice may contribute.
- Codes addressed to the public or a section of it: failure to comply with code as evidence of breach of legal duty. The most common type of provision giving legal effect to a code of practice is that making failure to comply with the code evidence of breach of some more general legal duty. The codes in relation to which such provision is made are normally addressed to the public at large or a section of it (for instance, road users or employers).
- The liability is not for breach of the code but for breach of a duty arising elsewhere.

- There is no essential difference between the two styles of provision to this effect. The first type of provision focuses on the effect of breach or compliance in establishing liability; the second focuses on the effect of the code's provisions in elaborating standards of conduct. Both types of provision produce substantially the same result: that in certain kinds of proceedings the code is an element in deciding the issue of liability or some other question, but is not itself decisive.
- In neither case does the provision directly shift the legal or evidential burden of proof. The significance of a failure to comply with a provision of a code cannot be assessed except in relation to the circumstances of a particular case. The evidential weight depends on the relevance and importance of the failure in relation to the matters to be proved in order to establish liability.
- When considering what evidential effect should be attributed to any particular code careful consideration should be given to identifying so far as possible what proceedings, and what issues, a breach of the code may be relevant to. The resulting statutory provision should be as specific as is possible.
- In general the first type of provision is preferable because it is more specific, but it cannot be regarded as universally applicable. It may be that some adaptation of it, or something more akin to the 'questions arising' form, is in particular circumstances more appropriate. For instance, it may not be 'liability' which is in issue but some other question; and the proceedings may not be ordinary legal proceedings.
- A form appropriate to the determination of issues in legal proceedings should not be stretched to cover the exercise of administrative functions which is more aptly dealt with by a duty to have regard. It may in some cases be necessary to provide for both types of effect in relation to the same code.
- There is a variant form of the evidential code provision in s.17 (1) and (2) of the Health & Safety at Work Act 1974 (c.37) which expressly shifts the burden of proof. It is not usual to attempt in legislation to modify the operation of general legal principles such as those relating to the evidential burden of proof whose impact in the nature of things varies from case to case. And to shift the legal (or 'persuasive') burden of proof would normally be regarded as

giving a code too much legal force. For these reasons, although this provision may be justified in its particular context, it should not in general be regarded as a precedent for future legislation.

Codes addressed to authorities and officers: duty to have regard to code

- Another type of code of practice is that relevant to the exercise of statutory functions by public authorities or officers.
- General principles of administrative law require public authorities or officers in exercising their functions to direct themselves properly and to take into account all relevant factors and not to take into account irrelevant factors. Failure to do so may result in a decision or other Act being challenged in proceedings for judicial review or simply being regarded as being legally ineffective.
- If the provisions of a code are intended to be included among the relevant factors in the exercise of a class of functions it will normally be desirable to make this clear by requiring the relevant authorities to have regard to the code, or, which amounts to the same thing, to take it into account. As indicated above, the consequences of their failing to do so are governed by general administrative law; ad hoc statutory provision as to the effect of failure is neither necessary nor desirable.
- The requirement that an authority or officer must have regard to the code means that the authority or officer must consider the provisions of the code and give them due weight in coming to their decision. They are not bound to follow the code if they properly conclude that the recommendations of the code are, in a particular case, either not relevant or are outweighed by other considerations.
- Careful consideration should be given to identifying the persons or authorities who are required to have regard to the code and the decisions or functions in relation to which the provisions of the code are to be taken into account. Again, the statutory provision should be as specific as the circumstances admit.

Codes administered by authorities having regulatory or disciplinary powers: Failure to comply with code leading to action by authority

- Another form of provision found is that failure to comply with the provisions of a code of practice is a ground for the exercise of regulatory or disciplinary powers by some supervisory authority or, which amounts to the same thing, that an authority shall exercise its general supervisory powers so as to secure compliance with the code. The code itself may be one issued by the authority in question, by Ministers or by some third party.
- This type of provision will not normally offend against the principle mentioned above (that a code of practice should not to be used to define specific legal obligations) because any legal liability arises as a result of the exercise of the authority's general powers and not simply from the failure to comply with the code. The authority will normally take action on some wider ground than breach of the code alone and will have a discretion as to how it exercises its regulatory powers.
- The effect of a breach of the code is in such cases broadly similar to that mentioned above in that it is a ground on which a sanction may, but need not, be imposed. However, similar considerations to those mentioned above (that a code of practice should not to be used to define specific legal obligations) apply if what is envisaged is a set of binding rules breach of which will, without anything else having to be shown or otherwise required, lead directly to the imposition of a sanction.

Statutory mention of codes having extra statutory effect

- The framing of codes of practice by trade associations, professional bodies and other self-regulatory organisations is commonplace and whatever legal effect they have is basically a matter of private law. There are a number of statutory provisions which confer duties on regulatory authorities to encourage the preparation and dissemination of codes by non-governmental bodies.

- These provisions do not confer any additional legal effect on the codes in question.

Drafting codes of practice

- Codes of practice are drawn up for a wide range of audiences and purposes and contain a variety of provisions. No general guidance is possible, or indeed necessary, as to the manner in which a code is expressed. The main purpose of a code of practice is to inform and guide and it will fail in that object if its provisions are not clear.
- Every code which is drawn up under statutory authority should refer to its authorising provision and recite or summarise the purposes for which it is issued.
- here a code is to have legal effect of any of the kinds mentioned above, it should also recite or summarise the provisions giving it that legal effect. Such a code must also be sufficiently precisely drafted for its intended purpose. In particular, where a code contains provisions of different kinds it should be arranged, so far as practicable, in such a way as to make it clear which passages are prescriptive and which contain only exhortation, explanation or information.
- Where use of a code of practice is contemplated as part of, or as an adjunct to, the scheme of an Act, the drafting of the code ought to begin early enough to enable a decision as to whether statutory provision is required, and if so what kind of provision is appropriate, to be made with a clear idea of the proposed contents of the code. Equally, if Parliament is to be asked to enact statutory provisions relating to a code, a draft of the proposed code should if at all possible be made available so that the appropriateness of the statutory provisions can be properly considered.
- Failure to do this can hinder the passage of the enabling legislation.

Parliamentary procedure for codes of practice

- Departments should ensure that there is appropriate provision for Parliamentary procedure where the nature and importance of the subject matter of a code warrants it. In the case of evidential codes (where the failure to comply with a code can be taken as evidence of breach of legal duty) and codes to which authorities are to have regard, there is a presumption in favour of parliamentary procedure of some kind; but this may not be appropriate for detailed technical documents. If it is envisaged that a code will be frequently amended, it may be sufficient to provide for parliamentary procedure only in relation to its original issue or revocation.
- The considerations involved in deciding between affirmative and negative procedure, or no procedure, are broadly similar to those applicable in the case of subordinate legislation. Parliament will wish to consider the substance of the code, so that provision for Parliamentary procedure should relate to the code itself and not, where there is one, to the order bringing the code into operation, even though that may be a statutory instrument. In the case of the approval by Ministers of a code drawn up by a third party it may be appropriate to provide for Parliamentary procedure in relation to the approval order, the code itself having been laid before Parliament.

Publication and commencement

- Departments should ensure that there are satisfactory arrangements for publication or other means of bringing the contents of a code of practice to the notice of those to whom it is directed.
- No special statutory provision is required, although it is sometimes found, for the publication and sale of codes. In the case of codes addressed to authorities or officers it should be borne in mind that others will have a legitimate interest in the contents of the code, for instance, in order to challenge a decision taken in breach of the code. In such cases other means of disseminating the necessary information may be appropriate, for instance, publishing the code on a website, as a circular in a series sold through TSO, or the

department's designated publisher including the code in a relevant annual report which is published. Every code issued under statutory authority ought to be made available to Parliament; if it is not otherwise available, by placing a copy in the Library of each House.

- It will often be important to know when a code, or an amendment of it, came into operation. There is no reason why this should not be stated in the code itself but it may be convenient to make provision in a separate order, particularly where it is necessary to include transitional provisions or savings. Where such orders are made by Ministers they should be made by statutory instrument.

Evidence: Admissibility and proof of document

- Provision is sometimes found that a code of practice is to be 'admissible' in certain kinds of legal proceedings. A code (whether expressed as a command or a statement of fact) is a statement of the opinion of the maker of the code as to what ought to be done. Such a statement would not normally be relevant to a court's consideration of what is legally required to be done. That may be simply a matter of law on which the court makes up its own mind after hearing argument; or it may involve questions of fact (such as, what is 'best practicable means' or 'reasonable care') on which expert witnesses may be called. The contents of a code of practice are a form of 'opinion evidence' of someone who is not a witness and may not be an expert in the sense under discussion (i.e. the code of practice is compiled by persons who are unidentified and who if identified might not count as experts). To provide that the code is admissible, therefore, means that the document can be put before the court despite these general rules of the law of evidence.
- Provision to this effect is unnecessary if the court is directed by the Act to take the code into account for some specified purpose. It must follow from such a duty that the court can look at the code whatever its status may be so far as the general rules of evidence are concerned.
- This question must be distinguished from the question of how the text of the code is proved. Assuming a code of practice is 'admissible'

or may be relied on in particular proceedings, there may in some cases be technical difficulties in proving that the document is in fact the code referred to in the Act or in establishing what the text of the code is. In criminal proceedings, in particular, the prosecution may find itself put to proof of a code not in common use or there may be a real dispute as to the correct text of a code at any material time. As well as the text, the party relying on a code may be required to prove when the code, or an amendment, was issued or came into operation.

- Codes and related documents issued by Government departments may have the benefit of the Documentary Evidence Act 1868 (c.37), as amended and extended, which enables the document to be proved by a copy purporting to be printed by, or under the superintendence or authority of, Her Majesty's Stationery Office. In other cases it will be necessary to consider whether provision should be made for facilitating the proof of the document, and of any order or other instrument approving it for the purposes of the statute, by creating a presumption that such a document is what it purports to be.

Index

A
Adverbial(s) 110, 112
Amendment(s) 31, 33, 84–86, 92, 94, 102, 103, 107, 108, 116, 125–127, 130, 132, 134, 187, 214, 215, 217, 220, 224, 227–232, 234, 242–244, 249, 250, 252, 255–258, 267, 268
Application 12, 26, 34–36, 60–62, 66, 90, 102–104, 106, 113–115, 122, 126, 128, 133, 136, 182, 184, 200, 225, 226, 240, 248, 249, 251, 259

C
Consequential 102, 103, 116, 125, 127, 128, 132, 134, 136, 249, 250, 252
Clarity 12, 26, 65–67, 94, 104, 168, 181, 191, 200
Comprehensibility 52, 57, 58, 63, 94, 104, 199, 200
Constraints 21
Context(s) 13, 17, 18, 23, 27, 28, 36, 37, 39, 41, 42, 44–46, 48–53, 59, 60, 65, 76, 82, 106, 108, 122, 139, 146, 148–150, 160, 161, 167, 168, 171, 173, 175, 176, 178, 180, 185, 189, 191, 193, 195–200, 242, 250, 263
Contextual 37, 41, 42, 44, 50–52, 196, 198
  analysis 12–14, 26, 27, 40, 41, 45, 49–52, 54, 58, 79, 96, 98–100, 123, 126, 141, 142, 146, 154, 156, 167, 168, 171, 195, 199, 200, 221, 235, 247, 249
Convention(s) 21, 25, 31, 32, 35, 36, 42, 46, 48–51, 54, 57, 59, 78, 84, 87, 113, 119–121, 142, 153, 155, 163–165, 169, 174, 197, 199, 214, 216, 221, 228, 253
  linguistic 12–14, 16, 17, 21, 23, 25–28, 36, 40–43, 46, 48–54, 58, 66, 96, 106, 112, 119, 122, 142, 150, 151, 156, 160, 166–168, 171–174, 178, 188, 195–197, 200

D
Deontic 119, 122
Discoursal features 40, 151, 197
Drafter(s) 12, 13, 22, 25–27, 29–32, 34–36, 39–41, 49,

51, 57, 63, 66, 92–94, 96, 98–102, 104, 105, 108, 119, 120, 123, 127, 131, 133, 135, 136, 142, 145, 146, 149–151, 168, 169, 181, 183, 184, 187, 193, 196–200, 237–245, 247, 249–254
Drafting 12–14, 22, 23, 25, 26–31, 33–36, 39, 41, 49–57, 61–63, 65–67, 88–94, 96–99, 101–105, 112, 113, 119, 121, 142, 144, 147, 149–151, 160, 167–169, 174, 175, 179–181, 183, 184, 186–193, 195–198, 214, 219, 220, 233, 237, 244, 245, 250, 252, 257, 259, 265

E
Easification 151–153, 160, 162, 164, 167, 200
  measures 152
  strategies 153, 160, 162, 164, 167
  techniques 162, 200
Effectiveness 36, 66, 100, 103, 144, 150, 168, 175, 200
Efficacy 63, 66, 183, 200
Enacting formula 20, 111, 113
English 9, 11, 12, 15–23, 26, 27, 50, 63–65, 69–71, 75, 77, 81, 82, 105, 119, 131, 143–145, 168–179, 181, 183–185, 191
Event,
  communicative 13, 28, 36, 40–42, 45, 48–50, 59, 59, 195
  situated 13, 28, 36, 49, 59, 195
Explanatory note(s) 32, 90, 136, 137, 139–141, 153, 214, 220, 221, 223, 226–231, 239, 255

F
Framework(s) 13, 14, 28, 36, 37, 42–49, 51–53, 61, 62, 98, 137, 138, 156, 195, 196, 198, 200
French 11, 17–21, 64, 71, 75, 145, 147, 170
  Norman 17, 64, 69, 75, 145, 147

G
Geographical extent 82, 113, 115
Gender,
  language(s) 169, 170, 174, 175
  neutral drafting 168, 174, 175, 179–181, 183, 184, 190–192
  neutrality 168, 175, 190
Germanic Old English 64
Good law 14, 93, 94, 192–194, 200

H
House,
  House of Commons 30, 70, 73, 75–78, 83–87, 90,

189, 215, 217, 219, 224, 231, 256, 257
House of Lords 32, 70, 74–78, 83, 85–87, 92, 113, 191, 215, 224, 230, 231, 246, 256, 257, 259

J
Jurisdiction(s) 17, 35, 39, 53, 81–83, 105, 108, 150, 161, 168, 169, 174, 175, 179, 183–185, 191, 196

K
Knowledge 13, 28, 33, 35, 36, 39, 41, 42, 55, 59–61, 65, 98, 135, 136, 167, 195, 197–199

L
Language(s),
community 48
Latin 11, 16–21, 64, 71, 75, 144–146
Law 12–15, 17–20, 22, 23, 25–27, 29, 31, 32, 34, 35, 39, 44, 49, 51–54, 59, 66, 71, 78, 80, 86, 89, 93, 94, 96–99, 101–106, 113, 115, 118, 119, 125, 126, 131, 133, 135, 137, 140, 141, 144–153, 157–161, 168, 184, 187–189, 192–194, 196, 199, 200, 215, 221, 222, 226, 232–234, 236, 238, 240–245, 247, 248, 251, 253, 256, 257, 263, 264, 267
Legal 9, 11–13, 15–30, 33, 34, 36, 39, 42, 44, 46, 47, 49–53, 55, 59, 62–64, 71, 78, 82, 89, 90, 95–98, 103, 104, 107–110, 119–121, 130, 131, 136, 140, 143–150, 156–161, 164–169, 184, 188, 189, 191–193, 195, 196, 199, 214, 217, 220–223, 226, 232, 234, 236, 238, 239, 241, 244, 245, 253, 256, 259–267
communication 143
knowledge 59, 167, 199
text(s) 11, 20–25, 145–148, 161, 168
Legislative,
drafting 12–14, 22, 23, 25–30, 34–36, 39, 41, 49–52, 54, 55, 59, 61, 63, 65–67, 90–92, 94, 96, 97, 102–105, 112, 121, 149–151, 168, 169, 179, 183, 184, 192, 193, 195–198
drafting process 52, 54, 55, 67, 91, 97, 104
Legislation 9, 12–14, 18, 19, 22, 23, 25–27, 30, 31, 33–36, 39, 40, 44, 46, 50, 51, 54, 55, 57, 59–61, 63, 65–67, 76, 78–84, 86–94, 97–100, 102–108, 111–124, 126, 128, 130–136, 139–142, 144, 145, 148, 150, 151, 153, 159–161, 168, 169,

174, 175, 180, 181, 184, 187, 189–194, 196, 197, 199, 200, 213–219, 221–226, 229, 232–234, 237, 242, 243, 246, 249, 254, 255, 257–263, 265, 266
Lexico,
  grammatical feature(s) 11, 21, 146
Lexico-grammatical 11, 21, 40, 105, 119, 142, 146, 151, 154, 168, 195, 197
  components 53, 93, 106
  structure(s) 119, 142, 168
Linguistic,
  constraint(s) 21
  convention(s) 21

M
Magna Carta 71
Modal(s) 24, 62, 119–123
Model 41, 44, 50, 57, 73, 78, 235
Multinomial(s) 166, 167

O
OPC 14, 89, 91–94, 96, 98, 119, 191, 192, 214, 237–239, 241, 243, 250, 252
Origins 15, 54, 69

P
Parliament 12–14, 17, 18, 20, 26, 27, 30–33, 54, 57–87, 89–95, 98, 102, 106–112, 119, 126, 136, 137, 179, 186, 189, 190, 192, 193, 213–220, 222–228, 230, 232–234, 236, 237, 239, 240, 246, 248–250, 253–259, 265–267
Phronesis 35, 41
Plain,
  English 15, 63, 119, 143, 144, 169
  language 11, 12, 14, 15, 26, 63–66, 102, 105, 112, 121, 143–149, 160, 181, 200
  movement 142, 147
Precision 22, 65–67, 145, 200
Professional(s),
  knowledge 28, 41, 195
  text(s) 58, 199
  writing 55, 56, 198
Provision(s),
  final 102, 103, 106, 125, 128, 130, 131, 135
  preliminary 40, 102, 106, 151, 197
  principal 101–103, 118, 119, 125
Provisional 120, 219

R
Repeal(s) 94, 101–103, 125–127, 130, 134, 135, 189, 215, 242, 249–252

S
Section(s) 13, 24, 61, 65, 82, 87, 88, 93, 100, 103, 108, 114–118, 120–128, 130, 132–135, 137, 139–141, 148,

149, 154, 156, 158, 159, 161, 165–167, 174, 182–187, 189–191, 213–216, 222, 233, 237, 258, 261
Schedule(s) 102–104, 122, 125, 126, 130–136, 140, 183, 187
Shall 18, 24, 62, 63, 119–121, 125, 144, 154–156, 158, 160, 161, 165, 174, 182, 189, 264
Simplicity 63, 65, 66, 147, 181, 200
Simplification 152, 153, 159, 167, 187, 188
Specialized,
  languages 119
Speech,
  community 55

T
Techniques 12, 14, 26, 32, 34, 94, 96, 104, 105, 144, 160, 162, 168, 169, 179, 180, 200
Text(s),
  legal 11, 20–25, 145–148, 161, 168
  legislative 9, 11, 14, 22, 32, 45, 49, 51, 52, 58–63, 66, 83, 95, 100–106, 109, 111, 113, 115, 118, 119, 121, 141, 142, 149, 153, 154, 156, 160, 161, 165, 168, 174, 175, 197, 199, 200, 259
Textual,
  structures 53
  components 53, 93, 106
Title,
  long 85, 102, 106, 108, 109, 111, 230, 256
  short 102, 103, 117, 125, 127–1300, 141, 227, 258

U
UK,
  legislation 51, 79, 107, 114, 159
  legislative drafting 192
  parliament 13, 27, 54, 69, 73, 74, 78–87, 92, 102, 111, 112, 136
Unambiguity 65–67, 200

V
Verb(s) 11, 21, 28, 41, 62, 85, 110, 112, 117, 125–127, 135, 141, 161, 169, 173, 182, 229

W
Westminster Palace 69

Linguistic Insights

Studies in Language and Communication

This series aims to promote specialist language studies in the fields of linguistic theory and applied linguistics, by publishing volumes that focus on specific aspects of language use in one or several languages and provide valuable insights into language and communication research. A cross-disciplinary approach is favoured and most European languages are accepted.

The series includes two types of books:

- Monographs – featuring in-depth studies on special aspects of language theory, language analysis or language teaching.
- Collected papers – assembling papers from workshops, conferences or symposia.

Each volume of the series is subjected to a double peer-reviewing process.

Vol. 1 Maurizio Gotti & Marina Dossena (eds)
Modality in Specialized Texts. Selected Papers of the 1st CERLIS Conference.
421 pages. 2001. ISBN 3-906767-10-8 · US-ISBN 0-8204-5340-4

Vol. 2 Giuseppina Cortese & Philip Riley (eds)
Domain-specific English. Textual Practices across Communities and Classrooms.
420 pages. 2002. ISBN 3-906768-98-8 · US-ISBN 0-8204-5884-8

Vol. 3 Maurizio Gotti, Dorothee Heller & Marina Dossena (eds)
Conflict and Negotiation in Specialized Texts. Selected Papers of the 2nd CERLIS Conference.
470 pages. 2002. ISBN 3-906769-12-7 · US-ISBN 0-8204-5887-2

Vol. 4 Maurizio Gotti, Marina Dossena, Richard Dury, Roberta Facchinetti & Maria Lima
Variation in Central Modals. A Repertoire of Forms and Types of Usage in Middle English and Early Modern English.
364 pages. 2002. ISBN 3-906769-84-4 · US-ISBN 0-8204-5898-8

Editorial address:

Prof. Maurizio Gotti Università di Bergamo, Dipartimento di Lingue, Letterature e Culture Straniere Piazza Rosate 2, 24129 Bergamo, Italy
Fax: +39 035 2052789, E-Mail: m.gotti@unibg.it

Vol. 5 Stefania Nuccorini (ed.)
Phrases and Phraseology. Data and Descriptions.
187 pages. 2002. ISBN 3-906770-08-7 · US-ISBN 0-8204-5933-X

Vol. 6 Vijay Bhatia, Christopher N. Candlin & Maurizio Gotti (eds)
Legal Discourse in Multilingual and Multicultural Contexts.
Arbitration Texts in Europe.
385 pages. 2003. ISBN 3-906770-85-0 · US-ISBN 0-8204-6254-3

Vol. 7 Marina Dossena & Charles Jones (eds)
Insights into Late Modern English. 2nd edition.
378 pages. 2003, 2007.
ISBN 978-3-03911-257-9 · US-ISBN 978-0-8204-8927-8

Vol. 8 Maurizio Gotti
Specialized Discourse. Linguistic Features and Changing Conventions.
351 pages. 2003, 2005.
ISBN 3-03910-606-6 · US-ISBN 0-8204-7000-7

Vol. 9 Alan Partington, John Morley & Louann Haarman (eds)
Corpora and Discourse.
420 pages. 2004. ISBN 3-03910-026-2 · US-ISBN 0-8204-6262-4

Vol. 10 Martina Möllering
The Acquisition of German Modal Particles. A Corpus-Based Approach.
290 pages. 2004. ISBN 3-03910-043-2 · US-ISBN 0-8204-6273-X

Vol. 11 David Hart (ed.)
English Modality in Context. Diachronic Perspectives.
261 pages. 2003. ISBN 3-03910-046-7 · US-ISBN 0-8204-6852-5

Vol. 12 Wendy Swanson
Modes of Co-reference as an Indicator of Genre.
430 pages. 2003. ISBN 3-03910-052-1 · US-ISBN 0-8204-6855-X

Vol. 13 Gina Poncini
Discursive Strategies in Multicultural Business Meetings.
2nd edition. 338 pages. 2004, 2007.
ISBN 978-3-03911-296-8 · US-ISBN 978-0-8204-8937-7

Vol. 14 Christopher N. Candlin & Maurizio Gotti (eds)
Intercultural Aspects of Specialized Communication. 2nd edition.
369 pages. 2004, 2007.
ISBN 978-3-03911-258-6 · US-ISBN 978-0-8204-8926-1

Vol. 15 Gabriella Del Lungo Camiciotti & Elena Tognini Bonelli (eds) Academic Discourse. New Insights into Evaluation.
234 pages. 2004. ISBN 3-03910-353-9 · US-ISBN 0-8204-7016-3

Vol. 16 Marina Dossena & Roger Lass (eds)
Methods and Data in English Historical Dialectology.
405 pages. 2004. ISBN 3-03910-362-8 · US-ISBN 0-8204-7018-X

Vol. 17 Judy Noguchi
The Science Review Article. An Opportune Genre in the Construction of Science.
274 pages. 2006. ISBN 3-03910-426-8 · US-ISBN 0-8204-7034-1

Vol. 18 Giuseppina Cortese & Anna Duszak (eds)
Identity, Community, Discourse. English in Intercultural Settings. 495 pages. 2005. ISBN 3-03910-632-5 · US-ISBN 0-8204-7163-1

Vol. 19 Anna Trosborg & Poul Erik Flyvholm Jørgensen (eds) Business Discourse. Texts and Contexts.
250 pages. 2005. ISBN 3-03910-606-6 · US-ISBN 0-8204-7000-7

Vol. 20 Christopher Williams
Tradition and Change in Legal English. Verbal Constructions in Prescriptive Texts.
2nd revised edition. 216 pages. 2005, 2007. ISBN 978-3-03911-444-3.

Vol. 21 Katarzyna Dziubalska-Kolaczyk & Joanna Przedlacka (eds) English Pronunciation Models: A Changing Scene.
2nd edition. 476 pages. 2005, 2008. ISBN 978-3-03911-682-9.

Vol. 22 Christián Abello-Contesse, Rubén Chacón-Beltrán,
M. Dolores López-Jiménez & M. Mar Torreblanca-López (eds) Age in L2 Acquisition and Teaching.
214 pages. 2006. ISBN 3-03910-668-6 · US-ISBN 0-8204-7174-7

Vol. 23 Vijay K. Bhatia, Maurizio Gotti, Jan Engberg & Dorothee Heller (eds) Vagueness in Normative Texts.
474 pages. 2005. ISBN 3-03910-653-8 · US-ISBN 0-8204-7169-0

Vol. 24 Paul Gillaerts & Maurizio Gotti (eds)
Genre Variation in Business Letters. 2nd printing. 407 pages. 2008. ISBN 978-3-03911-681-2.

Vol. 25 Ana María Hornero, María José Luzón & Silvia Murillo (eds) Corpus Linguistics. Applications for the Study of English.
2nd printing. 526 pages. 2006, 2008. ISBN 978-3-03911-726-0

Vol. 26 J. Lachlan Mackenzie & María de los Ángeles Gómez-González (eds) Studies in Functional Discourse Grammar.
259 pages. 2005. ISBN 3-03910-696-1 · US-ISBN 0-8204-7558-0

Vol. 27 Debbie G. E. Ho
Classroom Talk. Exploring the Sociocultural Structure of Formal ESL Learning. 2nd edition. 254 pages. 2006, 2007. ISBN 978-3-03911-434-4

Vol. 28 Javier Pérez-Guerra, Dolores González-Álvarez, Jorge L. Bueno-Alonso & Esperanza Rama-Martínez (eds)
'Of Varying Language and Opposing Creed'. New Insights into Late Modern English. 455 pages. 2007. ISBN 978-3-03910-788-9

Vol. 29 Francesca Bargiela-Chiappini & Maurizio Gotti (eds) Asian Business Discourse(s).
350 pages. 2005. ISBN 3-03910-804-2 · US-ISBN 0-8204-7574-2

Vol. 30 Nicholas Brownlees (ed.)
News Discourse in Early Modern Britain. Selected Papers of CHINED 2004. 300 pages. 2006. ISBN 3-03910-805-0 · US-ISBN 0-8204-8025-8

Vol. 31 Roberta Facchinetti & Matti Rissanen (eds) Corpus-based Studies of Diachronic English.
300 pages. 2006. ISBN 3-03910-851-4 · US-ISBN 0-8204-8040-1

Vol. 32 Marina Dossena & Susan M. Fitzmaurice (eds)
Business and Official Correspondence. Historical Investigations. 209 pages. 2006. ISBN 3-03910-880-8 · US-ISBN 0-8204-8352-4

Vol. 33 Giuliana Garzone & Srikant Sarangi (eds)
Discourse, Ideology and Specialized Communication. 494 pages. 2007. ISBN 978-3-03910-888-6

Vol. 34 Giuliana Garzone & Cornelia Ilie (eds)
The Use of English in Institutional and Business Settings. An Intercultural Perspective. 372 pages. 2007. ISBN 978-3-03910-889-3

Vol. 35 Vijay K. Bhatia & Maurizio Gotti (eds) Explorations in Specialized Genres. 316 pages. 2006. ISBN 3-03910-995-2 · US-ISBN 0-8204-8372-9

Vol. 36 Heribert Picht (ed.)
Modern Approaches to Terminological Theories and Applications. 432 pages. 2006. ISBN 3-03911-156-6 · US-ISBN 0-8204-8380-X

Vol. 37 Anne Wagner & Sophie Cacciaguidi-Fahy (eds)
Legal Language and the Search for Clarity / Le langage juridique et la quête de clarté. Practice and Tools / Pratiques et instruments.
487 pages. 2006. ISBN 3-03911-169-8 · US-ISBN 0-8204-8388-5

Vol. 38 Juan Carlos Palmer-Silveira, Miguel F. Ruiz-Garrido & Inmaculada Fortanet-Gómez (eds)
Intercultural and International Business Communication. Theory, Research and Teaching. 2nd edition. 343 pages. 2006, 2008. ISBN 978-3-03911-680-5

Vol. 39 Christiane Dalton-Puffer, Dieter Kastovsky, Nikolaus Ritt & Herbert Schendl (eds)
Syntax, Style and Grammatical Norms. English from 1500–2000. 250 pages. 2006. ISBN 3-03911-181-7 · US-ISBN 0-8204-8394-X

Vol. 40 Marina Dossena & Irma Taavitsainen (eds) Diachronic Perspectives on Domain-Specific English.
280 pages. 2006. ISBN 3-03910-176-0 · US-ISBN 0-8204-8391-5

Vol. 41 John Flowerdew & Maurizio Gotti (eds) Studies in Specialized Discourse.
293 pages. 2006. ISBN 3-03911-178-7

Vol. 42 Ken Hyland & Marina Bondi (eds) Academic Discourse Across Disciplines.
320 pages. 2006. ISBN 3-03911-183-3 · US-ISBN 0-8204-8396-6

Vol. 43 Paul Gillaerts & Philip Shaw (eds)
The Map and the Landscape. Norms and Practices in Genre. 256 pages. 2006. ISBN 3-03911-182-5 · US-ISBN 0-8204-8395-4

Vol. 44 Maurizio Gotti & Davide Giannoni (eds)
New Trends in Specialized Discourse Analysis.
301 pages. 2006. ISBN 3-03911-184-1 · US-ISBN 0-8204-8381-8

Vol. 45 Maurizio Gotti & Françoise Salager-Meyer (eds)
Advances in Medical Discourse Analysis. Oral and Written Contexts. 492 pages. 2006. ISBN 3-03911-185-X · US-ISBN 0-8204-8382-6

Vol. 46 Maurizio Gotti & Susan Šarcevic´ (eds) Insights into Specialized Translation.
396 pages. 2006. ISBN 3-03911-186-8 · US-ISBN 0-8204-8383-4

Vol. 47 Khurshid Ahmad & Margaret Rogers (eds)
Evidence-based LSP. Translation, Text and Terminology. 584 pages. 2007. ISBN 978-3-03911-187-9

Vol. 48 Hao Sun & Dániel Z. Kádár (eds)
It's the Dragon's Turn. Chinese Institutional Discourses. 262 pages. 2008. ISBN 978-3-03911-175-6

Vol. 49 Cristina Suárez-Gómez
Relativization in Early English (950-1250). the Position of Relative Clauses. 149 pages. 2006. ISBN 3-03911-203-1 · US-ISBN 0-8204-8904-2

Vol. 50 Maria Vittoria Calvi & Luisa Chierichetti (eds) Nuevas tendencias en el discurso de especialidad. 319 pages. 2006. ISBN 978-3-03911-261-6

Vol. 51 Mari Carmen Campoy & María José Luzón (eds) Spoken Corpora in Applied Linguistics. 274 pages. 2008. ISBN 978-3-03911-275-3

Vol. 52 Konrad Ehlich & Dorothee Heller (Hrsg.) Die Wissenschaft und ihre Sprachen. 323 pages. 2006. ISBN 978-3-03911-272-2

Vol. 53 Jingyu Zhang
The Semantic Salience Hierarchy Model. The L2 Acquisition of Psych Predicates 273 pages. 2007. ISBN 978-3-03911-300-2

Vol. 54 Norman Fairclough, Giuseppina Cortese & Patrizia Ardizzone (eds) Discourse and Contemporary Social Change.
555 pages. 2007. ISBN 978-3-03911-276-0

Vol. 55 Jan Engberg, Marianne Grove Ditlevsen, Peter Kastberg & Martin Stegu (eds) New Directions in LSP Teaching.
331 pages. 2007. ISBN 978-3-03911-433-7

Vol. 56 Dorothee Heller & Konrad Ehlich (Hrsg.) Studien zur Rechtskommunikation. 322 pages. 2007. ISBN 978-3-03911-436-8

Vol. 57 Teruhiro Ishiguro & Kang-kwong Luke (eds) Grammar in Cross-Linguistic Perspective. The Syntax, Semantics, and Pragmatics of Japanese and Chinese. 304 pages. 2012. ISBN 978-3-03911-445-0

Vol. 58 Carmen Frehner Email – SMS – MMS
294 pages. 2008. ISBN 978-3-03911-451-1

Vol. 59 Isabel Balteiro
The Directionality of Conversion in English. A Dia-Synchronic Study. 276 pages. 2007. ISBN 978-3-03911-241-8

Vol. 60 Maria Milagros Del Saz Rubio
English Discourse Markers of Reformulation. 237 pages. 2007. ISBN 978-3-03911-196-1

Vol. 61 Sally Burgess & Pedro Martín-Martín (eds)
English as an Additional Language in Research Publication and Communication. 259 pages. 2008. ISBN 978-3-03911-462-7

Vol. 62 Sandrine Onillon
Pratiques et représentations de l'écrit.
458 pages. 2008. ISBN 978-3-03911-464-1

Vol. 63 Hugo Bowles & Paul Seedhouse (eds)
Conversation Analysis and Language for Specific Purposes. 2nd edition. 337 pages. 2007, 2009. ISBN 978-3-0343-0045-2

Vol. 64 Vijay K. Bhatia, Christopher N. Candlin & Paola Evangelisti Allori (eds) Language, Culture and the Law.
The Formulation of Legal Concepts across Systems and Cultures. 342 pages. 2008. ISBN 978-3-03911-470-2

Vol. 65 Jonathan Culpeper & Dániel Z. Kádár (eds) Historical (Im)politeness.
300 pages. 2010. ISBN 978-3-03911-496-2

Vol. 66 Linda Lombardo (ed.)
Using Corpora to Learn about Language and Discourse. 237 pages. 2009. ISBN 978-3-03911-522-8

Vol. 67 Natsumi Wakamoto
Extroversion/Introversion in Foreign Language Learning. Interactions with Learner Strategy Use.
159 pages. 2009. ISBN 978-3-03911-596-9

Vol. 68 Eva Alcón-Soler (ed.)
Learning How to Request in an Instructed Language Learning Context. 260 pages. 2008. ISBN 978-3-03911-601-0

Vol. 69 Domenico Pezzini
The Translation of Religious Texts in the Middle Ages. 428 pages. 2008. ISBN 978-3-03911-600-3

Vol. 70 Tomoko Tode
Effects of Frequency in Classroom Second Language Learning. Quasi-experiment and stimulated-recall analysis.
195 pages. 2008. ISBN 978-3-03911-602-7

Vol. 71 Egor Tsedryk
Fusion symétrique et alternances ditransitives. 211 pages. 2009. ISBN 978-3-03911-609-6

Vol. 72 Cynthia J. Kellett Bidoli & Elana Ochse (eds) English in International Deaf Communication.
444 pages. 2008. ISBN 978-3-03911-610-2

Vol. 73 Joan C. Beal, Carmela Nocera & Massimo Sturiale (eds) Perspectives on Prescriptivism.
269 pages. 2008. ISBN 978-3-03911-632-4

Vol. 74 Carol Taylor Torsello, Katherine Ackerley & Erik Castello (eds) Corpora for University Language Teachers.
308 pages. 2008. ISBN 978-3-03911-639-3

Vol. 75 María Luisa Pérez Cañado (ed.)
English Language Teaching in the European Credit Transfer System. Facing the Challenge.
251 pages. 2009. ISBN 978-3-03911-654-6

Vol. 76 Marina Dossena & Ingrid Tieken-Boon van Ostade (eds)
Studies in Late Modern English Correspondence. Methodology and Data. 291 pages. 2008. ISBN 978-3-03911-658-4

Vol. 77 Ingrid Tieken-Boon van Ostade & Wim van der Wurff (eds) Current Issues in Late Modern English.
436 pages. 2009. ISBN 978-3-03911-660-7

Vol. 78 Marta Navarro Coy (ed.)
Practical Approaches to Foreign Language Teaching and Learning. 297 pages. 2009. ISBN 978-3-03911-661-4

Vol. 79 Qing Ma
Second Language Vocabulary Acquisition. 333 pages. 2009. ISBN 978-3-03911-666-9

Vol. 80 Martin Solly, Michelangelo Conoscenti & Sandra Campagna (eds) Verbal/Visual Narrative Texts in Higher Education.
384 pages. 2008. ISBN 978-3-03911-672-0

Vol. 81 Meiko Matsumoto
From Simple Verbs to Periphrastic Expressions:
The Historical Development of Composite Predicates, Phrasal Verbs, and Related Constructions in English.
235 pages. 2008. ISBN 978-3-03911-675-1

Vol. 82 Melinda Dooly
Doing Diversity. Teachers' Construction of Their Classroom Reality. 180 pages. 2009. ISBN 978-3-03911-687-4

Vol. 83 Victoria Guillén-Nieto, Carmen Marimón-Llorca & Chelo Vargas-Sierra (eds) Intercultural Business Communication and
Simulation and Gaming Methodology. 392 pages. 2009. ISBN 978-3-03911-688-1

Vol. 84 Maria Grazia Guido
English as a Lingua Franca in Cross-cultural Immigration Domains. 285 pages. 2008. ISBN 978-3-03911-689-8

Vol. 85 Erik Castello
Text Complexity and Reading Comprehension Tests. 352 pages. 2008. ISBN 978-3-03911-717-8

Vol. 86 Maria-Lluisa Gea-Valor, Isabel García-Izquierdo & Maria-José Esteve (eds) Linguistic and Translation Studies in Scientific Communication.
317 pages. 2010. ISBN 978-3-0343-0069-8

Vol. 87 Carmen Navarro, Rosa Ma Rodríguez Abella, Francesca Dalle Pezze & Renzo Miotti (eds) La comunicación especializada.
355 pages. 2008. ISBN 978-3-03911-733-8

Vol. 88 Kiriko Sato
The Development from Case-Forms to Prepositional Constructions in Old English Prose.
231 pages. 2009. ISBN 978-3-03911-763-5

Vol. 89 Dorothee Heller (Hrsg.)
Formulierungsmuster in deutscher und italienischer Fachkommunikation. Intra- und interlinguale Perspektiven.
315 pages. 2008. ISBN 978-3-03911-778-9

Vol. 90 Henning Bergenholtz, Sandro Nielsen & Sven Tarp (eds) Lexicography at a Crossroads. Dictionaries and Encyclopedias Today, Lexicographical Tools Tomorrow.
372 pages. 2009. ISBN 978-3-03911-799-4

Vol. 91 Manouchehr Moshtagh Khorasani
The Development of Controversies. From the Early Modern Period to Online Discussion Forums.
317 pages. 2009. ISBN 978-3-3911-711-6

Vol. 92 María Luisa Carrió-Pastor (ed.)
Content and Language Integrated Learning. Cultural Diversity. 178 pages. 2009. ISBN 978-3-3911-818-2

Vol. 93 Roger Berry
Terminology in English Language Teaching. Nature and Use. 262 pages. 2010.
ISBN 978-3-0343-0013-1

Vol. 94 Roberto Cagliero & Jennifer Jenkins (eds) Discourses, Communities, and Global Englishes 240 pages. 2010. ISBN 978-3-0343-0012-4

Vol. 95 Facchinetti Roberta, Crystal David, Seidlhofer Barbara (eds) From International to Local English – And Back Again.
268 pages. 2010. ISBN 978-3-0343-0011-7

Vol. 96 Cesare Gagliardi & Alan Maley (eds)
EIL, ELF, Global English. Teaching and Learning Issues 376 pages. 2010. ISBN 978-3-0343-0010-0

Vol. 97 Sylvie Hancil (ed.)
The Role of Prosody in Affective Speech. 403 pages. 2009. ISBN 978-3-03911-696-6

Vol. 98 Marina Dossena & Roger Lass (eds)
Studies in English and European Historical Dialectology. 257 pages. 2009. ISBN 978-3-0343-0024-7

Vol. 99 Christine Béal
Les interactions quotidiennes en français et en anglais.
De l'approche comparative à l'analyse des situations interculturelles. 424 pages. 2010. ISBN 978-3-0343-0027-8

Vol. 100 Maurizio Gotti (ed.)
Commonality and Individuality in Academic Discourse. 398 pages. 2009. ISBN 978-3-0343-0023-0

Vol. 101 Javier E. Díaz Vera & Rosario Caballero (eds)
Textual Healing. Studies in Medieval English Medical, Scientific and Technical Texts. 213 pages. 2009. ISBN 978-3-03911-822-9

Vol. 102 Nuria Edo Marzá
The Specialised Lexicographical Approach. A Step further in Dictionary-making. 316 pages. 2009. ISBN 978-3-0343-0043-8

Vol. 103 Carlos Prado-Alonso, Lidia Gómez-García, Iria Pastor-Gómez & David Tizón-Couto (eds)
New Trends and Methodologies in Applied English Language Research. Diachronic, Diatopic and Contrastive Studies.
348 pages. 2009. ISBN 978-3-0343-0046-9

Vol. 104 Françoise Salager-Meyer & Beverly A. Lewin Crossed Words. Criticism in Scholarly Writing?
371 pages. 2011. ISBN 978-3-0343-0049-0.

Vol. 105 Javier Ruano-García
Early Modern Northern English Lexis. A Literary Corpus-Based Study. 611 pages. 2010. ISBN 978-3-0343-0058-2

Vol. 106 Rafael Monroy-Casas
Systems for the Phonetic Transcription of English. Theory and Texts. 280 pages. 2011. ISBN 978-3-0343-0059-9

Vol. 107 Nicola T. Owtram
The Pragmatics of Academic Writing.
A Relevance Approach to the Analysis of Research Article Introductions. 311 pages. 2009. ISBN 978-3-0343-0060-5

Vol. 108 Yolanda Ruiz de Zarobe, Juan Manuel Sierra & Francisco Gallardo del Puerto (eds)
Content and Foreign Language Integrated Learning. Contributions to Multilingualism in European Contexts 343 pages. 2011. ISBN 978-3-0343-0074-2

Vol. 109 Ángeles Linde López & Rosalía Crespo Jiménez (eds)
Professional English in the European context. The EHEA challenge. 374 pages. 2010. ISBN 978-3-0343-0088-9

Vol. 110 Rosalía Rodríguez-Vázquez
The Rhythm of Speech, Verse and Vocal Music. A New Theory. 394 pages. 2010. ISBN 978-3-0343-0309-5

Vol. 111 Anastasios Tsangalidis & Roberta Facchinetti (eds) Studies on English Modality. In Honour of Frank Palmer. 392 pages. 2009. ISBN 978-3-0343-0310-1

Vol. 112 Jing Huang
Autonomy, Agency and Identity in Foreign Language Learning and Teaching. 400 pages. 2013. ISBN 978-3-0343-0370-5

Vol. 113 Mihhail Lotman & Maria-Kristiina Lotman (eds)
Frontiers in Comparative Prosody. In memoriam: Mikhail Gasparov. 426 pages. 2011. ISBN 978-3-0343-0373-6

Vol. 114 Merja Kytö, John Scahill & Harumi Tanabe (eds)
Language Change and Variation from Old English to Late Modern English. A Festschrift for Minoji Akimoto
422 pages. 2010. ISBN 978-3-0343-0372-9

Vol. 115 Giuliana Garzone & Paola Catenaccio (eds)
Identities across Media and Modes. Discursive Perspectives. 379 pages. 2009. ISBN 978-3-0343-0386-6

Vol. 116 Elena Landone
Los marcadores del discurso y cortesía verbal en español. 390 pages. 2010. ISBN 978-3-0343-0413-9

Vol. 117 Maurizio Gotti & Christopher Williams (eds) Legal Discourse across Languages and Cultures. 339 pages. 2010. ISBN 978-3-0343-0425-2

Vol. 118 David Hirsh
Academic Vocabulary in Context.
217 pages. 2010. ISBN 978-3-0343-0426-9

Vol. 119 Yvonne Dröschel
Lingua Franca English. The Role of Simplification and Transfer. 358 pages. 2011. ISBN 978-3-0343-0432-0

Vol. 120 Tengku Sepora Tengku Mahadi, Helia Vaezian & Mahmoud Akbari Corpora in Translation. A Practical Guide.
135 pages. 2010. ISBN 978-3-0343-0434-4

Vol. 121 Davide Simone Giannoni & Celina Frade (eds)
Researching Language and the Law. Textual Features and Translation Issues. 278 pages. 2010. ISBN 978-3-0343-0443-6

Vol. 122 Daniel Madrid & Stephen Hughes (eds) Studies in Bilingual Education.
472 pages. 2011. ISBN 978-3-0343-0474-0

Vol. 123 Vijay K. Bhatia, Christopher N. Candlin & Maurizio Gotti (eds) The Discourses of Dispute Resolution.
290 pages. 2010. ISBN 978-3-0343-0476-4

Vol. 124 Davide Simone Giannoni
Mapping Academic Values in the Disciplines. A Corpus-Based Approach. 288 pages. 2010. ISBN 978-3-0343-0488-7

Vol. 125 Giuliana Garzone & James Archibald (eds)
Discourse, Identities and Roles in Specialized Communication. 419 pages. 2010. ISBN 978-3-0343-0494-8

Vol. 126 Iria Pastor-Gómez
The Status and Development of N+N Sequences in Contemporary English Noun Phrases. 216 pages. 2011. ISBN 978-3-0343-0534-1

Vol. 127 Carlos Prado-Alonso
Full-verb Inversion in Written and Spoken English. 261 pages. 2011. ISBN 978-3-0343-0535-8

Vol. 128 Tony Harris & María Moreno Jaén (eds) Corpus Linguistics in Language Teaching. 214 pages. 2010. ISBN 978-3-0343-0524-2

Vol. 129 Tetsuji Oda & Hiroyuki Eto (eds)
Multiple Perspectives on English Philology and History of Linguistics. A Festschrift for Shoichi Watanabe on his 80th Birthday.
378 pages. 2010. ISBN 978-3-0343-0480-1

Vol. 130 Luisa Chierichetti & Giovanni Garofalo (eds)
Lengua y Derecho. líneas de investigación interdisciplinaria. 283 pages. 2010. 978-3-0343-0463-4

Vol. 131 Paola Evangelisti Allori & Giuliana Garzone (eds)
Discourse, Identities and Genres in Corporate Communication. Sponsorship, Advertising and Organizational Communication. 324 pages. 2011. 978-3-0343-0591-4

Vol. 132 Leyre Ruiz de Zarobe & Yolanda Ruiz de Zarobe (eds) Speech Acts and Politeness across Languages and Cultures. 402 pages. 2012. 978-3-0343-0611-9

Vol. 133 Thomas Christiansen
Cohesion. A Discourse Perspective. 387 pages. 2011. 978-3-0343-0619-5

Vol. 134 Giuliana Garzone & Maurizio Gotti
Discourse, Communication and the Enterprise. Genres and Trends. 451 pages. 2011. ISBN 978-3-0343-0620-1

Vol. 135 Zsuzsa Hoffmann
Ways of the World's Words.
Language Contact in the Age of Globalization. 334 pages 2011. ISBN 978-3-0343-0673-7

Vol. 136 Cecilia Varcasia (ed.) Becoming Multilingual.
Language Learning and Language Policy between Attitudes and Identities. 213 pages. 2011. ISBN 978-3-0343-0687-5

Vol. 137 Susy Macqueen
The Emergence of Patterns in Second Language Writing. A Sociocognitive Exploration of Lexical Trails.
325 pages. 2012. ISBN 978-3-0343-1010-9

Vol. 138 Maria Vittoria Calvi & Giovanna Mapelli (eds)
La lengua del turismo. Géneros discursivos y terminología. 365 pages. 2011.
ISBN 978-3-0343-1011-6

Vol. 139 Ken Lau
Learning to Become a Professional in a Textually-Mediated World. A Text-Oriented Study of Placement Practices.
261 pages. 2012. ISBN 978-3-0343-1016-1

Vol. 140 Sandra Campagna, Giuliana Garzone, Cornelia Ilie & Elizabeth Rowley-Jolivet (eds) Evolving Genres in Web-mediated Communication.
337 pages. 2012. ISBN 978-3-0343-1013-0

Vol. 141 Edith Esch & Martin Solly (eds)
The Sociolinguistics of Language Education in International Contexts. 263 pages. 2012. ISBN 978-3-0343-1009-3

Vol. 142 Forthcoming.

Vol. 143 David Tizón-Couto
Left Dislocation in English. A Functional-Discoursal Approach. 416 pages. 2012. ISBN 978-3-0343-1037-6

Vol. 144 Margrethe Petersen & Jan Engberg (eds)
Current Trends in LSP Research. Aims and Methods. 323 pages. 2011. ISBN 978-3-0343-1054-3

Vol. 145 David Tizón-Couto, Beatriz Tizón-Couto, Iria Pastor-Gómez & Paula Rodríguez-Puente (eds) New Trends and Methodologies in Applied English Language Research II.
Studies in Language Variation, Meaning and Learning. 283 pages. 2012. ISBN 978-3-0343-1061-1

Vol. 146 Rita Salvi & Hiromasa Tanaka (eds)
Intercultural Interactions in Business and Management. 306 pages. 2011. ISBN 978-3-0343-1039-0

Vol. 147 Francesco Straniero Sergio & Caterina Falbo (eds) Breaking Ground in Corpus-based Interpreting Studies. 254 pages. 2012. ISBN 978-3-0343-1071-0

Vol. 148 Forthcoming.

Vol. 149 Vijay K. Bhatia & Paola Evangelisti Allori (eds)
Discourse and Identity in the Professions. Legal, Corporate and Institutional Citizenship. 352 pages. 2011. ISBN 978-3-0343-1079-6

Vol. 150 Maurizio Gotti (ed.)
Academic Identity Traits. A Corpus-Based Investigation. 363 pages. 2012. ISBN 978-3-0343-1141-0

Vol. 151 Priscilla Heynderickx, Sylvain Dieltjens, Geert Jacobs, Paul Gillaerts & Elizabeth de Groot (eds)
The Language Factor in International Business.
New Perspectives on Research, Teaching and Practice. 320 pages. 2012. ISBN 978-3-0343-1090-1

Vol. 152 Paul Gillaerts, Elizabeth de Groot, Sylvain Dieltjens, Priscilla Heynderickx & Geert Jacobs (eds)
Researching Discourse in Business Genres. Cases and Corpora. 215 pages. 2012. ISBN 978-3-0343-1092-5

Vol. 153 Yongyan Zheng
Dynamic Vocabulary Development in a Foreign Language. 262 pages. 2012. ISBN 978-3-0343-1106-9

Vol. 154 Carmen Argondizzo (ed.)
Creativity and Innovation in Language Education. 357 pages. 2012. ISBN 978-3-0343-1080-2

Vol. 155 David Hirsh (ed.)
Current Perspectives in Second Language Vocabulary Research. 180 pages. 2012. ISBN 978-3-0343-1108-3

Vol. 156 Seiji Shinkawa
Unhistorical Gender Assignment in Lahamon's *Brut*. A Case Study of a Late Stage in the Development of Grammatical Gender toward its Ultimate Loss.
186 pages. 2012. ISBN 978-3-0343-1124-3

Vol. 157 Yeonkwon Jung
Basics of Organizational Writing: A Critical Reading Approach. 151 pages. 2014. ISBN 978-3-0343-1137-3.

Vol. 158 Bárbara Eizaga Rebollar (ed.) Studies in Linguistics and Cognition.
301 pages. 2012. ISBN 978-3-0343-1138-0

Vol. 159 Giuliana Garzone, Paola Catenaccio, Chiara Degano (eds)
Genre Change in the Contemporary World. Short-term Diachronic Perspectives. 329 pages. 2012. ISBN 978-3-0343-1214-1

Vol. 160 Carol Berkenkotter, Vijay K. Bhatia & Maurizio Gotti (eds) Insights into Academic Genres.
468 pages. 2012. ISBN 978-3-0343-1211-0

Vol. 161 Beatriz Tizón-Couto
Clausal Complements in Native and Learner Spoken English. A corpus-based study with Lindsei and Vicolse. 357 pages. 2013. ISBN 978-3-0343-1184-7

Vol. 162 Patrizia Anesa
Jury Trials and the Popularization of Legal Language. A Discourse Analytical Approach.
247 pages. 2012. ISBN 978-3-0343-1231-8

Vol. 163 David Hirsh
Endangered Languages, Knowledge Systems and Belief Systems. 153 pages. 2013. ISBN 978-3-0343-1232-5

Vol. 164 Eugenia Sainz (ed.)
De la estructura de la frase al tejido del discurso. Estudios contrastivos español/italiano.
305 pages. 2014. ISBN 978-3-0343-1253-0

Vol. 165 Julia Bamford, Franca Poppi & Davide Mazzi (eds) Space, Place and the Discursive Construction of Identity. 367 pages. 2014. ISBN 978-3-0343-1249-3

Vol. 166 Rita Salvi & Janet Bowker (eds)
Space, Time and the Construction of Identity.
Discursive Indexicality in Cultural, Institutional and Professional Fields. 324 pages. 2013. ISBN 978-3-0343-1254-7

Vol. 167 Shunji Yamazaki & Robert Sigley (eds)
Approaching Language Variation through Corpora. A Festschrift in Honour of Toshio Saito. 421 pages. 2013. ISBN 978-3-0343-1264-6

Vol. 168 Franca Poppi
Global Interactions in English as a Lingua Franca. How written communication is changing under the influence of electronic media and new contexts of use.
249 pages. 2012. ISBN 978-3-0343-1276-9

Vol. 169 Miguel A. Aijón Oliva & María José Serrano
Style in syntax. Investigating variation in Spanish pronoun subjects. 239 pages. 2013. ISBN 978-3-0343-1244-8

Vol. 170 Inés Olza, Óscar Loureda & Manuel Casado-Velarde (eds)
Language Use in the Public Sphere. Methodological Perspectives and Empirical Applications 564 pages. 2014. ISBN 978-3-0343-1286-8

Vol. 171 Aleksandra Matulewska
Legilinguistic Translatology. A Parametric Approach to Legal Translation. 279 pages. 2013. ISBN 978-3-0343-1287-5

Vol. 172 Maurizio Gotti & Carmen Sancho Guinda (eds) Narratives in Academic and Professional Genres. 513 pages. 2013. ISBN 978-3-0343-1371-1

Vol. 173 Madalina Chitez
Learner corpus profiles. The case of Romanian Learner English. 244 pages. 2014. ISBN 978-3-0343-1410-7

Vol. 174 Chihiro Inoue
Task Equivalence in Speaking Tests.
251 pages. 2013. ISBN 978-3-0343-1417-6

Vol. 175 Gabriel Quiroz & Pedro Patiño (eds.)
LSP in Colombia: advances and challenges. 339 pages. 2014. ISBN 978-3-0343-1434-3

Vol. 176 Catherine Resche
Economic Terms and Beyond: Capitalising on the Wealth of Notions.
How Researchers in Specialised Varieties of English Can Benefit from Focusing on Terms.
332 pages. 2013. ISBN 978-3-0343-1435-0

Vol. 177 Wei Wang
Media representation of migrant workers in China. Identities and stances 198 pages. 2018. 978-3-0343-1436-7

Vol. 178 Cécile Desoutter & Caroline Mellet (dir.)
Le discours rapporté: approches linguistiques et perspectives didactiques. 270 pages. 2013. ISBN 978-3-0343-1292-9

Vol. 179 Ana Díaz-Negrillo & Francisco Javier Díaz-Pérez (eds) Specialisation and Variation in Language Corpora.
341 pages. 2014. ISBN 978-3-0343-1316-2

Vol. 180 Pilar Alonso
A Multi-dimensional Approach to Discourse Coherence. From Standardness to Creativity.
247 pages. 2014. ISBN 978-3-0343-1325-4

Vol. 181 Alejandro Alcaraz-Sintes & Salvador Valera-Hernández (eds) Diachrony and Synchrony in English Corpus Linguistics.
393 pages. 2014. ISBN 978-3-0343-1326-1

Vol. 182 Runhan Zhang
Investigating Linguistic Knowledge of a Second Language. 207 pages. 2015. ISBN 978-3-0343-1330-8

Vol. 183 Hajar Abdul Rahim & Shakila Abdul Manan (eds.) English in Malaysia. Postcolonial and Beyond.
267 pages. 2014. ISBN 978-3-0343-1341-4

Vol. 184 Virginie Fasel Lauzon
Comprendre et apprendre dans l'interaction. Les séquences d'explication en classe de français langue seconde.
292 pages. 2014. ISBN 978-3-0343-1451-0

Vol. 185 Forthcoming.

Vol. 186 Wei Ren
L2 Pragmatic Development in Study Abroad Contexts 256 pages. 2015. ISBN 978-3-0343-1358-2

Vol. 187 Marina Bondi & Rosa Lorés Sanz (eds)
Abstracts in Academic Discourse. Variation and Change. 361 pages. 2014. ISBN 978-3-0343-1483-1

Vol. 188 Giuditta Caliendo
Rethinking Community. Discourse, Identity and Citizenship in the European Union. 240 pages. 2017. ISBN 978-3-0343-1561-6

Vol. 189 Paola Evangelisti Allori (ed.) Identities in and across Cultures.
315 pages. 2014. ISBN 978-3-0343-1458-9

Vol. 190 Erik Castello, Katherine Ackerley & Francesca Coccetta (eds).
Studies in Learner Corpus Linguistics. Research and Applications for Foreign Language Teaching and Assessment.
358 pages. 2015. ISBN 978-3-0343-1506-7

Vol. 191 Ruth Breeze, Maurizio Gotti & Carmen Sancho Guinda (eds) Interpersonality in Legal Genres.
389 pages. 2014. ISBN 978-3-0343-1524-1

Vol. 192 Paola Evangelisti Allori, John Bateman & Vijay K. Bhatia (eds) Evolution in Genre. Emergence, Variation, Multimodality.
364 pages. 2014. ISBN 978-3-0343-1533-3

Vol. 193 Jiyeon Kook
Agency in Arzt-Patient-Gesprächen. Zur interaktionistischen Konzeptualisierung von Agency 271 pages. 2015. ISBN 978-3-0343-1666-8

Vol. 194 Susana Nicolás Román & Juan José Torres Núñez (eds)
Drama and CLIL. A new challenge for the teaching approaches in bilingual education. 170 pages. 2015. ISBN 978-3-0343-1629-3

Vol. 195 Alessandra Molino & Serenella Zanotti (eds)
Observing Norm, Observing Usage. Lexis in Dictionaries and in the Media. 430 pages. 2015. ISBN 978-3-0343-1584-5

Vol. 196 Begoña Soneira
A Lexical Description of English for Architecture. A Corpus-based Approach. 267 pages. 2015. ISBN 978-3-0343-1602-6

Vol. 197 M Luisa Roca-Varela
False Friends in Learner Corpora. A corpus-based study of English false friends in the written and spoken production of Spanish learners.
348 pages. 2015. ISBN 978-3-0343-1620-0

Vol. 198 Rahma Al-Mahrooqi & Christopher Denman
Bridging the Gap between Education and Employment. English Language Instruction in EFL Contexts.
416 pages. 2015. ISBN 978-3-0343-1681-1

Vol. 199 Rita Salvi & Janet Bowker (eds)
The Dissemination of Contemporary Knowledge in English. Genres, discourse strategies and professional practices.
171 pages. 2015. ISBN 978-3-0343-1679-8

Vol. 200 Maurizio Gotti & Davide S. Giannoni (eds)
Corpus Analysis for Descriptive and Pedagogical Purposes. ESP Perspectives. 432 pages. 2014. ISBN 978-3-0343-1516-6

Vol. 201 Ida Ruffolo
The Perception of Nature in Travel Promotion Texts. A Corpus-based Discourse Analysis. 148 pages. 2015. ISBN 978-3-0343-1521-0

Vol. 202 Ives Trevian
English suffixes. Stress-assignment properties, productivity, selection and combinatorial processes.
471 pages. 2015. ISBN 978-3-0343-1576-0

Vol. 203 Maurizio Gotti, Stefania Maci & Michele Sala (eds) Insights into Medical Communication. 422 pages. 2015. ISBN 978-3-0343-1694-1

Vol. 204 Carmen Argondizzo (ed.)
European Projects in University Language Centres. Creativity, Dynamics, Best Practice. 371 pages. 2015. ISBN 978-3-0343-1696-5

Vol. 205 Aura Luz Duffé Montalván (ed.)
Estudios sobre el léxico. Puntos y contrapuntos. 502 pages. 2016. ISBN 978-3-0343-2011-5

Vol. 206 Maria Pavesi, Maicol Formentelli & Elisa Ghia (eds)
The Languages of Dubbing. Mainstream Audiovisual Translation in Italy. 275 pages. 2014. ISBN 978-3-0343-1646-0

Vol. 207 Ruth Breeze & Inés Olza (eds)
Evaluation in media discourse. European perspectives. 268 pages. 2017. ISBN 978-3-0343-2014-6

Vol. 208 Vijay K. Bhatia & Maurizio Gotti (eds) Arbitration Discourse in Asia.
331 pages. 2015. ISBN 978-3-0343-2032-0

Vol. 209 Sofía Bemposta-Rivas, Carla Bouzada-Jabois, Yolanda Fernández-Pena, Tamara Bouso, Yolanda J. Calvo-Benzies, Iván Tamaredo (eds)
New trends and methodologies in applied English language research III. Synchronic and diachronic studies on discourse, lexis and grammar processing. 280 pages. 2017. ISBN 978-3-0343-2039-9

Vol. 210 Francisco Alonso Almeida, Laura Cruz García & Víctor González Ruiz (eds) Corpus-based studies on language varieties.
285 pages. 2016. ISBN 978-3-0343-2044-3

Vol. 211 Juan Pedro Rica Peromingo
Aspectos lingüísticos y técnicos de la traducción audiovisual (TAV). 177 pages. 2016. ISBN 978-3-0343-2055-9

Vol. 212 Maria Vender
Disentangling Dyslexia. VenderPhonological and Processing Deficit in Developmental Dyslexia.
338 pages. 2017. ISBN 978-3-0343-2064-1

Vol. 213 Zhilong Xie
Bilingual Advantages. Contributions of Different Bilingual Experiences to Cognitive Control Differences Among Young-adult Bilinguals.
221 pages. 2016. ISBN 978-3-0343-2081-8

Vol. 214 Larissa D'Angelo
Academic posters. A textual and visual metadiscourse analysis. 367 pages. 2016. ISBN 978-3-0343-2083-2

Vol. 215 Evelyne Berger
Prendre la parole en L2. Regard sur la compétence d'interaction en classe de langue. 246 pages. 2016. ISBN 978-3-0343-2084-9

Vol. 216 David Lasagabaster and Aintzane Doiz (eds)
CLIL experiences in secondary and tertiary education: In search of good practices. 262 pages. 2016. ISBN 978-3-0343-2104-4

Vol. 217 Elena Kkese
Identifying Plosives in L2 English: The Case of L1 Cypriot Greek Speakers. 317 pages. 2016. ISBN 978-3-0343-2060-3

Vol. 218 Sandra Campagna, Elana Ochse, Virginia Pulcini & Martin Solly (eds)
Languaging in and across Communities: New Voices, New Identities. Studies in Honour of Giuseppina Cortese.
507 pages. 2016. ISBN 978-3-0343-2073-3

Vol. 219 Adriana Orlandi & Laura Giacomini (ed.)
Defining collocation for lexicographic purposes. From linguistic theory to lexicographic practice.
328 pages. 2016. ISBN 978-3-0343-2054-2

Vol. 220 Pietro Luigi Iaia
Analysing English as a Lingua Franca in Video Games. Linguistic Features, Experiential and Functional Dimensions of Online and Scripted Interactions. 139 pages. 2016. ISBN 978-3-0343-2138-9

Vol. 221 Dimitrinka G. Níkleva (ed.)
La formación de los docentes de español para inmigrantes en distintos contextos educativos. 390 pages. 2017. ISBN 978-3-0343-2135-8

Vol. 222 Katherine Ackerley, Marta Guarda & Francesca Helm (eds) Sharing Perspectives on English-Medium Instruction. 308 pages. 2017. ISBN 978-3-0343-2537-0

Vol. 223 Juana I. Marín-Arrese, Julia Lavid-López, Marta Carretero, Elena Domínguez Romero, Ma Victoria Martín de la Rosa & María Pérez Blanco (eds)
Evidentiality and Modality in European Languages. Discourse-pragmatic perspectives. 427 pages. 2017. ISBN 978-3-0343-2437-3

Vol. 224 Gilles Col
Construction du sens : un modèle instructionnel pour la sémantique. 292 pages. 2017. ISBN 978-3-0343-2572-1

Vol. 225 Ana Chiquito & Gabriel Quiroz (eds)
Pobreza, Lenguaje y Medios en América Latina. 362 pages. 2017. ISBN 978-3-0343-2142-6

Vol. 226 Xu Zhang
English Quasi-Numeral Classifiers. A Corpus-Based Cognitive-Typological Study. 360 pages. 2017. ISBN 978-3-0343-2818-0

Vol. 227 María Ángeles Orts, Ruth Breeze & Maurizio Gotti (eds)
Power, Persuasion and Manipulation in Specialised Genres. Providing Keys to the Rhetoric of Professional Communities.
368 pages. 2017. ISBN 978-3-0343-3010-7

Vol. 228 Maurizio Gotti, Stefania Maci & Michele Sala (eds)
Ways of Seeing, Ways of Being: Representing the Voices of Tourism. 453 pages. 2017. ISBN 978-3-0343-3031-2

Vol. 229 Dino Selvaggi
Plurilingual Code-Switching between Standard and Local Varieties. A Socio-Psycholinguistic Approach
371 pages. 2018. ISBN 978-3-0343-2663-6

Vol. 230 Anca-Cristina Sterie
Interprofessional interactions at the hospital. Nurses' requests and reports of problems in calls with physicians.
371 pages. 2017. ISBN 978-3-0343-2734-3

Vol. 231 Xiaodong Zhang
Understanding Chinese EFL Teachers' Beliefs and Practices in the Textbook-Based Classroom. 189 pages. 2017. ISBN 978-3-0343-3053-4

Vol. 232 Manuela Caterina Moroni & Federica Ricci Garotti (Hrsg.) Brücken schlagen zwischen Sprachwissenschaft und DaF-Didaktik. 345 pages. 2017. ISBN 978-3-0343-2667-4

Vol. 233 Dimitrinka Georgieva Níkleva
Necesidades y tendencias en la formación del profesorado de español como lengua extranjera
401 pages. 2017. ISBN 978-3-0343-2946-0

Vol. 234 Juan Santana-Lario & Salvador Valera (Hrsg.) Competing patterns in English affixation.
272 pages. 2017. ISBN 978-3-0343-2701-5

Vol. 235 Francisco Salgado-Robles
Desarrollo de la competencia sociolingüística por aprendices de español en un contexto de inmersión en el extranjero
241 pages. 2018. ISBN 978-3-0343-2323-9

Vol. 236 Maria Chiara Janner
Sguardi linguistici sulla marca. Analisi morfosintattica dei nomi commerciali in italiano
345 pages. 2017. ISBN 978-3-0343-2667-4

Vol. 237 Bárbara Herrero Muñoz-Cobo & Otman El Azami Zalachi La primavera del árabe marroquí.
192 pages. 2017. ISBN 978-3-0343-3104-3

Vol. 238 Consuelo Pascual Escagedo
El papel del oyente en la construcción de la conversación espontánea de estudiantes italianos en su interlengua y en su lengua materna
295 pages. 2017. ISBN 978-3-0343-3186-9

Vol. 239 Stefania M. Maci
The MS Digby 133 *Mary Magdalene*. Beyond scribal practices: language, discourse, values and attitudes.
336 pages. 2017. ISBN 978-3-0343-3256-9

Vol. 240 Eliecer Crespo-Fernández
Taboo in Discourse. Studies on Attenuation and Offence in Communication. 326 pages. 2018. ISBN 978-3-0343-3018-3

Vol. 241 Jana Altmanova, Maria Centrella, Katherine E. Russo (eds) Terminology & Discourse / Terminologie et discours.
424 pages. 2018. ISBN 978-3-0343-2417-5

Vol. 242 Xavier Blanco et Inès Sfar (dir.)
Lexicologie(s) : approches croisées en sémantique lexicale.
442 pages. 2018. ISBN 978-3-0343-3056-5

Vol. 243 Yunfeng Ge
Resolution of Conflict of Interest in Chinese Civil Court Hearings. A Perspective of Discourse Information Theory.
302 pages. 2018. ISBN 978-3-0343-3313-9

Vol. 244 Carla Vergaro
Illocutionary Shell Nouns in English
322 pages. 2018. ISBN 978-3-0343-3069-5

Vol. 245 Paolo Frassi
L'adjectif en français et sa définition lexicographique. 270 pages. 2018. ISBN 978-3-0343-3394-8

Vol. 246 Suwilai Premsrirat and David Hirsh (eds) Language Revitalization. Insights from Thailand
328 pages. 2018. ISBN 978-3-0343-3497-6

Vol. 247 Wei Wang
Researching Learning and Learners in Genre-based Academic Writing Instruction 282 pages. 2018. ISBN 978-3-0343-3297-2

Vol. 248 Isusi Alabarte, Alberto & Lahuerta Martínez, Ana Cristina (eds) La comprensión lectora de lengua extranjera
Estudio de los factores de familiaridad, interés, género y métodos de evaluación 336 pages. 2018. ISBN 978-3-0343-3493-8

Vol. 249 Mercedes Eurrutia Cavero
Approche didactique du langage techno-scientifique Terminologie et discours
374 pages. 2018. ISBN 978-3-0343-3512-6

Vol. 250 Aurora Ruiz Mezcua (ed.)
Approaches to Telephone Interpretation Research, Innovation, Teaching and Transference
268 pages. 2018. ISBN 978-3-0343-3330-6

Vol. 251 Morini Massimiliano A Day in the News
A Stylistic Analysis of Newsspeak
188 pages. 2018. ISBN 978-3-0343-3507-2

Vol. 252 Ignacio Guillén-Galve & Ignacio Vázquez-Orta (eds.)
English as a Lingua Franca and Intercultural Communication Implications and Applications in the Field of English Language Teaching 414 pages. 2018. ISBN 978-3-0343-2763-3

Vol. 253 Bianca Del Villano
Using the Devil with Courtesy
Shakespeare and the Language of (Im)Politeness 216 pages. 2018. ISBN 978-3-0343-2315-4

Vol. 254 David Hirsh (ed.)
Explorations in Second Language Vocabulary Research 252 pages. 2018. ISBN 978-3-0343-2940-8

Vol. 255 Tania Baumann (ed.)
Reiseführer - Sprach- und Kulturmittlung im Tourismus / Le guide turistiche - mediazione linguistica e culturale in ambito turistico
270 pages. 2018. ISBN 978-3-0343-3402-0

Vol. 256 Ariadna Sánchez-Hernández & Ana Herraiz-Martínez (eds) Learning second language pragmatics beyond traditional contexts 376 pages. 2018. ISBN 978-3-0343-3437-2

Vol. 257 Albert Bastardas-Boada, Emili Boix-Fuster, Rosa Maria Torrens (eds) Family Multilingualism in Medium-Sized Linguistic Communities 336 pages. 2019. ISBN 978-3-0343-2536-3

Vol. 258 Yuyang Cai
Examining the Interaction among Components of English for Specific Purposes Ability in Reading. The Triple-Decker Model
296 pages. 2020. 978-3-0343-2913-2

Vol. 259 Catia Nannoni
Participe présent et gérondif dans la presse française contemporaine 176 pages. 2019. ISBN 978-3-0343-3631-4

Vol. 260 Nieves Rodríguez Pérez & Bárbara Heinsch (eds.)
Contextos multilingües. Mediadores interculturales, formación del profesorado de lenguas extranjeras
289 pages. 2019. ISBN 978-3-0343-3768-7

Vol. 261 Giuliana Elena Garzone, Mara Logaldo, Francesca Santulli (eds.) Investigating Conflict Discourses in the Periodical Press
244 pages. 2020. ISBN 978-3-0343-3668-0

Vol. 262 Laura Nadal
Lingüística experimental y contraargumentación 233 pages. 2019. ISBN 978-3-0343-3791-5

Vol. 263 Claudia Claridge & Merja Kytö (eds.)
Punctuation in Context – Past and Present Perspectives 288 pages. 2019. ISBN 978-3-0343-3790-8

Vol. 264 Maurizio Gotti, Stefania Maci, Michele Sala (eds.) Scholarly Pathways
530 pages. 2020. ISBN 978-3-0343-3860-8

Vol. 265 Ruth Breeze, Ana M. Fernández Vallejo (eds.) Politics and populism across modes and media
350 pages. 2020. ISBN 978-3-0343-3707-6

Vol. 266 Jean Marguerite Jimenez
Understanding the Effects of Immediate Electronic Corrective Feedback on Second Language Development
252 pages. 2020. ISBN 978-3-0343-3815-8

Vol. 267 Sergio Rodríguez-Tapia, Adela González-Fernández (eds)
Lenguas y turismo: estudios en torno al discurso, la didáctica y la divulgación 380 pages. 2020. ISBN 978-3-0343-3881-3

Vol. 268 Ana Bocanegra-Valle (ed.)
Applied Linguistics and Knowledge Transfer. Employability, Internationalisation and Social Challenges
344 pages. 2020. ISBN 978-3-0343-3714-4

Vol. 269 Beatrice Garzelli
La traducción audiovisual español-italiano.Películas y cortos entre humor y habla soez 202 pages. 2020. ISBN 978-3-0343-4013-7

Vol. 270 Iván Tamaredo
Complexity, Efficiency, and Language Contact. Pronoun Omission in World Englishes 292 pages. 2020. ISBN 978-3-0343-3902-5

Vol. 271 Silvia Domenica Zollo,
Origine et histoire du vocabulaire des arts de la table. Analyse lexicale et exploitation de corpus textuels
239 pages. 2020. ISBN 978-3-0343-3890-5

Vol. 272 Paola Paissa, Michelangelo Conoscenti, Ruggero Druetta, Martin Solly (eds.) Metaphor and Conflict / Métaphore et conflit
385 pages. 2021. 978-3-0343-4068-7

Vol. 273 María Martínez-Atienza de Dios,
Entre el léxico y la sintaxis: las fases de los eventos 178 pages. 2021. 978-3-0343-4173-8

Vol. 274 Noelia Castro-Chao,
Argument Structure in Flux. The Development of Impersonal Constructions in Middle and Early Modern English, with Special Reference to Verbs of Desire.
300 pages. 2021. 978-3-0343-4189-9

Vol. 275 Gabriella Carobbio, Cécile Desoutter, Aurora Fragonara (eds.)
Macht, Ratio und Emotion: Diskurse im digitalen Zeitalter / Pouvoir, raison et émotion: les discours à l'ère du numérique
246 pages. 2020. 978-3-0343-4184-4

Vol. 276 Miguel Fuster-Márquez, José Santaemilia, Carmen Gregori-Signes, Paula Rodríguez-Abruñeiras (eds.)
Exploring discourse and ideology through corpora 293 pages. 2021. 978-3-0343-3969-8

Vol. 277 Tamara Bouso
Changes in Argument Structure
The Transitivizing Reaction Object Construction
392. 2021. 978-3-0343-4095-3

Vol. 278 Maria Luisa Maggioni, Amanda Murphy (eds.) Back to the Future. English from Past to Present 250 pages. 2021. 978-3-0343-4273-5

Vol. 279 Luisa Chierichetti
Diálogos de serie. Una aproximación a la construcción discursiva de personajes basada en corpus
246 pages. 2021. 978-3-0343-4274-2

Vol. 280 Cristina Lastres-López
From subordination to insubordination. A functional-pragmatic approach to if/si-constructions in English, French and Spanish spoken discourse
258 pages. 2021. 978-3-0343-4220-9

Vol. 281 Eleonora Federici, Stefania Maci (eds.)
Gender issues. Translating and mediating languages, cultures and societies 500 pages. 2021. 978-3-0343-4022-9

Vol. 282 José Mateo, Francisco Yus (eds.)
Metaphor in Economics and specialised Discourse 354 pages. 2021. 978-3-0343-4048-9

Vol. 283 Nicholas Brownlees (ed.)
The Role of Context in the Production and Reception of Historical News Discourse 376 pages. 2021. 978-3-0343-4181-3

Vol. 284 Catalina Fuentes Rodriguez, María Ester Brenes Peña, Víctor Pérez Béjar (eds.) Sintaxis discursiva: construcciones y operadores en español
396 pages. 2021. 978-3-0343-4306-0

Vol. 285 Dominic Stewart
Frequency in the dictionary. A corpus-assisted contrastive analysis of English and Italian
176 pages. 2021. 978-3-0343-4368-8

Vol. 286 Carla Bouzada-Jabois
Nonfinite supplements in the recent history of English 320 pages. 2021. 978-3-0343-4226-1

Vol. 287 Sofía Bemposta Rivas
Verb-governed infinitival complementation in the recent history of English 320 pages. 2021. 978-3-0343-4227-8

Vol. 288 Mirella Agorni
Translating Italy for the Nineteenth Century. Translators and an Imagined Nation in the Early Romantic Period 1816–1830s
180 pages. 2021. 978-3-0343-3612-3

Vol. 289 David Hirsh (ed.)
Research Perspectives in Language and Education 276 pages. 2021. 978-3-0343-4219-3

Vol. 290 Federica Vezzani
Terminologie numérique : conception, représentation et gestion 238 pages. 2022. 978-3-0343-4394-7

Vol. 291 Stefania M. Maci
Evidential verbs in the genre of medical posters. A corpus-based analysis 498 pages. 2022. 978-3-0343-4521-7

Vol. 292 Francisco J. Álvarez-Gil
Stance devices in tourism-related research articles: A corpus-based study 170 pages. 2022. 978-3-0343-4555-2

Vol. 293 Annalisa Baicchi / Stefania Biscetti (eds.)
The Language of Fashion. Linguistic, Cognitive, and Cultural Insights
190 pages. 2022. 978-3-0343-4428-9

Vol. 294 Ana Maria Piquer-Píriz
E-learning in EMI. Academic language for university students
200 pages. 2022. 978-3-0343-4589-7

Vol. 295 Geneviève Henrot Sostero (ed.)
Alle radici della fraseologia europea
400 pages. 2023. 978-3-0343-4645-0

Vol. 296 Klara Dankova
Les fibres textiles entre synchronie et diachronie: études terminologiques 300 pages. 2023. 978-3-0343-4587-3

Vol. 297 Marta Carretero, Juana I. Marín-Arrese, Elena Domínguez Romero, Mª Victoria Martín de la Rosa (eds.) Evidentiality and Epistemic Modality. Conceptual and Descriptive issues
350 pages. 2023. 978-3-0343-3993-3

Vol. 298 Kim Grego, Alessandra Vicentini, Virpi Ylänne (eds.) Age-Specific Issues. Language, Spaces, Technologies
300 pages. 2023. 978-3-0343-4411-1

Vol. 299 Giovanni Garofalo (ed.) Estudios de género asistidos por corpus. Enfoques multidisciplinarios
292 pages. 2022. 978-3-0343-4548-4

Vol. 300 Giuseppe Palumbo, Katia Peruzzo, Gianluca Pontrandolfo (eds.) What's Special About Specialised Translation? Essays in Honour of Federica Scarpa
296 pages. 2023. 978-3-0343-4411-1

Vol. 301 Raquel P. Romasanta Probabilistic variability in clausal verb complementation in World Englishes.
390 pages. 2023. 978-3-0343-4703-7

Vol. 302 Giulia Adriana Pennisi A linguistic Insight into Legislative Drafting. Tradition and Change in the UK Legislation
296 pages. 2024. 978-3-0343-4700-6

www.peterlang.com